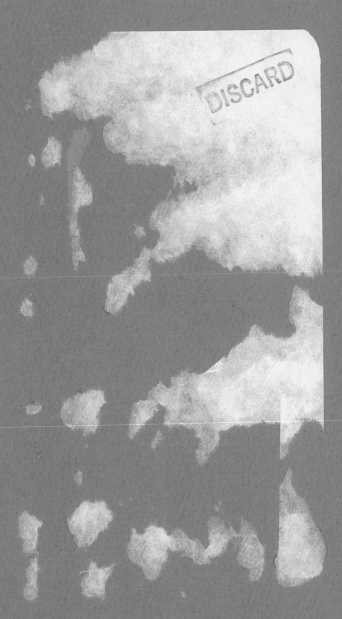

"MY DEAR ONES"

Other Books by the Authors

MY FATHER, CHARLIE CHAPLIN
1960

ACT YOUR WAY TO SUCCESSFUL LIVING
1966

"MY DEAR ONES"

BY NEIL AND MARGARET RAU

PRENTICE-HALL, INC.
Englewood Cliffs, N.J.

To
Betty Keniston
and
Jane Hill
who sparked our interest
in the Method

ACKNOWLEDGMENTS

It was Harry Nelson, medical writer of the Los Angeles *Times,* who first drew our attention to Recovery with a feature story in 1967 about the late Bertha Goldstein. At age seventy-seven, Mrs. Goldstein, a severe psychoneurotic for more than forty years, had been introduced to Recovery, Inc. Eleven years later, at the time of the Nelson story, she was attributing her cure and her resultant serene life to the Recovery Method developed by the late Dr. Abraham A. Low.

In our interview with Bertha Goldstein we began our research into the remarkable story of this physician. We are particularly indebted to his widow, Mae, for her protracted taped interviews, as well as for papers from Dr. Low's private files which revealed the depth and richness of the Recovery story. We are also grateful to her daughters, Mrs. David Cameron and Mrs. Tom Schmitt, to Dr. Low's sisters, Mrs. Jack Ditesheim and Mrs. Joe Alarado, to his sister-in-law, Mrs. Sol Low, and his nephew Leonard Low, as well as to all those others who shared with us Dr. Low's voluminous private correspondence and papers.

We wish to thank Miss Beatrice Wade, director of Curriculum in Occupational Therapy at the University of Illinois College of Medicine, who worked with Dr. Low in the early days of Recovery, and all those doctors and nurses and personal friends who, along with her, contributed their intimate recollections of him. We also wish to thank the physicians, directors of mental health clinics across the nation, and Mr. Herbert Rooney, chief of the Citizen Participation Branch of the National Institute of Mental Health, who have sent in their estimates of Recovery's usefulness as an adjunct to modern-day counseling. Mention must be made, too, of Wilma Troxel, director of the Library of Medical Sciences at the Medical Center of the University of Illinois in Chicago, who provided us with valuable information from her files.

We especially want to thank all the efficient and hardworking staff at Recovery National Headquarters in Chicago for their invaluable aid in helping us locate material, and those early members who knew Dr. Low as their physician and who, being freed of stigma, gave us their stories along with permission to use their full names. We wish to thank also all those hundreds of more recent Recoveryites across the country who sent us their detailed case histories. Length prohibits their inclusion in this book, but it was these touching histories that convinced us of the validity of the Method.

Last but not least, we owe a special debt of gratitude to Treasure Rice, who has painstakingly checked our manuscript for accuracy with regard to the organization.

Finally, we must point out that we have not presumed to try to explain Dr. Low's Method, since he himself said he couldn't. It is well demonstrated, however, in the true case histories in the book. Those who are further interested should either attend Recovery meetings or read Dr. Low's invaluable work, "Mental Health Through Will-Training," and, if possible, his more recent "Lectures to Relatives of Former Patients."

NO HOPELESS CASES
An Introduction

It was drawing to the close of the spring term at the University
of Strasbourg in Alsace that year of 1913, and a confident young
medical student who had made his mark as an outstanding
diagnostician during his four years at the school was preparing for
his final examination. One test required the student to diagnose a
patient. Young Abraham Low rendered what he was sure was a
masterly diagnosis, but to his chagrin he was informed that he
had failed the test. In anger he went to see his professor.

"Your diagnosis was brilliant," the professor told him, "but
you will never make a good physician with your present attitude,
for you said the case was hopeless in front of the patient. No good
doctor ever makes such a statement in the hearing of his patients.
But I will let you repeat the examination."

Out of this humiliating experience Abraham Low was later to
evolve the dictum which ruled his professional life: "There are
no hopeless cases—helpless perhaps, but not hopeless."

Abraham Low passed the second examination and went on to
Vienna, Austria, to complete his medical training, which included
courses in psychoanalysis. He moved to the United States and took
up residence in Chicago. Here within a few short years he re-
nounced psychoanalysis in favor of the socio-psycho-biological
approach to mental and emotional illness.

In 1925 he joined the staff of the University of Illinois Medical
School. And in 1931 he also served as assistant state alienist and
witnessed a sad parade of mentally and emotionally disturbed
patients during his visits to state hospitals. Their suffering stirred

him with an intense pity, but he refused to view the patients' fate as irrevocable, as long as there was no brain damage. Always there was the dictum from that long-ago diagnostic examination: "There are no hopeless cases."

By working with the patients he gradually developed a Method employing simple techniques, which proved to him conclusively that the patient could restore himself to health without enduring protracted—and costly—psychoanalytic sessions. Doctor and patients together evolved an organization called Recovery, Inc., which proved to be a potent form of group psychotherapy—a novel experiment for the Thirties.

That was the era when psychoanalysis was in its heyday, the doctor-to-patient relationship forming a tight little world in which it was unbelievable that the patient could do anything for himself. Upon this world Dr. Low's Method and his organization of laymen practicing simple psychotherapy techniques for themselves burst like a bombshell.

Most of Dr. Low's colleagues called his Method a crazy structure based on an impractical theory. And as so often happens to pioneers in any field, he had to pay for his audacity by suffering the persecution of those firmly entrenched powers with whom he took issue. They sealed him off in a vacuum of silence, refusing even to investigate his Method. Their antagonism was absolute and implacable.

Abraham Low was by nature no maverick. His years of training in European medical schools had given him a deep respect for medicine and psychiatry and for all his colleagues who were engaged with him in the work of healing minds and bodies. Over and over he tried the ways of reconciliation but to little effect. What his enemies wanted was not reconciliation but capitulation. He was given only one of two choices: a brilliant future as a conformist (his genius was widely recognized) or exile with his "unrealistic" dream, Recovery, Inc.

With his vision of the future as the dawning age of group psychotherapy, he chose Recovery, Inc. He was prepared to fight openly for it even though he knew that the penalty for such revolt might be the revocation of his license by his own profession. Yet for the sake of tens of thousands of sufferers in state hospitals who were being denied the benefits of the free group therapy service Recovery offered, he was prepared to make this ultimate sacrifice of his cherished career. But death closed the issue.

In the years that followed, few thought the vulnerable Recovery organization he left behind could survive. Certainly not his colleagues, most of whom believed that his charismatic personality, not his Method, was responsible for the high percentage of cures among his patients.

But Recovery did not die. Due to the heroic sacrifices of his widow, Mae Low, and his faithful lay lieutenants, all former patients, the little organization not only survived but began to spread. By 1971 some twenty-four years later, it was boasting branches in forty-five states. And membership lists show that tens of thousands of sufferers have joined it through the years.

Many of them have been cured and gone on their way. Others have stayed to act as leaders, motivated by a desire to help others as they were helped. What kind of people are these Recoveryites and what were their problems? The following four cases illustrate something of the range of disorders that have been helped through participation in Recovery and the application of Dr. Low's Method.

1.
The Case of Mary E.

"Could you deliberately harm someone?" Nine years ago this casual, speculative question was put by a girl friend to twenty-five-year-old bachelor girl, Mary E. Up until that time Mary had been suffering a variety of nervous symptoms: palpitations, air hunger, fatigue, a feeling of despair that expressed itself in protracted crying spells. The question oriented all these vague symptoms into one stark terror—the terror of committing suicide or of doing violence to others. Everywhere she looked she saw the instruments of death readily available: a harmless electric cord which she might use to hang herself, insecticides that might be dumped into food to poison herself or others. She stopped inviting guests to her home and she began avoiding people outside of it.

At the time Mary was working as a secretary for a doctor. She told him of her fears. It was just her nerves, he explained. She ought to get her mind off herself. Perhaps what she needed was a change of scenery.

Mary accepted the doctor's suggestion. She put her furniture in storage, sent a note of farewell to her mother and father, and left her home town under an assumed name so that she couldn't be traced. For two years she tried to flee her fears by moving around the United States, earning her way as she went. Every time the fears caught up with her, she would hurry on to a new place.

At last, however, the terrors subsided, and with a feeling of relief Mary returned home. Her family welcomed her. She got a new job, met a fine young man and was married.

Everything went well until her first child was born. Michael was two or three weeks old when Mary's mother came to visit. "Do you know how mothers used to kill their unwanted infants years ago?" she asked idly as she held Michael in her lap. "They used to stick a pin in the soft spot of the head."

The words reactivated the past and instantly the old terrors welled up in Mary. She couldn't trust herself to touch the baby. Even changing his diapers became torture for her. Most of all she didn't want to be left alone in the house with him.

She didn't dare confide in anyone, certainly not her husband. What would he think, married to a wife like this? A psychiatrist was out of the question—Mary was afraid he would have her committed.

Untreated, the terrors multiplied. Mary began spending most of the day crying in bed, or dragging herself around the house, forcing herself to do the simplest chores.

Then one day in 1962 she read an article in the paper. It was about a woman who also had been afraid of harming someone. This woman claimed to have conquered her fears through an organization known as Recovery, Inc. "That's been written for me," Mary thought. But it took her six months to make up her mind to attend her first Recovery meeting. Even then she didn't dare tell her husband where she was going. She just said she wanted to do some shopping downtown.

At the first meeting Mary bought Dr. Low's book, *Mental Health Through Will-Training*, and read it, though she didn't expect much help for herself. All the people at the meeting had looked too cheerful to her to have ever suffered the way she did.

By her third meeting Mary discovered that many of them had actually been worse off than she had ever been, and she became convinced that she could be helped too.

It took six more months before she could find the courage to tell her husband where she was going every Friday night. He worried about it because it sounded like such an offbeat organization to him. But whatever it was, he had to admit that things had happily changed for the better around the house.

The great test came when the second child, a girl, was born. Mary's training in Recovery had given her courage to confront any fears that might crop up. Not by a miracle but by her own effort she no longer had to live in despair and terror. And though today she doesn't need Recovery, she has remained in the organization to show her gratitude by helping newcomers back to health as once she was helped. And she is insuring her own continuing mental health at the same time.

2.
The Case of David S.

David S. of Duarte, California, was eighteen years old when he had his first breakdown. David, a high school senior, found himself in a state of confusion. Sometimes he would be filled with a sense of such excitement that he would roam the streets all night in his car. At other times he would retreat into a dream world where he could enjoy grandiose imaginary achievements. He would come out of this world into a life that looked so bleak and empty that he would entertain thoughts of suicide. He was afraid of people and suffered agonizing self-consciousness in their presence. He was frequently on the verge of tears. David's confusion became so serious he had to drop out of school and was taken to a psychiatrist by his family. The doctor diagnosed his illness as a schizophrenic breakdown. David was hospitalized for six weeks and went through a series of electroshock treatments.

After his hospitalization he began to withdraw more and more from the outside world. He keenly felt the stigma of his illness. He was constantly afraid of meeting people who might have heard about it. He feared encountering former acquaintances whose names and circumstances he could not now recall. He was sure his loss of memory was because of his illness. Even at home he felt the oppressive sense of stigma. A maternal uncle had once been in a mental hospital and the family had felt so ashamed of it that they had kept it a dark secret. Now David's mother tended to transfer the same feeling of disgrace to him.

So David left his family and went to live with a kindly couple. They gave him almost twenty-four-hour attention, encouraging him and employing him in the workshop they had established on their premises. So startling was his improvement under their devoted care that the doctor changed his diagnosis to "adolescent confusion" and pronounced him cured.

David wasn't really cured. He had fallen into a state of complete dependency on his friends and this bothered him. He consulted with a woman psychologist about his condition. Her diagnosis was also schizophrenia and she advised him to leave his friends and strive for his own independence.

David followed her advice but confusion remained a problem with him, so he went to see his third and last consultant, another psychiatrist. He diagnosed David's ailment as a neurosis with a tendency to schizophrenia at intervals. He gave David hope by telling him there was no need to fear a permanent handicap. Through the use of will power, David could learn to stand on his own two feet and deal with setbacks. The doctor also recommended Recovery.

David attended his first Recovery meeting in nearby Pasadena in 1967. The people he found there came from different backgrounds —clerks, housewives, attorneys, secretaries—but they all had one thing in common: they had suffered like himself and some had been much worse off than he was. They spoke openly of their illnesses in a matter-of-fact way.

Contact with these people helped David lose his own feeling of stigma. The self-respect he gained from disciplining himself kept him from wallowing in a feeling of rejection. He cultivated new friendships and became self-assured and confident. In place of the dream fantasies he learned to substitute realistic goals. Although a professional gardener, he had always wanted to be a machinist, but had never found the stability within himself to take the demanding courses required for this trade. With the help of the

Recovery Method, he returned to school to complete his training, and now is happily employed as a machinist.

3.
The Case of Glory K.

Glory K. lives in New Orleans, Louisiana. She was still in her teens when she had to be taken to the state hospital in Jackson, Louisiana. Glory's illness took a violent form. She would change suddenly from a normally sweet-tempered person into a screaming, irrational cyclone of fury. At such times she was terrified of what she would do. She had a constant fear that she would choke her mother, or use picks or similar sharp objects to harm others.

Sometimes Glory was pronounced cured and then she would be discharged from the hospital. But these discharges never lasted long. During one of them she married and had a son. Shortly after his birth she had to be taken back to the hospital. From then on she had no share in his upbringing.

As the years passed Glory slipped steadily downhill. She became untidy in dress. At times she had to be cuffed, hand and foot, to keep her from biting herself or punching in a window and using the glass to cut her arms in her rage against herself. Over and over Glory tried to commit suicide with bits of broken window panes. Sometimes she became so unmanageable that she had to be placed in a padded cell which had only one small window through which an attendant could keep an eye on her. The cell was furnished only with a mattress. Glory was allowed a dress but she would not wear it.

She was given many forms of therapy from hydrotherapy to a series of electroshock treatments. Nothing brought her more than temporary sanity. Then after some twenty-two years in the hospital, Glory picked up a magazine called *Catholic Action* which she found in the ward and came upon a story in it about Recovery, Inc. Glory became interested and wrote to the address listed. By return mail she received pamphlets describing the organization. Presently a woman member of Recovery came to call on her to tell her more about it. The chaplain of the hospital also talked to Glory about the possibility of leading a normal life.

Something changed in Glory. She made up her mind that if others could find sanity she could too. She showed such progress in the next twelve months that she was released to her family— twenty-three long years from the time she had first been hospitalized. Such releases had happened before but Glory intended to make this one permanent. She began attending Recovery meetings, going to as many as three a week.

Glory has never returned to the hospital as a patient. By the end of her first year in the outside world she had recovered sufficiently to start work. For the past eleven years she has been self-supporting. She also attends night school and has completed courses in typing, public speaking, and salesmanship. Today she's working on getting that long coveted high school diploma.

Glory was never able to care for or enjoy her son during his childhood. But she has learned through Recovery not to mourn a lost past. She is just grateful for the present. She says, "I don't think I will ever go back to the hospital. My son is a man now and I love him very much."

4.

The Case of Jack D.

Jack D. is forty-eight years old. He lives in Yonkers, New York. His father was a dedicated physician, applying himself almost entirely to his medical practice and leaving the management of the home to his wife. Jack had little paternal supervision or discipline. He was always an all-or-nothing individual and was allowed to give free vent to this personality characteristic. He would take up a project, work on it compulsively for a while, and then let it drop. His grades in high school revealed this tendency. One year he might stand at the top of his class in a given subject; the next he might be at the bottom in the same subject. He went through college, then enlisted for overseas duty during World War II. When he was discharged from the Army he entered law school. A year before his graduation he married an English girl whom he had met while stationed in England.

Jack took his first drink at the age of nineteen. It was a glass of ale which he couldn't even finish. But by the age of thirty-three he was a confirmed alcoholic, drinking great quantities of beer a day in addition to much hard liquor.

With a wife and two small children to support he was by this time heavily in debt to his father. His law practice was a shambles and his home life was threatened. He knew that something had to be done, so he joined Alcoholics Anonymous and quit drinking. But presently he discovered that giving up alcohol was not enough. Alcohol had alleviated many frightening symptoms. Now these began to come painfully to the fore.

One day when Jack had to sign twenty-four affidavits in front of four witnesses his hand began to shake. From then on he developed a phobia about signing his name in the presence of others. He began avoiding situations where he might be called upon to do so in public. Clients started complaining about his apparent procrastination. His practice began to dwindle away.

Jack was going to a psychiatrist who gave him helpful insights into the reasons for his fears and phobias. But somehow Jack wasn't able to translate these insights into practical action. Then one day in the fall of 1958 Jack heard about Recovery, Inc. He ordered literature from it and also bought Dr. Low's book. When he came to page 141 in the book he read of a patient who had also suffered the problem of being unable to write. The Recovery Method had cured this man, why couldn't it help him too?

Jack began going to Recovery meetings. There he learned the various simple techniques, or tools, which make up the Method. He began to put them into use, and was rewarded with changes in his life as time went by. Presently he was able to sign his name without difficulty. He dropped psychiatric counseling. It had already served its purpose in giving him insights into his behavior. Now he had the tools to act on those insights.

As he became more confident in himself, Jack's annual income began to increase until it had more than doubled the income of any of his troubled years. His wife, always loyal and cooperative, was now freed of the tension his former illness had caused. His two sons, eleven and eight, were benefiting from a more understanding, attentive father, an advantage Jack had not enjoyed in his childhood.

Such is the quality of the testimony for Recovery. But this

testimony no longer stops with the patients. Today group psychotherapy has come into its own. And Recovery is at last being recognized by professionals for the great aid it can be as an adjunct to their own counseling. Many of these psychiatrists hadn't even heard of the existence of the organization until years after Dr. Low's death.

In the past two or three years, important medical publications, such as *World Medical News, Medical Tribune, Your Health* (the official A.M.A. magazine), along with many others, have carried favorable articles on Recovery.

Mental health clinics, too, are introducing Recovery to the patients in their charge. And the organization is spreading by word of mouth and by articles in popular magazines and newspapers, which serve to bring the troubled layman in off the street to investigate for himself. Yet little is known of the man who was responsible for it all, a pioneer so far ahead of his time in the field of group psychotherapy that the world today is only just beginning to recognize the unique merits of his Method.

Once a small boy, the son of a Recovery member, asked his mother if Dr. Low was famous. When she laughingly passed his question along to the doctor, he didn't answer for a minute. Then with that whimsical smile so characteristic of him, he replied, "Tell your son that I just may be standing in the outer foyer of the Hall of Fame."

If he had been left standing there much longer, the world, including the members of his own organization, would have known little of the beginnings of this amazing man or the circumstances of his childhood which helped contribute to his extraordinary understanding of human nature. He himself talked but little of his past, and of the immediate family of his childhood only two sisters are left to reminisce.

CONTENTS

ONE

On February 28, 1891, in Baranow, Poland, a son was born to Lazar Low and his wife, the former Bluma Wahl. They called him Abraham. He was their fifth child and fourth boy.

Both Lazar and Bluma came from strict Orthodox Jewish families that had been longtime citizens of that section of Poland which, as part of the Austrian Empire, was known as Silesia. They were not without claim to fame.

Back in the Middle Ages when the king of Poland had died suddenly, Bluma Wahl's ancestor, Saul Wahl, minister of the exchequer, had been named temporary ruler until a new king could be selected. Thus Saul Wahl's kingship of a single day provided Bluma's children with an opportunity to list royalty among their ancestors.

Lazar's father had also had his importance. A very rich man, he had been mayor of the Polish town of Sczendishow, while his wife had acted as banker for the peasants. It was the custom for the Jewish people to have their big meal Friday night. Since payday was on a Sunday or Monday, few Jewish families in the village had the money to spend on a feast. So, Friday morning they would leave their jewelry with the mayor's wife and she would lend them money. Sunday or Monday, when they were paid, they would come back to redeem their valuables. One day, however, when everyone was in the synagogue, the Low house burned down. There was great lamentation over the lost jewelry, but Mrs. Low, who had suffered the greatest loss, said calmly, putting first things first, "Thank God, no child got hurt. We can always get back jewelry."

Such was the ancestry of the little boy born that 28th of February as the nineteenth century entered its last decade. Of his immediate parentage his father, Lazar Low, was one of nine children. The oldest, Nachum, was in real estate. Another brother owned a flour mill. The girls had all made more or less successful marriages. Lazar alone seemed destined for failure in everything he attempted. Well-versed in Jewish law, he knew little of the ways of the world. He drifted from occupation to occupation, trying his hand at everything and being subsidized in all his unfortunate ventures by his wealthy brother Nachum.

Perhaps a faded daguerreotype in the possession of Theresa, his youngest daughter, contains a clue to Lazar Low's perennial failures. It shows an old-fashioned European Jew with braided earlocks and a thick waist-length beard. The thin austere face wears a stern, set expression. But the deep-sunk eyes have a haunted, suffering look.

Lazar was an excitable man, given to sudden violent temper outbursts. They were often unleashed against the children, who unnerved him. They lived in terror of his physical brutality. "I think nobody understood it then," his daughter Fanny was to explain without rancor in later years. "Nobody analyzed why he was acting as he did. Jewish people, as you know, usually scold their children to correct them. They don't abuse them physically. We know now that our father was different because he was a nervous patient and needed help. We learned that from Abraham."

Lazar had another demoralizing failing: a propensity for drink, which might have formed the basis of his bad temper and which grew with the passage of years and the bombardment of disappointments.

Bluma, Lazar's wife, was one of six children—four girls and two boys. She was beautiful, as were all the women in her family, which was both affluent and socially prominent. The Wahls were known as the Rothschilds of the town where they lived.

Bluma endured her husband's succession of failures with resigned fortitude, following him loyally as he drifted across Europe all the way from Poland to Alsace-Lorraine in France. Year after year she bore him children, thirteen in all, nine of whom lived, five boys and four girls. They ranged from Ed, the oldest, through

Selma, Nat, Ben, Abraham, Rebekka, Sol, Fanny, and Theresa. Except for brunette Rebekka, they were all blue-eyed, blond children. None of them possessed a middle name, one given name being considered sufficient in Poland.

Bluma Low cherished her children, but she wasn't a demonstrative woman. Not one of them ever experienced a mother's kiss in childhood. This was because Bluma, like so many others of orthodox Polish families of the day, firmly believed in the superstition that to kiss a child was to bring it ill fortune.

Of all the Low children, young Abraham was the most imaginative, the liveliest. He was always the ringleader in their childish escapades. And he was a born storyteller. His fanciful yarns often held his brothers and sisters spellbound for hours at a time. He also showed a youthful acquisitiveness in the field of business which he was, to all appearances, to lose in later life. At one point during his childhood, his mother, beginning to miss all kinds of household commodities such as flour, sugar, milk, sweets, made a search of the premises and finally discovered the solution to the mystery in the attic. There stood Abraham surrounded by a cluster of neighborhood children to whom he was dispensing his mother's pilfered goods at a penny apiece.

In Strasbourg, where the family finally settled, it seemed as though at last the bad luck which had been dogging them had changed for the good. Lazar started a chicken farm outside the city and was proving that he had real talent in this work. By 1902 the chicken farm was well launched. Hundreds of fryers were almost ready for the market. They would bring in a substantial profit that would enable the family to enlarge its business. Bluma Low, whose health had not been of the best the last few years, was happier than she had been at any time of her married life.

Then one night an enemy stole into the hatchery and strewed poison meal in the chicken pens. Most of the chickens died in a single night. Lazar was bankrupted. The weight of that final loss was more than Bluma could bear. Shortly afterwards she died, at only thirty-nine years of age. The autopsy listed her death simply as heart failure. But the family diagnosed it differently. "We knew she died of a broken heart," her daughter Fanny was to maintain.

While the death of a mother is always a tragic event, it was far worse for the Lows. Separated from other relatives and im-

poverished in a foreign land, Lazar Low found himself with a
brood of small children to care for. Fortunately Selma, the oldest
girl, was eighteen. Lazar called her home from Switzerland, where
she was attending a home economics school, to help him with the
household.

Shortly afterwards, Ed, the oldest boy, made his way to America
where he was helped by an uncle on his mother's side who was in
the surgical appliance business. Nat, the second boy, became an
apprentice at a brace and truss manufacturing plant in Germany
to learn the mechanics of the surgical appliance business so that
he could join his brother later.

Remaining in Strasbourg was impossible for Lazar. He had to
return to Poland, where his brother had offered him the management of one of his large estates. But Poland was far away and it
would be too much for Selma to handle the numerous children
on the long trek back. Lazar decided to take with him only Selma,
Theresa, and Sol. Eleven-year-old Rebekka and four-year-old
Fanny were left in an orphanage just outside Strasbourg. Thirteen-
year-old Ben and twelve-year-old Abraham, who were attending
the Lyceum in Strasbourg, were placed in another orphanage so
that they could complete their studies.

2.

Those years were difficult for Abraham. He had lost first his
mother and then his family and home, and he now found himself
among strangers with only Ben to remind him of all the past large
circle of intimate life of which his mother had been the hub.
Beautiful and lost to him forever, wrapped in the mythology of a
child's memory, Abraham's mother haunted his dreams, as she
was to haunt the memory of her daughter Fanny for years.

It was a form of psychic amputation that left the young boy
self-conscious and high-strung. He developed a compulsion to bite
his fingernails and kept them always chewed to the quick. He
would explode with temper tantrums whenever he met with frustrations. Sometimes he had difficulty sleeping and tossed and
turned much of the night. At other times spasms would knot his
stomach, doubling him up in agony. A shy boy to begin with, he

developed an acute self-consciousness that expressed itself in pain-ful blushes.

When Ben left the orphanage to study electrical engineering, Abraham was also taken out of it and boarded with a rich local family, the Benzingers, to complete his high school education and act as tutor to their young sons. He proved himself so apt a teacher that the sons of the Benzingers' friends also began coming to him. The Benzingers had an affectionate regard for their brilliant young tutor and treated him as a member of their own family. They followed an elegant and gracious way of life made possible by generations of wealth, and it was these values and norms which governed Abraham's outlook in those early years.

As he entered puberty, however, he must have been made pain-fully aware of the wide gap that suddenly seemed to stretch be-tween the well-ordered environment of the Benzinger household and his own tumultuous inner situation. He began to be tor-mented by dreams, erotic dreams of his lost mother. He would wake from them drenched in sweat, lying sleepless in the dark night, loathing himself for what he regarded as his bestial nature. How else could he account for such dreadful visitations? He strove to banish the dreams, but they became increasingly re-alistic. Eventually, horrifying impulses began to invade his waking hours as well. Lascivious, lustful, obscene, murderous, they surged across the screen of his mind, leaving him exhausted. The more he tried to fight them off, the more rapidly they grew in number and variety. Sometimes his heart would start racing or an agonizing pressure would build in his head and a tight band would seem to be squeezing his chest, making it difficult for him to breathe.

In later years he was to describe those adolescent experiences to his patients with remarkable candor: "And then there are sex impulses, particularly things that happened in the dream . . . the fact of sleeping with one's mother or with one's father. And people in general, if they have such dreams, are thoroughly ashamed of them. Well, there is nothing to be ashamed of. I remember distinctly having had such dreams and at that time they scared me no end and today, of course, I have gone through the mill of training and I know there's nothing to it, and I am ready to admit that I had such dreams and had them fre-quently. . . ."

But no training was available to that young boy of long ago, caught in the mesh of his terrifying impulses. As he grew more and more preoccupied with his condition, his self-consciousness increased. His blushing became so acute that the least criticism or fancied slur would send the hot crimson tide flooding up his neck to his forehead. Beads of perspiration would break out. He was sure all eyes were curiously upon him.

Finally, after one particularly embarrassing incident, he decided he'd had enough of such torment. He began to withdraw from the company of his friends until he became almost a recluse. Isolation only increased his suffering, and he had nowhere to turn, no one to whom he could talk.

At last he decided to see the Benzingers' family physician. But once in the doctor's office he sat tongue-tied, afraid to tell his troubles even to this grave, attentive man who sat across the desk from him. If he were so indiscreet as to do so, wouldn't he be judged insane and committed? So he complained instead of the pain in his chest and voiced a fear of tuberculosis. It was for this that the doctor examined him and wrote out a prescription which he instructed Abraham to take faithfully. Abraham was always to feel gratitude to that long-ago doctor whose calm, authoritative manner and whose refusal to launch into windy dissertations on his vague illness had spared him further confusion.

That visit seemed to be the turning point in the young boy's condition. He took the prescription faithfully, and his courage to face life grew. A gregarious, fun-loving boy by nature, he decided he'd had enough of his self-imposed isolation. He made up his mind to rejoin his schoolmates. And if he blushed, well, then he would just blush—what difference did it make!

The decision was easier made than followed. At first Abraham had to fight his own inclinations to run and hide whenever he felt his face reddening. But he stood his ground, and gradually he realized the blushing was diminishing until he wasn't much bothered by it any more, and then only in strange surroundings or unfamiliar situations. The racing thoughts and shocking dreams had faded too. He had come out of that dark land, in which for a brief spell he had wandered, a bewildered traveler. Had he been suffering just the pangs of puberty, more intense in himself than in others? Or had it been the shadow of an illness that he was to become more and more acquainted with in later years as a psychiatrist?

In 1910 Abraham was in his last year of high school at Strasbourg's famous Lyceum. The talents of this brilliant young student were recognized by all his professors, but especially those in language and philosophy. He had acquired a fine mastery of English, French, Latin, and classical Greek. And he was a voracious reader for whom philosophers held a special attraction. His favorite at that time was Nietzsche.

His mathematics course might not have fared so well except for the Prussian instructor who taught it. Though Abraham preferred the other subjects, he didn't dare go to this man's class unprepared. "My math teacher would have booted me if I didn't know my lesson," he was to tell his wife in later years.

3.

It was sometime in 1910 that Abraham paid his first visit to his family in Poland. Much had changed. Several years before, Lazar had remarried. The new wife, Chaja, came from Bluma's home village. Selma, no longer needed at home, had been forced into an arranged marriage, and full of bitterness, she had left with her new husband. Rebekka and Fanny had been brought home from the orphanage. But then Rebekka had been sent to Lemberg, Poland, to be a companion to her maternal grandmother, and shortly afterwards Sol joined her there. Sol had such an active dislike for his stepmother that it was impossible for the two to stay under the same roof. The only children left in the home then were Fanny and Theresa and a little half-brother, Nutek.

As manager for his brother Nachum, Lazar Low collected the rents from the peasants who leased the surrounding farmlands. But he had had such indifferent success that to augment his income he had rented a house and established a small tavern and general store in the little village of Niedary, where the family lived.

The tavern business had worsened Lazar's drinking problem. He now began every day with a glass of something alcoholic and his temper was roused by his daughters' smallest offenses, even imagined ones. One time when Fanny was dutifully peeling potatoes, a fist was suddenly driven into her face. Her father had stopped to supervise her work and felt she was cutting the peelings too thick.

The girls' stepmother had little affection for them either. She flogged them on occasion, but for the most part she heaped work on them. The girls were always late for school because they first had to finish the morning housekeeping chores. When they came home in the afternoon there were mountains of beer glasses to be washed and dried.

There were many tempestuous quarrels between Lazar and his wife, making life even more miserable for the girls. They soon discovered a barometer though, by which they could check the temper of the household and conduct themselves accordingly. There were twin beds in the room which their father and stepmother shared. When the beds were shoved together, the girls knew peace prevailed. When the beds were pulled to opposite sides of the room, they knew that another conjugal fight was in progress and the house would be an armed camp.

It was to this unhappy home that Abraham was making his way, arriving on a Friday afternoon. All the Jewish women in the village were preparing food for the Sabbath, carrying the dishes they had fixed to the large communal oven provided by the village bakery. The dishes would cook through the night and could be removed the following day when needed without breaking the prohibition against working on the holy day.

Heads must have craned to see the handsome stranger in his school uniform walking jauntily down the dusty village street. "Lazar Low's son," the whisper went around. People took notice, too, of how halfway home the young man fell in with one of the lovely village girls. Soon he was gallantly carrying her bundle of food to the bakery for her. Together they strolled along, chattering and laughing. He was at the age where every girl wore a magical aura of mysterious promise for him, and this chance encounter made his day complete. By the time he reached home the story of his chivalry, buzzing along as though on wings, had already preceded him.

His father greeted him formally in the front room which had been taken over by the combined tavern and general store. Abraham's stepmother and little Nutek, to whom he was introduced, were complete strangers to him. His sisters, Theresa and Fanny, might as well have been, because it was so long since he had last seen them and they had grown so much. At the time of his visit, Theresa was about eight, and Fanny, eleven.

The two children were as different in personality as two people could be. Theresa was full of fire and would risk a flogging or any other punishment to assert her independence. Her one fear was of being broken as, when only a child of two, she had seen Selma, broken and crying. "I hope you never have to cry like this," Selma had told her.

Fanny, by contrast, withdrew into herself as if to become as unobtrusive as possible. She had been like this even in the orphanage. Once while removing a dress being fitted on the child, a seamstress was shocked to discover that she had pinned a pinch of the girl's skin to the material. It must have been very painful but Fanny had not so much as whimpered.

The two children reacted characteristically to Abraham's homecoming. To both he was a mysterious messenger from the free outside world. That world was expressed in everything about him: his confident and easy manner, the carefree expression of his warm blue eyes, his infectious laughter. Fanny was fearful of giving her heart to this engaging stranger and greeted him with blushing, tongue-tied shyness. Theresa clung to him, chattering away, completely at ease. Since Fanny seemed to avoid him, Abraham saw more of Theresa during those few days of his first visit.

His relationship with the little girl alternated between warm affection and sparring hostility. He could never be sure when he might rouse her to one of her sudden flares of temper. Once when he refused her something she threw an inkwell at him. Another time she tore up the term paper upon which he had been working. He lost his temper, of course. She always saw to that. It was her one victory in a world in which she felt beset on every hand, in which the fear of physical pain could no longer cow her. She wouldn't give up teasing until she had him shouting, berating her, stamping around, shaking his finger in her face in a paroxysm of exasperation. But he never struck her, no matter how much she provoked him. This was the greatest miracle about her older brother to Theresa, in whose world blows and cuffs were a common occurrence.

Then there was the magical day when Abraham took her by horse and buggy to the town of Bochnia seven miles away. She was beside herself with delight when he ushered her into a restaurant. She had never eaten out before. Trembling, she let Abraham help her to a seat at a table. But she couldn't sit still. She kept wriggling and squirming as she tried to take in everything. When the waitress arrived with a loaded tray, Theresa bounced up suddenly and upset it, sending food flying in all directions. People turned to stare, to laugh, to gossip. The waitress glared. The old embarrassment flooded up in Abraham. Crimson mottled his face and he cast a long, stern look of accusation at the little girl who sat huddled in her chair, mute and chagrined. The day was now irrevocably spoiled.

Abraham was soon made painfully aware of a more poignant side to this strange little sister. It showed itself only at night at the end of yet another loveless day. Then she would come stealing softly into his room and crawl into his bed. Hungry to be close to someone, to love and be loved in turn, she would press against him and spill out her grievances in a rush of tears—all that she and Fanny suffered: the beatings, the scoldings, the hunger when there wasn't enough food in the house, the cold when there was no coal and their clothing too light to provide warmth, the dull drudgery.

Abraham would put his arms around his little sister and hold her tight as she talked. What more could he do? For he was only a schoolboy and didn't count for much in this family where each member's importance was judged by his earning capacity. When Theresa ended her recital of griefs, he would whisper encouragement to her until, comforted and heavy with sleep, she would slip back again to her own bed.

TWO

~

The Lows were a clan made up of striking individualities. Scattered at an early age, they had no opportunity to build up deep affections for one another. But there was a fierce loyalty among them which expressed itself in tangible aid, not only to family members but even to distant cousins in need.

It was this loyalty that motivated Ed when he first came to the United States. He would never rest content until he had brought to the New Country all those Lows whom he felt would benefit from the emigration. It wasn't easy for him at first. Wages were low for unskilled labor. But Ed was determined that out of those low wages he would save enough money for Nat's fare over. This was accomplished by sleeping on rooftops during the humid summers, by stinting himself on food, and by washing his own clothes. At last in 1907 he was able to send for his brother.

When Nat came, his technical knowledge of surgical supply manufacturing enabled him to obtain a lucrative job in a Brooklyn firm. He stayed there just long enough to build up a little capital. Then he and Ed established their own business in New York City. Their success was phenomenal. By 1909 Ed could contemplate marriage and the young men were sending allowances to their brothers and sisters in Europe and preparing to bring them over one by one. Ben, Selma and her husband, and Sol were the first to come. Generous allowances were provided Theresa and Fanny in Niedary and Abraham also received his share.

It had finally been decided that Abraham should be a doctor.

11

That fall he enrolled at the University of Strasbourg Medical College, and to help with expenses he still did tutoring.

At the University of Strasbourg a whole new and exciting life was opened up to him. In the intellectual milieu of the ancient university, Abraham felt completely at home. His reading widened to include such philosophers as Fichte, Kant, Schopenhauer, and Hegel. His knowledge of classical Greek and Latin enabled him to read the ancient philosophers in their own tongue. His knowledge of English and French gave him an equal advantage with the literature of those countries. He was early and lastingly to be affected by the writings of Shakespeare.

Religions interested him deeply too. He not only pursued the study of his own Hebrew faith, but also made a close acquaintance with the writings of such men as Meister Eckhart, the mystic; Thomas Aquinas, the Dominican Scholastic, and Ignatius Loyola, militant founder of the Jesuits. In later years he was to express great admiration for Loyola's system of disciplines.

In those days Abraham would certainly have been numbered among the intellectual elite of the great university. But he was no glib young sophisticate cramming his head with knowledge to be spun out of an almost photographic memory when the occasion called for erudite showmanship. It had come to him early that all the wisdom he was garnering could be translated into terms of everyday living and that this, rather than the practice of a hollow etiquette, was the mark of true culture. In the light of this awareness he could no longer indulge in his childish outbursts of temper and began working on himself to restrain them. He also started cultivating a humorous attitude toward his own foibles and sense of importance—later defined by him as "the inner smile."

By nature he was primarily a teacher, and the urge that had prompted him to amuse his brothers and sisters with storytelling, that had made tutoring such an enjoyable occupation for him in his high school days, now expressed itself in bull sessions with his fellow students at the university. He liked to gather them around him to discuss the extracurricular subjects which he was investigating. So fascinating did they find these discussions that he was always surrounded by an admiring group.

His professors quickly recognized the young man's brilliance and his academic enthusiasms. One, a man of some prominence, offered to be his sponsor in his climb up. "You must make one concession, though," the professor warned him. "You must be realistic. There's a great deal of anti-Semitism in the world today. You won't have much of a chance with a name like Abraham. If you'll change it, I can push you all the way to the top."

Abraham knew that he could and would back his word. But he shook his head. "I'm sorry," he responded firmly. "But I would never change my name for any reason."

He wore that name like a banner all his life, and when older members of the family often shortened it to Abe, it was without his approval.

Toward another professor, an ardent Zionist, Abraham was more responsive. It was during the era when Jews all over the world were working to establish a nation in Israel, the Promised Land. And to prepare for that day, funds were being collected to buy land in Palestine and to build hospitals, schools, and other public buldings. The professor's enthusiasm for this cause was so infectious that soon young Abraham was spending his spare time traveling with him through France and Switzerland, lecturing on Zionism and appealing for funds. That his intellectualism was only half of Abraham's character, that he was also a man of deep warmth and passionate convictions, is revealed by his devotion to the Zionist cause.

This same naive, almost unreasoning warmth, he brought to his relationships with the opposite sex. He enjoyed the company of pretty girls and often fell in love with them. Those were the slow-paced days of old courtly customs and frozen social attitudes. The young women he met in the Benzingers' drawing room or the homes of other families led sheltered lives. Few sought or even dreamed of a higher education. Their schooling consisted mainly of learning the social graces, acquiring fluency in French, and proficiency at the piano. This became Abraham's ideal of a well brought-up young lady, an anachronism to which he would cling all his life.

As for clothes, he never paid much attention to them. His wardrobe was simple, because to him being well-dressed was to be clad in a dark blue or black, conservatively styled business suit. He allowed himself one luxury item—a tuxedo, an absolute necessity for almost any social gathering in the prewar upper-class life of Europe.

2.

During the summer another facet of Abraham's nature was given full play. He was an ardent outdoor man and loved such sports as hiking, skiing, and skating, but skiing in particular was a rich man's sport in those days. Abraham could indulge in it by accompanying his tutorial charges on skiing expeditions in the Alps. He also chaperoned them on hiking trips around Europe, getting paid for his services.

These vacations were packed with robust fun and the Rabelaisian jokes indulged in by young men on a lark. There were beer bouts in German taverns along the way. There were nights in the open in lonely forests or on long, sloping meadowlands above Alpine lakes. Visions of those clear blue lakes, cupped in their amphitheaters of great snow mountains, would haunt him forever.

In the summer of 1912 Abraham stopped to visit his family again in Niedary. Now twenty-one, he was wearing a different kind of uniform. To fulfill the required military training he had enlisted in the Army under the special classification of medical student. For the next four years he would be expected to serve three months of every year as a medic either on the field or in the hospital, with the rank of a junior officer.

In his Austrian uniform with his heavily accented Polish speech and his Germanic ways and gestures, he stood out in the tight-knit little community of Niedary. And although he was Polish by blood, he came to be known by the nickname "German."

Abraham's ardor for the Zionist movement was still as strong as ever and was one of the reasons he had stopped off at Niedary. He had brought a dozen blue boxes with him, and now Theresa scurried around at his bidding summoning all the Jews in the village to the Low home. Soon the tavern was crowded with people.

Standing before them, Abraham described in glowing terms the hardship which Dr. Theodor Herzl, the founder of the Zionist organization, had suffered. He asked the peasants to take the little blue boxes home and use them to collect change to aid Herzl's dream of the new nation. Although the peasants of Niedary were not rich, so eloquent was young Abraham that they accepted all the little boxes. Abraham did more than rouse the peasants—he kindled Theresa's enthusiasm for a reunited Israel, an enthusiasm which was to stay with her all her life.

3.

Abraham returned to his last year at the University of Strasbourg and was graduated from there in the spring of 1913. That fall he entered the medical school of the University of Vienna. He no longer had to tutor to support himself, for sufficient money was now coming in from America to supply all his needs. He boarded with his cousin, Max Low, and began his final years of training.

It was a time of tension in Europe. The continent seethed with conflicting power drives that exploded into World War I the summer of 1914. All over Europe young men were being conscripted, and Abraham was called into active service with the Austrian Army.

The captain to whose unit he was assigned was anti-Semitic and would not recognize the young medic's training because of his Jewish birth. Abraham, shorn of his special-officer rating, found himself a private on the eastern front. There he learned firsthand all the dangers, the loneliness, the bone weariness that can un-nerve a common soldier in the trenches.

There was one three-month period on the front during which his whole unit had no time to bathe or shave or even to remove their clothing. Finally, when the corps was relieved, the men found that the long johns they had on had completely disinte-grated, leaving only tattered remnants in their boots.

It wasn't all grime and horror, however. There were deep belly laughs over many a comedy of error, and simple jokes. Just to be alive was worth a laugh in itself. There were clandestine dates with girls in the villages through which the troops passed. And there was the close companionship of men bound together by danger and hardship. Abraham came to realize that the suffering the common soldiers endured was balanced by the sense of security they shared when led by a commander who exuded self-confidence. Then the sense of solidarity among them was so strong that they often ignored their own safety in the thick of battle to come to the aid of some fallen companion. That was the bitter-sweet draught of war.

Abraham spent more than four months as a private. Then one day an emergency arose and the unit found itself short of medics. A young lieutenant, discovering Abraham's training, restored him to his rightful rank. From then on he was to see the war through a doctor's eyes.

At times he traveled along roads lined with peasant women wizened from starvation because foraging troops had left no food behind. In shrill, pitiful voices they begged for scraps from the passing soldiers. Some of the women were in the last stages of pregnancy and Abraham stopped to deliver their babies, who were surprisingly fat and healthy in stark contrast to their emaciated mothers. But he knew, sorrowfully, that these babies could not live long, for there would be no milk for them in their mothers' withered breasts. Though he was not yet a licensed physician, surgeons were so scarce on the front that he had to do his share of operating, tending, and repairing the mutilated bodies of fine young men, often seeing them die despite all he could do. The waste of human life by war appalled him.

For long months Abraham's family in Niedary received no word of him. When finally he came to visit them on a short furlough, he was a different young man, more mature, his eyes old with the peculiar knowledge which war brings. A picture of the time shows him in a wrinkled uniform, his beard matted, his face lined beneath the peak of his worn cap.

He stayed only a little while in Niedary. Then he returned to the front, leaving behind a family feeling the pinch of want. The generous allowances which the brothers from America had been faithfully sending had been cut off by the fighting, and as the war continued even the family home was jeopardized. With the Russians advancing into Poland, the Lows fled to Prague, Czecho-slovakia, where they stayed for the remainder of the war.

4.

Then at last it was over. With the signing of the Armistice on
November 11, 1918, the whole world seemed to go mad with joy.
Everywhere there were celebrations, dancing in the streets, the
pure intoxication of peace, of the conviction that the war to end
all wars had just been concluded. Nowhere else, perhaps, was
there such abandon as in conquered Austria, where an Empire
had been smashed and with it the stability of century-old customs.
Vienna society abandoned itself to a frenzied postwar whirl of
partying. It was into this wild sophisticated gaiety that Abraham
was plunged when he returned to his studies. He joined the madness, danced and drank and played with the revelers and often
saw in the dawn, usually with a different woman companion.

Despite all these distractions, he finished his medical schooling
and in 1919 began his two years of internship at the Allgemeines
Krankenhaus, the foremost hospital in Vienna.

To his medical studies he had added courses in psychoanalysis.
This new therapy, that focused like a giant spotlight on the psyche
of emotionally and mentally disturbed patients, was a fascinating
science to him. He undertook the new study enthusiastically,
reading the textbooks and attending lectures by the Freudians,
including Dr. Sigmund Freud himself. He also studied Dr. Carl
Gustav Jung's theories, which he felt were too mystical for practical purposes, and Dr. Alfred Adler's conclusions, which impressed him with their emphasis on the human being's desire
for domination.

It was as a psychiatrist practicing Freudian psychoanalysis that
he was to begin his career. And no one was more conscientious
than he as he probed into the dark thoughts and the incestuous
and violent and even seemingly innocuous dreams of his patients.
No one pursued more doggedly the dark hidden urges and desires
that lay under even the most innocent sounding expressions. And
once found, no one showed greater zeal in exorcising them from
the patients prostrate before him.

In later years, reminiscing with rare humility and humor about those days of his psychoanalytic fervor, he was to tell his patients, "In former days I was a big professional. I was the official, well, and the patient—what is a patient anyhow, you know! When I was the official opposite a patient, I had to show smartness, cleverness, knowledge. I had to impress the patient with my professional art. That was about the situation, until here in this group the patient became the supreme object of my work—not only my smartness but the patient's suffering."

5.

After the war was over, allowances began coming in once more from America, and Nat resumed his yearly trips to Europe to visit the various members of the family. Probably it was through Nat that Abraham learned of the move his sisters had made because life at home had become more intolerable than ever for them.

Taken out of school, they had been forced to work full time in their father's tavern. Now in their teens and old enough to be independent, they had decided that their situation could be changed only by running away to their relatives in Kraków. Here Nat had visited them and made arrangements to send them their allowances directly.

The following year, some time in the late summer or early fall of 1919, Abraham's father, an ill, bitter old man, full of anger toward his daughters, arrived in Vienna to put himself under the care of his intern son. Abraham's examination revealed cancer of the lymph glands of the neck. It was already in the terminal stage and all Abraham could do was to make him as comfortable as possible during his last days.

The lonely isolation of this man, sealed within his violent temper, his life of perennial failure, and his tragic lack of communication with his children, must have affected Abraham deeply. How little he had known his father in life, and now he was dying, a stranger still. Abraham was with him at his death, only a few months after his arrival in Vienna. And it was Abraham who saw that he received a proper burial in a Viennese cemetery.

Shortly afterwards, Nat returned to Europe, this time to take care of his father's estate. He was surprised to find that Lazar Low, who had lived most of his life in penury, had left behind a legacy that amounted to more than one hundred thousand dollars. Generously, Nat decided to give all the inheritance to the widow with her small son to support. He offered to invest it for her in the United States, but Chaja Low could not bring herself to entrust it to anyone. Six months later the fortune was wiped out by inflation. Still the brothers could not ignore their relationship to their half-brother Nutek. They continued sending allowances to the widow and her son. It was their money which also put Nutek through medical school.

THREE

In 1921 Abraham finished his internship in Vienna and was ready
for the trip to America. Theresa had made the journey the year
before, Fanny was going now. On Nat's next European visit he
made the necessary arrangements and took her with him for a
reunion with Abraham.

While Nat returned to America, Abraham and Fanny prepared
themselves for the journey, buying themselves new wardrobes with
the generous allowances Nat had left them. The gay, sophisticated
city of Vienna awed Fanny, who had grown up in the country,
and in this new setting her brother seemed like a stranger to her.
She was twenty-three and he was thirty, a mature young physician now.

By this time he had fallen in love with a beautiful Viennese
girl and the parting was painful. Abraham consoled her by promising there would be a reunion once he had established himself
in the new world. And then he and Fanny were off, with a brief
stop at Munich for a last visit with the kindly Benzinger family
who had moved to that city.

Hospitable as usual, they invited their former tutor and his
sister to dinner. Fanny went reluctantly. The fine home to which
the butler admitted them filled her with dismay. She felt awk-
ward and self-conscious before the poised family who greeted her
so graciously.

Abraham, on the other hand, moved at ease among them, saying just the right things, doing the right things. She marveled
at him. More than ever he seemed like a stranger to her. Hoping

she wouldn't embarrass him, she retreated into a corner where she made herself as inconspicuous as possible. And everything seemed to be going well until dinner was announced.

Fanny was not prepared for the sight that met her eyes when she followed her host and hostess into the dining room. The table, spread with expensive linen, sparkled with crystal and silverware. Three glasses to every place, several forks, knives and spoons of various sizes and shapes at every plate. How would she ever be able to make her way through this array of silverware? She looked at Abraham. He didn't seem at all concerned. She edged to his side.

"What shall I do, Abraham?" she whispered in desperation. "I don't know how to behave in such company. I never have been to such a house."

She was afraid he might be ashamed by her confusion, but his blue eyes smiled encouragement. He was no longer the callow youth of nineteen who had been embarrassed and angry because a little girl had upset a tray of food.

"Just sit down, Fanny," he advised her. "Watch the others. Do what they do."

Fanny followed his advice. She kept an alert eye on those around her, but most of all she watched Abraham. How skillfully he picked up the right forks, knives, and spoons. He knew the mysterious purpose of each, when to use it and when to discard it for another. He had grown up knowing. But his simple advice enabled her, the novice, to make her way through the elegant dinner without disgracing herself.

2.

From Munich Fanny and Abraham traveled on to Le Havre, where they boarded the French steamer, the *France*. It was a plush crossing and Abraham enjoyed it. Fanny saw little of her brother because, although he had left behind a deathless love in Vienna, crossing the Atlantic without participating in the social activities aboard ship would have been dull. And Abraham, by nature too gregarious to enforce solitude upon himself, quickly struck up an acquaintance with a pretty Romanian girl. It was just a light-hearted companionship and both of them knew that when the ship docked it would all be over. But meanwhile it was pleasant to dine and dance together and to stroll hand-in-hand around the deck.

Fanny didn't take part in any of the activities. Her cabin was an excellent hiding place and she spent most of her time there where she felt comfortable. Subject to the same embarrassing spells of blushing that Abraham had once suffered, there were periods in her life when she felt so vulnerable to the outside world that she simply withdrew into her shell.

She did not dream of discussing her problems with Abraham. He had her admiration but not her confidence; too many years of separation lay between them. They never spoke of the tragic past which they had shared, or of their mother lost to them so early in childhood.

To Fanny that mother was at best a beautiful shadow whose appearance she knew only from memory, because no pictures of her existed. Fanny had never been sure of her mother's love since the day a family acquaintance had come to the orphanage to take her walking. During the course of the walk, the woman had suddenly gossiped to the child, "You know your mother never liked you. When you were only a few months old she sent you away to your father's mother to be cared for." Unable to weigh the woman's malicious stupid remarks, the shy little girl had simply accepted her words at face value. But the shock would linger for years and give her the feeling that she was on earth by sufferance only.

Abraham must have been aware of his sister's excessive shyness. Yet he never spoke to her about it, nor tried to draw her out, though he was very fond of her. But he was not a man to give advice unless asked and his medical training had taught him the inadvisability of counseling family members.

April 15, a year to the day from the time that Theresa had arrived in America, the *France* docked in the New York harbor. Fanny and Abraham found their brothers waiting to greet them: Ed, a big man, tallest of the whole family; Nat much smaller, carefully and expensively groomed; Sol, never one to pay much attention to fashion, dressed in casual slacks and open shirt; and Ben, handsome and debonair, irresponsible and utterly delightful.

Besides the brothers, a group of American Zionists had come to greet Abraham. Among them was Louis Lipsky, one of the biggest names in the Zionist movement. Their coming signified the important place Abraham had earned for himself in the organization.

After the greetings were over, Abraham and Fanny were driven to the family flat on Faile Street in the Bronx. There Selma and Theresa were waiting. For the first time since their mother's death, the Low family was reunited with the exception of Rebekka in faraway Poland. Ed, of course, being married, had his own home. The others lived together in the flat. There were Sol, Abraham, Fanny, Ben, Nat, Theresa, and Selma. Selma's little boy Harry also stayed with them and sometimes her second husband, William Coteus. Selma and Willy often quarreled and then Willy would move away, but they always got back together again. In addition to the brothers and sisters, cousin Max also shared the flat. That made ten in all.

3.

Abraham had to wait six months before he could take the medical examinations that would qualify him to practice in the state. And this gave him time to acquaint himself with New York. In the Twenties it was a razzle-dazzle, fast-moving city. The fastest city in the world, the New Yorkers liked to boast. Almost everything excited Abraham's wonder: skyscrapers, steep canyon streets down which people rushed, the sea of humanity in Times Square day and night, milling beneath the flashing, winking electric signs that blossomed into life with the dusk. Everything seemed geared to frenzied action. The city, dedicated to mechanical perfection and streamlined efficiency, with no deep roots in the past, bewildered Abraham.

He was bewildered, too, by many other seeming peculiarities in the American way of doing things. There were the drugstores, for instance. In Europe their sole purpose was to dispense drugs. In New York they were not only catchalls for every kind of household equipment, but also housed soda fountains and lunch counters. Subways with their crowding, shoving swarms of commuters, all fighting to get into the train at the same time, astonished him. Then there was the fad of chewing gum. It was the era of Wrigley's glory and everywhere Abraham looked he saw the frantic motion of hundreds of jaws, young and old, male and female, chomping lustily with now and then a loud snap.

American schools nonplused him with their emphasis on splendid buildings, swimming pools, and the latest athletic equipment. Everything seemed to be geared to comfort. He felt that the drab European schools with their strict disciplines were a far better preparation for life than these plush buildings. And he noted that children who graduated from the European grammar schools of that day seemed to know as much as the high school graduates in the United States.

Plunged into this strange new world in which he was still feeling his way, Abraham found it pleasant to be surrounded at home by family members who were rooted in the familiar Old World way of living. Dinners in the Low flat were delightful affairs. Selma did the cooking, and every night from six to ten o'clock, the brothers and sisters gathered at the big round table standing in the center of the room. When dinner was over, the family didn't separate immediately. For an hour or two they would sit around the table telling jokes and laughing, the room rocking with their merriment.

Abraham's was a special kind of laughter—the same laughter which had so brightened Theresa's and Fanny's life in the dreary house in Poland. It was more an infectious chuckle than an out-and-out guffaw, but it was so wholehearted that as he laughed tears would stream down his face.

Selma, a stout woman with a domineering manner and a kind heart, was the matriarch of the family. She ran it along lines of deeply ingrained thrift and was concerned over the tendency of all her brothers, but most especially Ben, to pay little attention to the value of money. Ben, who was of a convivial nature, was imposed upon by his friends. They so often made off with his underwear, several pairs at a time, that he began buying it in lots. Selma couldn't bear such squandering of goods. So when Ben brought home his stack of new underwear, she would put most of it away in her capacious trunk, which also engulfed the excess clothing that other members of the family might purchase on a buying spree. Should loss of fortune visit the family, Selma reasoned, she would have enough outfits to tide everyone over. But since the Lows continued amazingly prosperous, Selma's trunk became packed to overflowing with articles that no one ever saw again.   ———

4.

Early in 1922 Abraham obtained his license and was ready to start practicing psychoanalysis in New York. During that time the family split up. Nat got married, Max moved to California, and Selma went to the Catskills to do the cooking at an old people's home.

Sol, Abraham, Ben, Fanny, and Theresa moved into an apartment on the second floor of a building on Seventy-first Street and Broadway. The apartment also provided Abraham with office space. The front door opened on a large foyer which he could use for a reception room. His office was to the left. The brothers generously fixed it up for him, having it painted white at Abraham's directions and equipping it with office furniture.

To the right of the foyer was a big living room which could be used to seat any overflow of patients from the waiting room. The kitchen was in the rear and there were three bedrooms. The two girls shared one and there was one each for Sol and Abraham. Ben slept in a little room which had previously been used as a maid's room. But preferring to go his own way, he didn't stay long.

At first Theresa and Fanny shared the housework in their new quarters, taking turns cooking the meals. But when Fanny developed a persistent cough which was diagnosed as incipient tuberculosis, she was sent to the Catskills to be looked after by Selma until her health returned. This left Theresa to take care of the housekeeping, the laundry, and the cooking for the family. A lot of her time went into cleaning, dusting, and polishing the office which Abraham liked to have spotless.

He soon had a busy medical practice, but he didn't confine himself to work. He still enjoyed lecturing before groups, and he gave many talks to the Zionist organizations in New York. He was also a frequent guest speaker at a club of German intellectuals. He could converse in seven languages, but he was of course most proficient in German, which he had spoken from childhood. It was in this tongue that he gave his brilliant dissertations on the subject of psychoanalysis. One of the papers he read to a fascinated audience was a psychoanalytic study of Shakespeare's *Hamlet*.

There were many social evenings in the Low apartment, too. Friends and associates of the family would drift in and out for drinks and refreshments, and stimulating conversations would last well into the night. Abraham enjoyed drinking with friends, but alcohol wasn't necessary to his well-being. Like his cousin Max he had one addiction—he enjoyed fine cigars. He smoked them almost chain fashion and the aroma of expensive tobacco became an integral part of the apartment.

By New World standards Abraham was a shy man, but he had an innate self-respect which transformed his shyness into a dignified reserve that gave confidence to his patients. There were other things that made him stand out: the genuine understanding and kindness which was part of his nature and which people quickly divined; his strong Viennese accent of which he himself seemed almost totally unaware; the Old World courtliness to which he still faithfully adhered and which struck bluff New Yorkers as charming. Yet the New World had also been subtly at work fashioning him, too. His use of the English language was precise and beautiful, especially for a foreigner, yet he was not adverse to sprinkling it with Brooklynese and Yiddish idioms if they expressed his meaning.

While he still corresponded with the girl he had left behind, the separation from her had given him perspective and the magic he had felt in her presence was not communicated by her letters. There was something disappointingly shallow about them and he felt disillusioned. The girl, too, seemed to be losing interest. Her letters grew more and more infrequent. Before Abraham had been in New York a year, their correspondence had stopped completely.

By this time the young physician's talents as a neurologist had been recognized and he was given a grant by the Rockefeller Foundation to do further research on the subject. It was during this period of his life that he met and fell in love with a beautiful brunette. So deep were his feelings for this girl that, when he finished his research project, he followed her to Buffalo where she had moved. He stayed in Buffalo practicing psychoanalysis. But his romance with the girl gradually cooled and by the end of the year it, too, was over.

There was nothing now to hold him in Buffalo. But he would not even consider returning to New York with its dizzy pace and brittle manners. In fact, the whole East Coast had lost its charm for him. For some time he had been looking westward to Chicago, where his sister Selma and her husband had moved. Selma had been writing him encouraging letters about the prospects of this Midwest city, and Abraham finally made up his mind to join her there.

FOUR

Selma had a big home on the north side of Chicago in the Clark-Diversy Parkway area. Abraham moved in with her and opened an office in rooms above a drugstore across the street from Selma's. He was interested in becoming affiliated with a university and continuing his research in neurology, but it was difficult in those years for a foreign-born physician to be accepted at a university. Meanwhile he engaged in general practice and psychoanalysis.

He liked Chicago. The massive gray buildings and somber streets had a flavor of the Old World cities he had known. The Lake Michigan shoreline with the glittering expanse of blue water beyond gave an added dimension to the city. The bracing winds that blew across the lake from the north, even the bitter winters, were not new to him. He had known such weather from childhood. And in contrast to scintillating New York, haunted by a sense of the ephemeral, Chicago was stolid and dependable, moving at a far slower, more comfortable tempo.

Living with Selma and Willy and their family was pleasant. Selma and Willy now had a son, and Willy was doing well as a mechanic. He was a pleasant, unassuming man who left Selma to run the home, which she did with an iron hand. She wasn't well in those years. A deficiency of iodine in childhood had given her a thyroid condition, and a goiter had begun forming which would become huge over the years.

But beneath Selma's homely appearance and her domineering ways, there was a warm, generous disposition that Abraham recognized and appreciated. He was very fond of her and tolerant

28

of her idiosyncrasies. He introduced her to all his friends and she welcomed them as guests.

Shortly after Abraham's arrival in Chicago, his two younger sisters, Theresa and Fanny, stopped off for a visit on their way to a hiking vacation in Colorado. They paid another visit on their way home. And it was here that Theresa made her first big experiment in modern fashions. Because of her adventurous nature, there wasn't a new fad she wasn't willing to try. So one day she came home with her hair cut like a boy's, wearing one of the mannish suits for women then in vogue.

Abraham was standing on the steps of Selma's home when this petite apparition swung into the driveway. He couldn't believe his eyes at first. His sister's appearance was a far cry from his idealized version of young womanhood as he had conceived it in the Benzinger drawing room. His first response was one of shock. This was followed by the familiar flush of exasperation which had characterized his relationships with his sister in their younger days. In his famous Method he was later to call such simple reactions "reminder symptoms." But he wasn't caught unaware this time—he had been working on curbing his temper outbursts, and remembering those futile quarrels of the past, he simply fled the scene and sought out Selma and Fanny. Through them he relayed his blunt opinion of Theresa's new get-up and a request that she alter it.

Of course Abraham's brotherly dictate was like waving a red flag in front of Theresa. Just as the little girl of Niedary had delighted in teasing her brother, so now the young woman in Chicago continued to needle him by wearing her hair short and going around in the mannish clothes. Today she admits the silliness of her gesture of independence. "I was the stupidest thing," she laughs. "I was followed by all kinds of women. It was just purgatory."

Theresa soon returned to New York where she began working as a fitter in her brothers' surgical supply business. But she often made quick visits to Chicago where Jules Bisno, a Chicago realtor and family friend, recalls her as a fun-loving, happy-go-lucky girl.

Fanny chose to stay in Chicago with Selma because the security of her sister's home and the quieter pace of Chicago living appealed to her. For years she was to remember the long walks she

took with Abraham in the nearby park after dinner. Their conversations were never profound. Sometimes there was no talk at
all. But Abraham seemed to take a deep pleasure in those hours
of relaxation after a busy day.

He had a great admiration for nature—plants, insects, birds,
animals—and he brought a childlike curiosity to many things
which most people take for granted. Although he had been
brought up in the Orthodox Jewish faith, his belief in God as a
Creative Power was rapidly superseding all organized religion.

In later years he was to express this belief to his wife, when
she asked him the direct question, "Do you believe in God?"

With a smile he replied, "There's a beautiful higher power.
All you have to do is go out and watch nature."

His admiration of Shakespeare's works increased the more he
studied them. He continued to make detailed psychiatric studies
of the playwright's major characters. Not only Hamlet, but Ophelia, Polonius, Macbeth, Lady Macbeth, Richard III, and many
others went, one by one, through the crucible of intensive psychoanalysis. To his amazed delight he found them all well-rounded
personalities that emerged from the printed page to become as
real to him as the patients on his couch.

Because he remembered the pleasures of the old bull sessions
in Strasbourg and the lectures in New York, he began to hold
seminars in Chicago. Every Sunday evening the doors of Selma's
home were thrown open to family friends and professional acquaintances—doctors, university professors, patients. Thirty to
fifty people gathered weekly in her living room to listen spellbound to Abraham's lectures on Shakespearean characters.

2.

Abraham was not just a bookworm. The romantic side of his
nature was keeping an even pace with his intellectualism. And
it was this charming combination that made the thirty-three-year-
old doctor so popular with the young women of Chicago. In fact
he was such an eligible bachelor that he was also pursued by
ambitious mothers who wanted to match him up with their
daughters.

One of these women, a stately matron of German descent, was a patient of his and a friend of the family. She had the eccentric habit of fainting dead away in Selma's home when she knew Abraham was nearby. There, stretched out on a bed in one of the bedrooms, she would babble about intimate family secrets, the prime one of which was that her daughter was madly in love with Abraham.

The first time it happened, Fanny and Selma were terrified and summoned their brother. He came and looked at her, listened a few minutes, and then remarked calmly, "Don't touch her, do nothing at all. She'll wake up and be normal again."

For a time Abraham became involved with a young girl from one of the wealthiest families in Chicago. Things went so far that he was invited to her home to meet her parents, and from his confidences to Selma and Fanny, it began to look as though a marriage would soon take place. But this romance, too, faded.

It was that year that Abraham made the acquaintance of two young women, the Willetts. In 1924 twenty-year-old Mae and her older sister Lillian had moved from the south side of Chicago to the north side. Their father had just died, and in the loneliness that followed, their mother had gone to visit relatives in Wisconsin. Mae and Lillian decided they wanted to start a new life in a different section of town, and Lillian had friends on the north side who helped them find a place there.

One afternoon Mae and her sister were visiting their friends who lived near Selma. They were sitting on the porch when Abraham strolled by. The friends called to him and he came up and was introduced. It was such a chance meeting that he might have been entirely forgotten by the sisters had not Lillian fallen and injured her knee a short while later. When infection set in, the girls remembered the young doctor they had met and went together to his unpretentious office above the drugstore. It was the beginning of a patient-physician relationship that continued even after Lillian married, and that included both Lillian and her husband as well as Mae and the girls' mother when she returned from Wisconsin.

The family's first social contact with young Dr. Low was at a function which Mae attended with her sister and brother-in-law. When, at the end of the evening, Abraham offered to drive them home, they were delighted. They had little idea of what was in store for them as they got into the car and Abraham settled himself jauntily in the front seat. But as soon as he'd turned on the ignition they realized what a mistake they had made. Only then it was too late to change their minds.

Abraham took off with a shrieking of tires and with bursts from the exhaust pipe. It seemed to his three companions that every rule in the book was broken that night. They held their breath and wondered if they would ever see home again. They did, however, and as they clambered out, their young physician told them proudly, "You know I got this car last week. I've just learned to drive."

Abraham's driving improved with the years, but not by much. Poor driving seemed to be a weakness of the Low family. Fanny never learned to drive, and Ben gave it up after stepping on the accelerator instead of the brake one day and going right through the back of the garage. Selma also had her troubles behind the wheel. There was one memorable occasion when she offered to chauffeur Mrs. Jules Bisno to New York to visit her son there. The two women managed to get as far as New Jersey before Selma ran into a tree and wrecked the car. Mrs. Bisno phoned her son to come for her, and Selma returned to Chicago minus the car. Theresa still drives today, but does so with extreme caution. She avoids large cities and seldom goes faster than thirty miles an hour. Rather than pass a slow-moving vehicle, she prefers to pull over to the side of the road and let the other traffic go by.

The funny thing about Abraham's driving was that, even when he wasn't at fault, mishaps just seemed to befall him. There was the time, for instance, when Fanny and he took a trip south to get a respite from the cold. "We were driving back home," Fanny recalls, "and there was ice on the road and all at once we skidded and he made a complete circle with the car over the ice. Well, perhaps because of the ice you couldn't say it's bad driving. But you certainly couldn't say it's good driving either."

On another occasion Abraham and his three sisters were taking a simple pleasure jaunt through suburban Chicago when suddenly a car driven by a drunken man careened out of a side street. There was a terrific crash and both cars turned over before finally uprighting themselves again. Miraculously no one was hurt and

Abraham's new car wasn't seriously damaged. Neither was the car of the other driver. He staggered out, waving his card and shouting, "Don't worry, I'm insured. Here's my card."

Abraham, shaken and white-faced, climbed out of his car and approached the drunk sternly. "Don't you know that someone could have been seriously hurt?" he demanded.

But the man, unimpressed, only repeated cheerfully, "Don't worry. Don't worry. I'm insured."

In stiff silence Abraham exchanged cards and license numbers. The experience hadn't intimidated him. He continued driving but Theresa, usually so adventurous, was too terrified to ride in anybody's car. For a whole year she went by bus, trolley, or elevated train. And when finally she overcame her phobia about automobile travel in general, she would never get into a car with Abraham at the wheel.

"When he was learning to drive," she says, recalling those past experiences, "he took all the horses, all the cows, all the telephone poles with him. He got into everything. And he wasn't much better with practice."

One reason Abraham never made a prompt takeoff at stoplights and often had to be jarred into action by drivers honking behind him was because he usually had a book on the front seat with him. Every time he had to stop for a red light he would take the opportunity to get in a few snatches of reading.

3.

By 1925 young Dr. Low's reputation in the field of neurology had come to the attention of Dr. George Boris Hassin, of the Neurological Department at the University of Illinois Medical School in Chicago. Dr. Hassin invited young Abraham to join his staff at the university where he was to teach neurology and do research in the field of histopathology.

This meant that Abraham would have to give up his private practice. In the next few days he notified his patients that he could no longer be their personal physician. The Willetts, among others, were given the names of three physicians, with one being singled out as the best of the three. His name was Dr. Eugene

Grosz, an internist from Budapest, Hungary. Actually, Gene Grosz was more than a professional associate. He was one of Abraham's first friends in Chicago and the two men were to remain close throughout life.

In the years ahead, the Willetts didn't see their former physician, but they heard of him through Dr. Grosz, who saw Dr. Low now and then at the research hospital and clinic. He had nothing but good reports to give of the strides forward his friend was making in his study of histopathology, and of his success as a professor. But he never had anything personal to relate about him. It seemed that Abraham Low was still successfully avoiding matrimony.

FIVE

‾‾‾‾‿‾‾‾‾

Shortly after his appointment to the staff of the Neurological Department at the University of Illinois Medical School, Abraham moved from Selma's home into quarters of his own. He took a hotel apartment at 500 Fullerton Street and soon it bore the imprint of what had become his life's chief passion: books. He was already a devoted bibliophile—he knew all the rare-book dealers in Chicago and haunted their shops. He bought books by the dozen, by the score. It was his one extravagance.

One day Theresa visited him and looked around his apartment. It was a litter of books. They were not only stacked in every conceivable corner and on tables and chairs in the living room and bedroom—they were piled high on the kitchen sink board and in the dish cupboards. Even the stove was heaped with pillars of books.

"Abraham," Theresa exclaimed with a gesture of her hand, "how are you ever going to fix your coffee?"

"Oh, I can always move them when I need to," he answered vaguely.

As a matter of fact, there was no room even for food in the apartment, as a book dealer friend once testified. He had gone to visit the young doctor, and feeling thirsty, he had asked for a drink of ice water. Abraham had directed him to the icebox. He had opened it and discovered it filled with books. Abraham, seeing his astonishment and always ready for a joke on himself, had explained laughingly, "They're my hot sex books. I put them on ice to cool off."

35

Actually no cooking was done in the apartment—except for coffee. Abraham would make a huge pot of it on Monday and keep it for the rest of the week, warming it up now and then when he wanted a cup. When his office staff heard about it, they laughed and scolded him, shuddering at how the coffee must taste by the end of the week. But nothing could make him change his ways.

Most of the time Abraham spent in his hotel room was confined to reading, often with a cup of his awful coffee by his side to keep him company. He had difficulty sleeping and did a lot of tossing and turning with much twisting of the bedclothes during the course of the night. He never slept more than six hours at a time. Usually four or five hours with several catnaps throughout the day were sufficient for him.

He liked to rise around four or five o'clock and those morning hours were the most precious of the whole day to him. He did the major portion of his reading then when his mind was fresh and bright. Most of his reading was concerned with keeping abreast of the voluminous medical literature being published. But he always found time for his favorite philosophers and also for doing some writing of his own.

When the rest of the world began to stir, he would go out for a long walk, get the morning paper, and finally drop in at a neighborhood restaurant, where he would read his paper while he ate breakfast. He always had a few words with the news vendor and perhaps with a fellow diner in the restaurant or some early morning worker whom he met on his walk.

Contacts with ordinary people were becoming more and more of a delight to him. They gave savor to his intellectual pursuits. He enjoyed their down-to-earth philosophies and their rich choice of words. These humble people, he realized, often had a more vital contact with reality than many of the sophisticates he knew. All were part of the well-rounded education he sought.

The course this education was to follow through the years is delineated in a compact series of notes which his widow compiled from his sayings: "I had early recognized that the standardized descriptions of academic teaching were woefully deficient. All along, the burning desire was to escape the pressure of textbook formulation. A striving for new insight was always driving me into new pathways—research. It was one continuous effort, never slumbering, inevitably driving toward the sources and springs of knowledge. The main source seemed to be Shakespeare. To him I reverted unerringly. And Kant, Schopenhauer, Nietzsche. I started with Nietzsche, proceeded to Schopenhauer, met the Freudians at college, and finally landed with Kant and Shakespeare who were my final mentors. Much I owe to Schopenhauer. His emphasis on intuition has decisively influenced my thought."

Abraham's talks on Shakespeare ended when he moved from Selma's place, but he quickly substituted another series of lectures. The venture began by chance one Saturday night when he accompanied Jules Bisno to an open house conducted regularly by a prominent Chicagoan.

The evening proved to be a lively one of philosophic discussion. Abraham was in his element and as usual was soon surrounded by an interested audience. Those who heard him were so impressed that they begged him to give a series of lectures on any topics he chose. The idea delighted him, only he insisted that the entertainment be all at his expense. He rented a modest hall and invited his friends, allowing each one to bring a guest. There were always twenty and usually more in his select little audience. They came from all walks of life and among them were such diversified professionals as a well-known woman pediatrician, two general practitioners, three or four business men, a newspaper columnist, a dentist, and Jules Bisno, the real estate broker.

The weekly event was Abraham's show. He gave impromptu lectures on any subject that came to mind. And he asked only one thing of his audience: its complete and undivided attention. Once when a member of the audience was asked by a friend what went on at the weekly sessions, he replied, "Well, Dr. Low talks to himself for about an hour and nobody must interrupt him."

One of the delights of the series was the varied menu he offered. Over the ten years of these remarkable lectures he never seemed to run out of themes. One evening he talked on the importance of "being in character," using as examples Flaubert's *Madame Bovary* and Ibsen's *A Doll's House*. He had great admiration for Flaubert's craftsmanship and pointed out that the novelist had not described Emma by standing on the sidelines and interpreting her. Rather, he had allowed Emma to project her own character through words and actions. He also analyzed all the characters in Ibsen's *A Doll's House*. Nora was to him the first completely modern woman to appear on the printed page. But although he praised many writers, he always came back to Shakespeare—Shakespeare the master, whose characters were the most completely drawn in the world of fiction.

Sometimes his lectures concerned the science of language, for he felt it played a far more crucial role in human behavior than people realized. Most quarrels, he pointed out, were not due to overt actions such as blows but to misunderstandings during the exchange of words. He explained that though disputants might use the same vernacular, the words they employed often connoted different things to different people. And he spoke of the need for a basic language in which there would be only one interpretation for each word, thus removing the possibility of misunderstanding.

Words themselves were of such vital importance to him that he was most meticulous in choosing the right ones. When he couldn't find a suitable word in the dictionary, he would coin one. For instance, he created two new words out of the root word "scotoma," meaning blindness: "scotophobe" and "scotophile." A scotophobe, he said, was an individual who had a blind spot for his own shortcomings. A scotophile, on the other hand, was one who did not suffer from such self-blindness. His habit of coining words raised objections among certain members of the audience, especially the newspaper columnist. But Abraham would only smile his acknowledgment of the right of anyone to disagree with what he was doing, and then continue doing it.

Sometimes his lecture concerned some article he had read in a newspaper. Once he brought a clipping from the Chicago *Tribune* to the meeting. After pointing out that the paper referred to itself as the "World's Greatest Newspaper," he announced that the title of his talk was, "Things are not what they seem." He began by explaining to his listeners the need for a definite method to arrive at the truth which underlies appearances. For instance, the article he had brought described Chicago as a city of great learning and culture. It had many fine schools and churches. It had nurtured many famous writers, philosophers, and men of science. Its libraries were among the most complete in the world. But after going through the points in the article, he began to show the other side of the city. He pointed out that gangsterism was rife, with massacres, bootlegging, and terrorism, that newspapers hired ruthless killers to do away with competitors, and that the officers who were supposed to enforce law and order often worked hand-in-hand with criminals and were corrupted by them.

Another of his favorite subjects for an evening's discussion was Immanuel Kant and his philosophy. Jules Bisno remembers the startling prophecy with which Abraham concluded one of his lectures on Kant, and which he had arrived at from his study of Kant's basic theories. It had to do with the future of gangsterism which was then rife in Chicago and other big cities of the East. "This I can tell you will occur," he assured his audience. "The gangsters who are now involved in bootlegging will not stop after Prohibition. They will go into other fields of endeavor."

2.

In those years Jules Bisno looked upon his friend Abraham as a confirmed bachelor, well-settled in his ways and not wanting to have his life disrupted by the added responsibilities of marriage. He did not really know the character of the Low family. Theresa says of them, "The Lows don't talk about marriage. They just get married one day."

So it was not surprising that Abraham should again become interested in an attractive young woman, this one from Australia, whom he met at a friend's home. Her name was Estelle Mendelsohn and she was a divorcée with a twelve-year-old son. She and the boy had come over from Australia alone and had no relatives in America.

Estelle, who was working as a copywriter for an advertising firm, found the young doctor refreshingly different from the business men with whom she came in contact. She saw him frequently after their first meeting, and she was flattered to feel that he was interested in her and her son. Occasionally he invited her to social affairs where he impressed her with his impeccable manners and his sense of true culture that went deeper than the outward veneer. He wouldn't allow himself to get drawn into fruitless arguments. Sometimes when a guest would take him aside to expound some theory, Dr. Low would listen attentively. And although often the theory was diametrically opposed to his own, he would only smile and say equably, "Perhaps you are right."

Fascinated, Estelle began attending his weekly lectures. And although she never got beyond the stage of addressing him as Dr. Low, she was immensely pleased when one day he invited her to spend a Sunday with him at the Indiana Dunes, a park on Lake Michigan. Estelle's son was away at boarding school and the thought of herself and the charming doctor spending a whole day together in a quiet rustic setting filled her with romantic dreams. She prepared a picnic lunch and they traveled by train to the Dunes. It was a warm, fair day, just the kind of day for swimming, sunning, and a picnic.

But that wasn't the kind of outing Estelle was to experience. No sooner were they on the lakeshore, sitting on their beach towels, than Abraham brought out a volume of Kant and began to read aloud from it. Once started he never even seemed to be aware of the inviting water and the shapely woman at his side. He paused only briefly to eat some of the picnic lunch which Estelle had prepared with such care.

Then it was back to his book again. His voice rolled on and on through the long golden afternoon, sometimes reading, sometimes explaining the philosopher's views in his own words. Estelle understood little either of Kant's philosophy or of the doctor's explanations. The warm sun, Dr. Low's Viennese voice with its rich accent and hypnotically sonorous cadence made her drowsier and drowsier until presently she fell asleep.

She was roused by the doctor who made no mention of the fact that she had slept the afternoon away, though he couldn't have helped noticing it. He merely said, "We just have time to catch the five o'clock train back."

No romance blossomed between Estelle and Abraham. And before long she met and fell madly in love with a young musician named Sol Nemkov, another member of the seminars. They were married before too long, and when, a month later, Estelle sought out Abraham, it was with a serious problem concerning her son. She had once made a promise to the boy that if she ever planned remarriage, he would be the first to know about it. She had forgotten that promise and her son had learned of the marriage only after the event.

The boy had become so rebellious that after one short month of battling with him, Estelle was about to break up her marriage just to find a little peace. There didn't seem to be anything else to do, because all her friends had tried reasoning with the boy but without success. They had pointed out his selfishness, his disregard for his mother's happiness, his spitefulness. They had urged him to mend his ways and start showing a little consideration for others, but he had only become worse.

Now Estelle was asking the child's old friend, the doctor, to see what he could do about it. Abraham agreed to talk to the boy and there followed one of the most unique conferences ever held between an adult and a child.

They sat facing each other, the boy perched on the edge of his chair quivering with indignation and prepared to fight off another self-righteous admonition. The doctor sat opposite him watching him sympathetically for a few minutes. Finally he said gravely, "Your mother has done you a great wrong, Sonny. She broke a promise she made to you."

The boy stared, his defenses going down. At last someone was seeing his viewpoint.

"You have every right to be sore at her," the doctor continued. The boy leaned forward eagerly, grateful for this understanding friendship. A moment of intimacy linked the two.

"But you know, Sonny," the doctor concluded after a pause, "it is not always wise to exercise your personal rights. Indeed, often it is best to forget them."

With a few understanding words, he had made contact. The boy began to change, gradually the house returned to normal, and the marriage was saved. Of course it didn't happen all at once. Abraham hadn't expected an immediate transformation. He was not a man to believe in any miracles but one—the miracle of the strange and wonderful and flawed human being who inhabits the world and whose very imperfections made him more beautiful to Abraham than all the efficient and amazing machines that modern science could produce.

He saw those marvels of science all around him, and he didn't completely disapprove of them. He could recognize the utility value of automatic dishwashers, vacuum cleaners, and washing machines. Only when these comforts were elevated into supreme values did he object. They were wants, he liked to point out, but not needs.

3.

In 1927 Abraham and Fanny became naturalized citizens. About this time he made one concession regarding his name in compliance with American custom. A doctor at the medical school suggested that he adopt a middle initial for himself and proposed "A" as being the most euphonious. Abraham liked the sound of that—Abraham A. Low. He chose the name Adolph to go with the initial.

Since the beginning of his stay in America, Abraham had been changing in many ways. The youthful ardor with which he had worked for Zionism in Europe had gradually diminished, occupying less of his time and effort, though he continued to make contributions of money to the cause.

The psychoanalytic method—that method in which he had placed so much faith in his early days—was also gradually losing its luster for him. He had seen so many patients returning so many times to his office to dredge up the bilge from their psyches without showing any visible improvement. He had discovered how mercurial a patient's reactions were. It was even easy to hoodwink some of them into health.

Once he had explained to Fanny, "As long as a patient wants to be fooled, that is his cure. He believes and is cured." He was referring to electrical equipment he had acquired early in his practice. Freud had used similar equipment to demonstrate the power of suggestion. The equipment consists of an imposing-looking machine which gives off an electric spark when brought in contact with something. Although it has no therapeutic value of its own, a patient suffering from hysterical paralysis sometimes responds to its powerful suggestion and after its application is able to move his limbs.

Abraham recognized the instrument's value as a form of hypnosis. But, he asked himself, did this method of fooling people into a cure achieve lasting results? He began to make other tests of suggestibility on his patients. It started one day when he asked a man on his couch to tell him the color eyes the cow in his dream had had.

The man hesitated and Dr. Low prompted, "Did the cow have blue eyes?"

"Yes," the man replied, accepting the suggestion with alacrity.

In the days and weeks that followed, Dr. Low began making all kinds of similar suggestions to his patients. Instead of refuting them, they would usually respond with a, "How did you know that, Doctor?"

He began to wonder how the validity of a therapy could be proved on the basis of such universally fluid responses. He wondered, too, about the value of a cure that required so many long and costly sessions, with a successful outcome always in serious doubt. Meanwhile, his work in neurology and histopathology was convincing him more and more that much of the answer lay not in childhood traumas but in physiological causes. Finally, he became so disillusioned that he dropped the psychoanalytic method completely and for the rest of his life referred to himself as a clinical psychiatrist.

4.

During her frequent visits to Chicago, Theresa often took her brother to task for his betrayal of the glamorous new science which had achieved such prominence in the Twenties. Strong words passed between them on the subject until finally, in brotherly pique, Abraham told her that she talked too much and was too independent ever to risk marriage.

Theresa did marry, however. In 1931 Abraham received an invitation to the wedding which was to take place in New York to tall, distinguished-looking Jack Ditesheim, a wealthy executive of a Swiss watch factory with distribution centers in America. The wedding was to be a private affair with only relatives in attendance because Jack wanted it that way. But it was to be a fashion-able event with the women in formal gowns and the men in tuxedos.

Abraham wouldn't have missed the wedding of his youngest sister for the world. But he was working hard and couldn't leave until the last minute. To save time he put on his tuxedo in Chicago and drove straight to the New York apartment which was shared by cousin Max and Selma's son Harry, now grown and working in his uncles' surgical supply business. Abraham planned to spend Saturday night with them, attend Theresa's wedding on Sunday, and then head back for home.

When, late Saturday afternoon, Max and Henry opened the door in answer to Abraham's ring, they could only stare. The tuxedo Abraham was wearing was the one he'd bought during his university days in Europe. Since that time he'd grown taller—though he was never to be more than five feet seven inches in height—and had also put on weight. The ill-fitting suit now hung high above his ankles and wrists and was fusty with age. Max and Henry were horrified and told him bluntly that he would have to buy a new one.

It was Abraham's turn to be shocked. Tuxedos were expensive and his salary as a university professor was modest. He saw all the money he'd been saving for books taking wing in one dark moment of extravagance, and he couldn't believe the suit looked as bad as his cousin and nephew insisted it did.

Finally he made a deal with his two harassers. He would go out with them and buy a new suit, but only if Theresa requested it of him. With this promise Henry rushed to the phone and got Theresa at work and told her the story. She dropped everything she was doing and hurried over to the apartment because there really wasn't much time before the stores closed. There stood Abraham in the too-short, too-tight suit, anxiously awaiting her.

The boys were right, of course. She could see that at a glance. All that remained was for her to make the decision.

"Look, Abraham," she asked him, "do you ever wear these things in Chicago?"

"No," he answered her. "I've had it twenty years. It was hanging up in the closet and I took it out for your wedding."

Theresa thought it over. He had broken a busy schedule and

had come all the way from Chicago for her wedding. Why should she make him spend money for something he would probably never use again?

"You're perfectly all right for me," she told him. "I'm the one getting married, not you."

So Abraham came to the wedding in the old-fashioned, too-tight suit. Some of the party, it's true, were scandalized by his appearance and annoyed with Theresa for allowing it. But the rabbi, who was Theresa's special friend, wasn't among them. Because there were only thirteen relatives attending the wedding party, Theresa invited the rabbi to join the festivities to relieve the minds of any superstitious guests.

Abraham and the rabbi turned out to be kindred souls. They had the best time of anyone there, drinking together and expounding philosophies and views and ending the evening in the warm glow of a mild inebriation.

SIX

~

Dr. George Hassin was an elderly man who was so dedicated to his work that he didn't mince matters where his colleagues were concerned. He was a taskmaster and the members of his staff who didn't measure up to his standards could expect a blunt reprimand from him for their failings.

But Dr. Hassin never had cause to complain about the new histopathology and neurology researcher and professor he had brought into his fold. He deeply admired Dr. Low's dedication and the tenacity and thoroughness with which he pursued his investigations. There was in his feeling for the young doctor something of a fatherly affection.

Another important figure in the neurological-psychiatric field of the time was also beginning to take an interest in Abraham Low. He was Dr. Harold Douglas Singer, a tall, angular Englishman with a middle-class Englishman's sense of propriety. He had come to America in 1906, and in 1907 had been called to Illinois to become director of the Illinois State Psychopathic Institute. When the office of state alienist was created in 1917, he held it for four years, going on to a professorship in psychiatry at the University of Illinois College of Medicine where he eventually became head of the Department of Neurology and Psychiatry. He also was president of the American Neurological Association and as such was editor-in-chief of the professional journal of that body, *The Archives in Neurology and Psychiatry.* Dr. Singer's achievements were unusual in those days of discrimination against foreign doctors. They testified to the fine reputation he had earned for himself in his field.

46

It was as editor of the *Archives* that he first became aware of Dr. Low. Two brilliant papers on histopathology written by the young doctor had come to his desk and were printed in his magazine. The papers were very well received in medical circles and later were published by the university.

In January of 1931, Dr. Singer opened the Psychiatric Institute which was housed in a wing of the Research and Educational Hospital and was to be used for research on patients with various mental illnesses who had been selected from hospitals around the state. Since Dr. Singer preferred to do only the administrative work of the Institute, he cast around for a capable doctor to develop the medical side of it. Cool to the psychoanalytic method himself, he could think of no better physician for the job than the brilliant young researcher from Vienna. He asked Dr. Low to head the staff of the new Psychiatric Institute.

In 1932 Harry Horner was elected Governor of Illinois. And with the idea of bringing much needed reforms to the psychiatric wards of the state hospitals he asked Dr. Singer to resume the office of state alienist. Dr. Singer accepted under one condition— that Dr. Low be named his assistant. So it was that Dr. Low, with his penchant for research, was placed in a position which enabled him to study numbers of human beings suffering mental illness. But if it was Fate that put him in this sensitive position, it was the doctor's own inventiveness and charisma that enabled him to use it to the fullest to develop his great curative Method of self-help.

2.

Dr. Low went at his new tasks with ardor. In his daily rounds in state hospitals, he came across all kinds and degrees of illness. He quickly discovered that with the less disturbed patients the right choice of words had the power to mobilize their will to health. He who had spent so much time in the study of language now used every interview to make a search for the most effective words.

Then it came to him that he could give more counseling if he could meet with his patients collectively. This would save time in his already overcrowded schedule. By 1933 he was gathering the patients together and holding group sessions for staff conferences. He quickly discovered that such group conferences not only enabled him to present a richer background of material to his staff, but that they also proved to be a potent form of psychotherapy for the patients.

Actually, he was practicing an early form of group psychotherapy, though he was not the first in the field; Dr. Edward W. Lazell and Dr. L. C. Marsh had preceded him by a number of years. Most of the few group psychotherapists of the day relied on lectures. A few had combined lectures with interviews. Dr. Paul Schilder of New York City seems to have been the only one who relied on interviews entirely. As the years went by, however, group psychotherapists began one by one to drop the lecture method as unsatisfactory.

Dr. Low himself had early discovered that lectures could not hold the attention of his patients and began to use the single interview method. While the rest of the class listened, he would interview one of the patients and interpolate his replies with explanations. These explanations were simple and to the point, and they were always kept in a fluid state of experimentation. If one word or group of words didn't register, he would try others until he had found the proper combination.

The young doctor's novel approach was proving effective with the small group of less disturbed patients on the hospital wards. But what of those others, that dismal array of humanity whom words could not reach? As assistant state alienist, he was becoming more and more familiar with those tragic victims. In every hospital he visited, and he visited all of them in the state of Illinois, he saw the same dreary spectacle: people who were more like vegetables than human beings or who were suffering the delusions and hallucinations of paranoia or who were living in the agonizing seesaw world of the manic depressive.

Illness of this kind had no regard for age. It equally struck teenagers, young mothers, husbands, successful professionals, the old and the young, the rich and the poor. Though many of them had squandered their life's savings on extensive psychoanalysis or other forms of mental therapy, they had become progressively worse. Once admitted to the hospital, few of them ever left it again until death released them.

Now that shock treatments and an array of modern drugs have succeeded in drastically reducing the numbers of those condemned to a living death, it is hard to imagine the utter helplessness that the dedicated physicians of an earlier day felt in the face of such tragedy. Abraham Low was one of these physicians. Each time he left the hospital wards he was visibly shaken by the plight of the lost ones he had visited.

Yet he, along with other doctors, had noticed a phenomenon among these tragically-ill people. A few of them did recover and return to a normal life in the outer world. Their recovery seemed always to be spontaneous. There was no uniformity even in the way the cure was effected. In some it was gradual, in others sudden. In some it seemed to occur after a dramatic incident in the life of the patient. In others there was no such stimulating outer environment. Sometimes it would follow an acute ailment characterized by high fever. At other times the cure would take place in the absence of such an ailment.

Such spontaneous cures pointed to a physiological basis for the illness—an illness that like pneumonia or meningitis ran a predestined course from which, when untreated, some recovered and others did not. This theory seemed quite plausible to Dr. Low. In giving a thorough examination to every patient brought to the hospital, he would sometimes discover that an illness that had been diagnosed as psychological was in reality physiological in origin—perhaps some disease of the spinal cord or brain. If a physical ailment could be confused with a psychological one in this way, couldn't the serious mental ailments really be physiological in origin? he asked himself. If this were so, then surely a synthetic product could be developed that would duplicate the spontaneous cures of nature.

Dr. Low was not alone in his quest for a solution to the problem. Other psychiatrists had been working on it for some time and he studied all their findings. He was also engaged in research of his own on the behavioral patterns of the psychiatric patients in the state hospitals. To do this he trained nurses to observe carefully the patients under their care and to jot down their findings in detail. Out of these voluminous statistics, he hoped eventually to discover clues that would guide him in the treatment of the sick.

Another of his research projects was triggered by his work

with young victims of aphasia in the children's hospital. Aphasia, or the loss of the power to use words due to a brain lesion, interested him deeply, for it seemed to be duplicated in the speech patterns of the mentally ill. With other researchers in the field he felt that the dissolution of the powers of speech and thought in these sufferers was paralleled by the evolution of speech and thought in infants. To provide a basis for future investigations he launched into a quantitative study of the evolution of speech, obtaining his material with the cooperation of three mothers of young children. For two years and three months, these mothers collected every word their children uttered, presenting Dr. Low with some twenty-five thousand utterances to discuss with his staff and evaluate. This exhaustive study was published by the *University of Illinois Bulletin* in May of 1936.

Besides his various research projects, he was spending a great deal of time at the clinic training the fathers and mothers of the emotionally ill children who were brought there. Such instruction was very important to him because he believed that parents had to learn to guard even their unconscious gestures and voice intonations and facial expressions if they wanted to help their children get well. Dr. Singer, delighted by the young doctor's painstaking program of education, once confided to a colleague, Dr. Samuel Henry Kraines, that he was "immensely impressed with the detail, the specificity, and the thoroughness of Dr. Low's instructions to the parents."

3.

Despite his heavy work load, Abraham was still continuing his Saturday night lectures because his highly sensitive audience provided a valuable sounding board for the many experiments he was engaged in. But all other social engagements were drastically curtailed, and his scant hours of sleep were cut even further.

Addicted to his work as he was, he seemed to be bearing out Jules Bisno's prophecy of perennial bachelorhood. Then one day a chance encounter on Michigan Boulevard changed the course of his life. He suddenly found himself face to face with a former patient: Mae Willett, the blonde young woman whom he had attended in his days of general practice. Nine years had gone by

since then, but she was just as vivacious as ever. And her friendly
gray-green eyes sparkled with pleasure as she recognized him.

There was no mistaking that erect jaunty figure that came
walking down the street toward her with an almost martial pre-
cision. Heavier than when she had seen him last—his weight
hovering around 178 pounds—he still was not fat. The dark blond
hair, which had been thick before, was beginning to thin. But his
eyes were still the same clear blue: the Low eyes that did not
fade with age.

Mae greeted him warmly, "It's so good to see you."

There was something so spontaneous in the way she said it
that the doctor was completely caught up in that magical moment.
"I'm just on my way to dinner," he exclaimed. "Would you join
me?"

He was both pleased and amused at her breathless reply, "Yes,
yes."

They had dinner together and spent it reminiscing about old
times and telling each other what they were doing now. Mae, he
learned, had left her sister's home and was rooming with a girl
named Kay Dixon in an apartment that was only a couple of miles
from his own hotel.

The evening passed quickly and made such an impression on
Mae that the next time she visited her mother and sister she had
to tell about the encounter in detail. Her mother must have detected something in her daughter's manner and tone of voice of
which Mae herself was unaware. "Now don't get ideas," she suddenly advised firmly. "He's married to his science."

"I haven't any ideas," Mae replied hotly. And she really believed it. In childhood she'd made up her mind not to marry
anyone, and after all the quarreling contentious couples she'd seen
around her since, she hadn't changed her mind.

The doctor didn't seem particularly interested either. He
didn't call Mae again for two weeks. When he did, it was to ask
her for a second dinner date. From then on their dates were
sporadic. Sometimes there would be no word from him for a
month or so. Then suddenly he would be back on the phone
again. He always called at the last minute, so that on a couple of
occasions Mae regretfully couldn't accept, and noticed how disappointed he seemed about it.

Later she was to learn that his weeks of silence were because of

his out-of-town trips to the various state hospitals. But his last-minute phone calls were designed as a test to see how truly interested
she was in him. She was to say to him then, a little piqued, a little
amused, "I feel as though I was always in a test tube."

But at the time she thought little of his strange absences or his
last-minute phone calls. She only knew she was always overjoyed to
hear from him, that she looked forward to evenings spent with
him.

"I felt like a queen with him. Whatever compliment he paid
me, I knew he meant it," she was to say in later life.

Finally he asked her if she would dine with him every night.
Then the Saturday night lectures stopped and his friends began
hearing a great deal about the new young lady he had met. It
wasn't hard for Estelle Nemkov to realize that he was at last falling
in love.

"What do you like so much about her?" she asked him finally,
wondering what kind of girl would appeal to this man who had
spent the afternoon reading Kant to his date.

"She is natural, simple," Abraham replied without a moment's
hesitation. "I feel very comfortable with her."

And this, Estelle knew, was the highest form of praise that could
come from a man whose penetrating insight made him aware of
pretentiousness of any kind.

The courtship was not without its humorous moments. When
Mae expressed a fondness for dancing, Abraham cheerfully complied, but his dancing had grown as fusty as his tuxedo. He had
little sense of rhythm and he persisted in pumping his arm up and
down in the European manner of fifteen years back.

"Let's hold your arm still," Mae would suggest gently, not
wanting to hurt his feelings.

But it was impossible to offend him because by this time he had
developed such a tremendous sense of humor about himself that
he would merely throw back his head and laugh. Then he would
hold his arm still for a little while, but before long it would start
pumping once more. After two such evenings Mae never suggested dancing again.

In February when Abraham's birthday was nearing, she felt a
gift was in order. Although he smoked a pipe now and then, he
was still addicted to cigars. So one night after dinner when he took

one from his pocket and removed the gold band from it, Mae surreptitiously retrieved it and slipped it into her purse. Later she bought him a humidor and filled it with cigars of the same brand. It seemed to her that they were very cheap, but then who could account for the tastes of a cigar smoker?

The night of his birthday she presented the humidor to Abraham. "They are your brand, aren't they?" she asked confidently.

To her surprise he shook his head. "No," he answered with the candor that characterized him.

"But you were smoking them one evening we had dinner together," she protested.

"Oh, that," he said. "Some patient brought in some very cheap cigars. I didn't have any others so I smoked one of them."

4.

Abraham's proposal, which took place in May of 1935, was as whimsical as his courtship had been. It came about just a few days after Mae and her roommate Kay moved to another apartment. The very night of their moving a messenger arrived at the door with a bouquet of flowers and a note from Abraham inquiring when Mae was going to cook him a meal in her new place.

Mae read the note in consternation. She was a career girl who didn't know the first thing about cooking. But how could you refuse a man whom you'd grown to love, especially when his request was made with a bouquet of flowers? She took her courage in both hands and phoned him.

"How about next Monday night?" she asked, trying hard to keep the tremor from her voice.

"Fine," he answered.

Mae's roommate Kay conveniently left the apartment that Monday afternoon so that Mae could entertain her guest in privacy. It was only after she'd gone that Mae discovered she couldn't find anything in the kitchen because it was Kay who'd arranged things there. Pots, kitchenware, and the usual basic commodities seemed to be all hidden away, and the new stove smoked.

The doctor arrived promptly, to find the dinner unprepared.

But he seemed unperturbed. He just sat puffing on his pipe, an amused smile on his face as he watched Mae flying around, growing more and more flustered. Sometimes when she rattled in kettle closets or strewed seasoning shakers around, he would break into a friendly chuckle that seemed to be encouraging Mae to relax and laugh about it with him.

But to Mae the situation was really too serious for that. By the time dinner was on the table she was exhausted, and the meal was a failure, overcooked and poorly seasoned. Abraham began eating as though it were the best meal in the world. Afterwards he put his question to her. He loved her. Would she marry him?

Although Mae always claimed not to have any humor about her own foibles, she quipped back, "Not on the strength of this dinner, I hope."

"No, not at all," he answered gravely, but there was a twinkle in his blue eyes.

Mae's green eyes met his. Bit by bit, he had made her change her opinions of marriage. But the words she spoke were an almost childlike rebuke that came straight from her practical nature.

"Now you ask me!" she exclaimed. "I just signed the lease."

He smiled as if it were a private joke between them. "We'll pay your half of it off," he told her equably.

"We'll have to wait a couple of months at least," she still protested, "because I'll have to train somebody for my job."

He didn't like the thought of delay but reluctantly he agreed to it. And they decided to wait until September or October when he'd be free to take a vacation and they could have a proper honeymoon.

But the fall was a long way off for a man in love and two or three weeks later Abraham was asking her if she wouldn't reconsider and marry him in June. He'd been invited to go east that month and hold some clinics in various hospitals and he wished her to go along with him. It would be a kind of honeymoon and at the same time she could meet the rest of his family in New York.

By this time Mae had fairly well broken in her replacement, so she agreed to his proposal and on June 18 they were married in a simple ceremony performed by a judge. One of Abraham's friends, Dr. A. Federman, and Mae's roommate, Kay, were the witnesses. After the wedding, followed by the congratulations of their friends, the newlyweds got into their car and drove off for New York. The honeymoon had begun.

They spent the night in Cambridge, Ohio, and next day resumed their journey eastward, Abraham at the wheel. The road wound over a high incline flanked on either side by higher hills, obscuring the view. They were on the downward slope when a truck suddenly appeared as though out of nowhere. The driver, thinking he could make it in time, gunned his motor, but he wasn't fast enough and there was a collision.

The Low car went over a thirty-foot enbankment and was wrecked. Abraham and his bride were fortunate to have escaped with their lives but they were both in critical condition and had to be taken to the hospital in Cambridge. Abraham had a couple of fractured ribs and his front teeth were driven through his lower left jaw, requiring dental surgery and a bridge. Mae was in far worse shape. Her skull was cracked and her face, arms, and chest were a mass of lacerations. By the time the doctor finished with surgery, stitches, and bandaging she looked like an Egyptian mummy.

Since Abraham hadn't been able to bring Mae to the Lows in New York, Nat flew in to Cambridge to see what the new sister-in-law looked like. He had to go back with a negative report. "I really don't know," he told the family. "She was covered with bandages. All her exposed parts—her face, everything."

Mae and Abraham stayed in the hospital for two weeks. Abraham made a quick recovery, but Mae's injuries were more serious. When she was well enough to be moved, they returned to Chicago by train. Lillian, who came down to meet her sister, was shocked to see Mae, still covered with bandages, being escorted off the train in a wheel chair.

Mae quipped, "You should have taken a picture of us leaving and then coming back and titled it, 'Before and After Marriage.'"

SEVEN

Abraham, his fractured ribs strapped in place, was able to go back to work almost immediately. But for weeks after the disastrous honeymoon Mae had to stay in bed. Wherever she looked in the little apartment, she saw the books piled high. When guests came, the books had to be removed to provide a place to sit. She chided herself because she couldn't get up to straighten the place. She couldn't even make breakfast for her husband.

At last after two weeks, Mae was able to drag herself around a little. One thing she'd have to get used to was Abraham's early rising, because she was a night person herself. She loved the luxury of a good morning sleep and here he was always up in the predawn darkness bustling with energy.

When she heard him whistling in the shower, she'd slip into her bathrobe and, her eyes heavy-lidded with sleep, she'd stumble around the kitchen percolating coffee, fixing oatmeal, bacon, eggs, toast. By the time he was out of the shower, everything was ready for him. He'd go for the paper and return for breakfast. And after he'd eaten and gone, she would creep back to bed exhausted.

The first day he expressed his appreciation warmly. But as the days went by, he became less and less communicative. Finally there came a morning when he simply buried himself behind his paper and said nothing at all. Mae felt something was very wrong between them.

"Just what is it?" she asked him frankly.

He looked at her squarely.

"You know," he said, "I prefer to have breakfast alone."

She stared at him disbelievingly. The great sacrifice was no longer necessary.

"Then I can sleep?" she asked eagerly.

"Yes," he assured her.

Far from feeling neglected by an incapacitated wife, he had actually been enjoying those meals at the little Greek restaurant on the corner. He'd struck up a fine friendship with Fred, the taxi driver, who by prearrangement came every morning to take him to work. They always had breakfast, or at least coffee together, while Fred regaled him with his philosophical and political opinions. The inquisitive doctor, versed in medical research, appreciated Fred's insights, uncontaminated by the sophisticated jargon of the learned and fresh with the very stuff of living. The taxi driver's homely philosophy went straight to the heart of things, and the doctor began making careful notes of everything his companion said. It was part of the great research he had been conducting for years among average people, ever since he had come to the conclusion that the textbooks of the intellectuals could contribute little to a real understanding of human beings.

Perhaps Mae's first weeks of confinement, which weighed on her so heavily, were really a blessing which she didn't recognize at the time. They gave her a chance gradually to become accustomed to this eccentric European-born scholar, some twelve years her senior, to whom she was now married. They were so opposite in temperament that though they were both very much in love it didn't bode well for an easy first year of marriage.

Mae had been a typical American career girl, enjoying her freedom and leading a carefree social life. She was well-versed in the requisite small talk for cocktail parties. But such talk had became a lost art with Abraham, immersed as he was in his study and work.

Mae took for granted all the new conveniences which made life easy. Abraham still deplored the modern emphasis on speed and efficiency, the constant search for the easy way of doing things. In every push-button innovation he saw a threat to man's self-sufficiency and self-discipline.

There was about him, too, an air of formal reserve that Mae quickly learned couldn't be easily breached. Once she tried calling him Abe—Abraham seemed so formal to her. But he gravely corrected her, "My name is Abraham." From then on Mae always called him either Abraham, or, in public, The Doctor. In private they usually addressed each other in endearing terms.

It was natural that the apartment with which Abraham had never found any fault should depress Mae with its drabness. When she was able to get around a little more, she began renovating it with soap, paint, and gay shelf paper. She couldn't do much at a time because she was still weak. But gradually, as the apartment became transformed under her busy hands, her strength came back. Even after she had completely recuperated from the accident, however, her facial disfigurements still made her unpresentable to friends and associates. This was difficult for the fun-loving young woman who up until then had led such an outgoing life.

Yet when eventually the scars disappeared, it was Mae herself who held back when Abraham brought her their first invitation to dinner with a group of his colleagues from the University of Chicago. As a child Mae had been quite shy. She had overcome that shyness as far as her own social set was concerned. But the people she was going to meet now were totally different—professors and scholars, all erudite thinkers. How could she possibly enter into their profound discussions?

"What can I talk about with these men?" she wailed in despair to Abraham. "I'd rather not go."

But he wouldn't hear of it. "Oh, no, you just be yourself," he advised her.

Mae went to the dinner in trepidation but it wasn't long before she was completely at ease. She became engrossed in conversation with the professors beside whom she found herself seated at dinner, and discovered that they were just as attentive to what she had to say as if she had had a college degree. After that she never worried over what she was going to talk about with her husband's colleagues.

Later from a mutual friend she learned of Abraham's attitude toward education. When someone asked him how many degrees his new wife had, assuming that, after all, a man as learned as he would want a partner of equal erudition, he had replied, "Heavens, I'd never marry anyone who had a lot of degrees. I couldn't stand an intellectual wife. I want someone with common sense, someone who knows how to manage life. And Mae knows how to do that."

Mae was to treasure that statement as one of the finest compliments she was ever to receive from her husband. During the first year of marriage, when she found herself plunged into a completely different and more exacting milieu than she had ever known before, it gave her a feeling of confidence in herself as the wife of this brilliant doctor.

She needed this feeling of confidence because, considerate as Abraham was, he was not an easy man to live with. He could in some instances be strict and demanding. He also had to change many of his bachelor ways, the habits and modes of behavior to which he had become accustomed through long years of living alone.

It took Mae a while to master the art of cooking, but presently she became so successful in the kitchen that her new husband began to prefer her meals to any he could get outside. The most difficult item she had to prepare was coffee. No coffee she brewed seemed to please him. She bought the most expensive brands and he still complained about it.

She appealed to her mother, who was Norwegian by nationality. Like most Norwegians she always had a pot of coffee on, and it was always delicious. Her mother taught her the secrets of good coffee making—the egg shell, the brand, the split-second of brewing. Mae's coffee came out clear and wonderfully fragrant. But still her husband found fault with it.

Finally one day he returned from the university with what he was sure would be the solution to the problem. "You know my secretary, Miss Goodman, makes wonderful coffee," he told his wife. "Would you please phone her and ask her how she does it?"

So Mae phoned Grace Goodman. The secretary replied in some astonishment, "Mrs. Low, I don't know anything about coffee making. I put it on and who turns it off I don't know. It just perks and perks."

"What kind of coffee do you get?" Mae asked, thinking that the solution lay in the brand.

"We get the A & P Eight O'Clock coffee," Grace answered.

Mae knew all about Eight O'Clock coffee. That year, selling
for fourteen cents a pound, it was just about the cheapest coffee
on the market. She took the enigma to her mother again. And
this time something clicked in her mother's head.

"Has he been eating in Greek restaurants?" she demanded.

Mae remembered the little Greek restaurant on the corner where
Abraham had been taking his meals for years, and nodded.

"Then he's just used to old boiled coffee," her mother said
scornfully.

2.

Mae was determined to be a good wife, the kind she'd read about
who help their husbands' careers along. So at first she tried to
please Abraham in everything, keeping her grievances bottled up
until, unable to stand it any longer, she would finally explode
with them. Only then would Abraham become aware that something was wrong and say in surprise, "Now what?"

He always saw the justice of Mae's complaint once it was out in
the open. "You know you're right," he'd agree. "I'll watch that.
I'll try not to do it again."

In some ways Abraham was incredibly naive where women were
concerned. That first year of marriage he would receive letters
now and then from girls he had dated in former times. One day
after receiving such a letter he asked Mae, "Would you mind if I
invited her here for a visit?" and he went on to confide that she
was an old sweetheart.

Mae couldn't believe her ears. But this time she didn't explode.
Instinctively she realized that it wasn't a situation in which to
show anger. So instead she replied with a smile, "Tell you what,
I'll invite a couple of my old sweethearts, too, and we'll all have a
ball."

He stared back at her stunned, the enormity of his request
finally dawning on him. He never made it again or even brought
up the subject and presently the letters, too, stopped coming.

As for Mae, it was her intuitive qualities which Abraham held
in the highest regard. She had, he told her, a fine intuition which
needed only to be trained and channeled. And he began teaching

her how to apply rational judgments to her feelings. When meeting someone for the first time she learned to go beyond saying, "Well, there's something not just right here," to analyzing what it was in the person's voice or manner that made her suspicious of his sincerity.

Mae didn't need any training, however, where her husband's feelings were concerned. So great was the rapport between them that she was able to divine these at once. Sometimes when men were more gallant toward her than common courtesy called for she would realize his annoyance without his having said a word. When this happened she would take care not to see the offending person again so as not to give Abraham cause for unhappiness.

She wanted no estrangement between them to mar their companionship. She had so little time really to be with him, so little of life to share with him, immersed as he was in his work. Before their marriage he had explained to her the importance of that work. He had told her that it had to come first, that there wouldn't be much room for social activities. He'd asked her anxiously if this mattered to her. And Mae had replied that it didn't, that she'd had her fill of frivolity.

So instead of the parties of former days, Mae spent as much time as possible accompanying her husband in his work. When he went on tours of the out-of-town hospitals, she would go with him. She would sit through the tedious hours while he diagnosed patients in the clinics for the benefit of the hospital staff and the young medical students. From these out-of-town clinics he would select the most unique patients and have them transferred to the Research Hospital in Chicago for further study by himself.

Only rarely might a patient throw something at him during his inspections of the wards. But he was not afraid of violence. Though he was not a big man, he was strong. And there was an air of quiet authority, even of sternness about him at such times that kept the patients in check.

And, always, Mae was to see him leaving the wards with the tears running down his cheeks. "Poor wretches, poor wretches," he would be muttering. "Something has to be done for them."

He was upset by more than the illness of these patients. As assistant alienist his duty was to inspect the state hospitals, and much of what he found shocked him. Many doctors, long in charge, were getting rusty and indifferent to their patients' needs. Ensconsed in a sinecure, they showed litle interest in keeping up with modern treatments.

Dr. Low returned from his visits with the recommendation that the doctors in state hospitals be ordered to come in to the Psychiatric Institute from time to time to take refresher courses. Dr. Singer, an ardent reformer himself, with Governor Horner behind him, backed his assistant, and the disgruntled doctors had to attend the courses set up for them. It was not likely they would look with affection on their blunt, outspoken younger colleague. But Dr. Low didn't care for their personal opinions of him. It was the welfare of his patients which was always closest to his heart.

3.

In his private affairs, there was the promise of new life. Mae was expecting their first child. A bigger apartment would be needed which would provide more privacy and better accommodations than the small hotel rooms, although it must have been with some reluctance that Abraham left his bachelor quarters where he had lived for so long. The new place into which he and his young wife moved that April of 1936 was situated on Arlington Place.

By the standards of the time it was far more modern than had been the hotel apartment on Fullerton, and there were innovations in it that actually shocked Abraham. He couldn't believe his eyes the first day he strolled into the kitchen and saw Mae lighting the gas burners of the stove with a pilot light.

"This modern business!" he scolded, while Mae, who hadn't given the pilot light a thought, stared at him in disbelief. "Everywhere you turn there's something to take the challenge out of life and make it easy. Now you can't even scratch a match to light a fire."

But presently Abraham became used to the new place, even the pilot light. He and Mae were both looking forward to the coming child. They talked a lot about it.

Of course it would be a boy. That was what Abraham wanted more than anything—a boy to accompany him on camping and hiking trips, to roughhouse with him, to carry on his name, and perhaps to follow in his footsteps. He was so confident it would be a boy that he picked the name Philip for it. But when finally on October 3 the child was born, it was a girl. So they called her Phyllis instead of Philip.

There was little time those days for the new father to devote to his child. Important changes were taking place in the treatment of the mentally ill. It had begun in 1933 when Dr. Manfred Sakel of Vienna had published his report on his daring treatment of schizophrenia, then called dementia praecox. He had been giving his patients heavy doses of insulin—doses which up until that time had been considered dangerous to life. Not only was he administering those supposedly lethal doses, but he was administering them at intervals, producing a comatose state in the patient which might last over a considerable period. In the beginning most psychiatrists regarded Dr. Sakel's treatments as bordering on the homicidal. But by 1936 several leading clinics in Europe were trying the new treatment and reporting favorable, even startling results.

Meanwhile another physician, Dr. Ladislas J. Meduna of Budapest, had been experimenting with intravenous Metrazol injections. Metrazol produced temporary convulsions but matched the curative powers of the insulin treatment. Three years of intensive Metrazol testing bore out the positive results of the first experiments.

Finally, by June of 1936, with the approval of Dr. Singer, Dr. Low began treating his patients with insulin and Metrazol shock treatments. Both the Metrazol and insulin treatments of that day were not without danger to the patient's life, and Dr. Low always administered them himself. But he also needed skilled nurses to keep the patient under constant surveillance and to act quickly should the need arise.

This required thorough training which he would not entrust to anyone else. Student nurses at the hospital were rotated every several months and the head of the nurses' training program refused to allow even Dr. Low to keep any of them in his department beyond that length of time. So he had to retrain new recruits at short intervals. It was an exhaustive process that took up much of his precious time.

4.

The dramatic improvements which resulted from the shock treatments were to Dr. Low the final proof of the inherent error in the psychoanalytic school, which had been claiming for years that mental illness was due solely to psychological causes such as childhood traumas and fixations.

In his enthusiasm he wrote an article with this as its thesis and sent it around to his colleagues, hopeful that his incisive essay would show them the new era into which psychiatry was now entering. But instead of being convinced by the proofs he offered, the psychoanalysts merely resented the article which cast such doubt on the validity of their own theories. It was the beginning of a rupture between the pioneering doctor and the well-entrenched psychoanalysts in the state universities and it was to widen with the years.

Meanwhile, the shock treatments were to open up a whole new world of contact between Dr. Low and the patients he had longed so much to help. Unlike many psychiatrists of his day, he was not disillusioned when shock treatments turned out not to be the panacea hoped for, but only a form of temporary relief. He was not surprised when statistics showed that a high percentage of the patients who had been returned to normalcy by this method were soon back in the hospital.

He realized that while the shock treatments restored the physiological functions, enabling the patient to reason, to feel, to memorize, and to concentrate again, the personality traits usually remained deficient. These important traits, which include a sympathetic attitude to others, a sense of fairness and of humor, an overall ability to adjust to the group, had to be acquired before the patient could live a normal life in the outside community. Shock treatments, which broke the circuit of obsessive thoughts and habits, gave the patient a respite during which he could be trained. If he was not trained, he was likely to revert to his former unrealistic adjustment to life.

It was such training that Dr. Low now began to inaugurate among the patients at the Psychiatric Institute. From his years of study he had evolved the conception of the duality operating in nature. Everything that had life and movement was made up of a pair of opposites, he had discovered. Even language was so constructed that the meaning of one of the pair could not be understood until it was linked to the other. How could "Above" be understood without its counterpart "Below," or "Right" without "Wrong," or "Comfort" unless contrasted to "Effort"?

"All human thinking is built on the twosome principle," he would explain to his staff. "You can't have love without hate."

The opposites, he would continue, were always in a state of tension, and whenever one moved to meet the other, a tug of war would ensue which would result in victory for one or the other. In his efforts to bring understanding to his patients he made full use of this basic law of opposites. He discovered that so engrained was the concept of opposites in the human psyche that explanations couched in terms of simple contrast were easily grasped by the patient. Once the patient realized that for every negative force there was a positive tool with which to combat it, he could overcome abnormality with sanity. This was later to be an integral part of the Method he was to evolve: a positive force to overcome every negative condition. That is why the techniques of the Method consist of such homely tools as: "Excuse don't accuse," to keep one's feelings of aggression in control; "Move your muscles" to overcome inertia; "Control your muscles" to control impulse; "Take the secure thought in place of the insecure"; "Do the thing you fear to do."

He acknowledged his adherence to the tenets of semantics by insisting on accurate statements from his patients. He had come to realize that it was the faulty interpretations they put on their experiences that was the basis of most of their mental and emotional maladjustments. That was why he cautioned them against using flamboyant phrases such as "I can't bear it," "This headache is killing me," "I just knew I was dying." With him "depressions" became "lowered feelings," "discouragement" became "self-defeatism," "a crying spell" became "a crying habit."

He looked on wordiness as a sign of the intellectuality which he had come to abhor and which he carefully differentiated from intelligence. "Keep it simple," he was always telling his patients. One of the most important tenets of his Method was the dictum,

"Simple but not easy." He never promised them a magic pill, but only that if they continued doggedly through difficulties and failures to practice the rules he was giving them they would achieve health. A complete cure was the goal he set for all his patients.

He was intrinsically a man of action despite the long hours he spent in philosophical studies. He always made it clear to his patients that insight alone was not enough. To be cured it was necessary to put that insight into practice in everyday life. And if there was a choice between practicing new constructive behavior patterns and merely understanding why they ought to be developed, the emphasis should be placed on practice, which would eventually bring understanding in its wake. His greatest successes came, surprisingly enough, when he coupled a minimum of explanations with an authoritative order, "Do this, whether you understand or not, whether you believe or not. Substitute my diagnosis for yours. Substitute my positive belief in your ability to get well for your own negative fears."

In that day, when permissiveness was the hallmark of most psychiatric counseling, Dr. Low's approach was looked at askance. There were complaints that he had brought a Prussian attitude into the field of psychiatry. His "Do it because I say it is right" struck many in his profession as too arbitrary. They even compared the jaunty upright stride with which he marched down corridors, his back straight as a ramrod, to Prussian militarism.

The young student nurses who worked under him were filled with awe, not unmixed with fear, because this forthright doctor wouldn't accept slackness in the least particular, especially where his patients were concerned. They were the most important persons in the world to him and his main goal in life was to return them cured to the outside world. He was most exacting in the therapy he gave them, and expected the same exactitude from his staff, especially during those dangerous hours that followed the shock treatments.

The young nurses whispered among themselves that he had eyes in the back of his head. Little escaped his attention. And his creed made a deep impression on at least one of them, Lorraine Bagby.

"He never believed that a patient was incurable," she was to

recall, "and we didn't believe so either, or let him know our
thoughts if we did."

"There are no hopeless cases—helpless perhaps, but not hopeless." This was the foremost law by which the wards were run.

5.

At night Abraham would come home, tired from an arduous day
but glowing with enthusiasm and full of reports of the patients
who were being returned whole to their families. His life was
wrapped up in those patients. After twenty minutes or so of play
with his baby daughter and conversation with his wife he would
retire to his study where he would spend the evenings immersed
in his work. Then to bed and up again for another early morning
session with his books and papers.

It was lucky for Mae that she had the child to occupy her time,
because she was seeing even less of Abraham than before. She
had other household chores to keep her busy too. Her husband's
salary was too meager to pay for a housekeeper, and until he could
bring in more money, frugality in the home had to be practiced.
It would be a number of years before Mae could afford help.

Meanwhile, with a family to support, Abraham, who had never
given much thought to the amassing of money, realized he would
have to do something to augment his income. So in addition to
his work at the medical school, he went back to private psychiatric
practice. He rented an office and equipped it with the furniture
he had put into storage when he had joined the university teaching staff. Out came the couch which had figured so prominently
in his psychoanalytic days. It was with a sense of wry self-humor
that Abraham restored it to a place in his consultation room. But
it was never again used for a patient. Occasionally when he needed
rest he would stretch out on it for a few moments, lying motionless, his usual way of relaxing nervous tension.

As for his patients, he met them face to face now and he talked
to them in the same forthright, authoritative way which he used
in the hospital. He would allow no difference of opinion or questioning of his views in matters in which he regarded himself as
an authority. But underneath his bluntness lay a depth of sincere

concern for his patients' welfare that they felt. In later years one of them was to say of him, "He was always very kind, but never sympathetic." In his office a patient was not permitted to pour out endless complaints.

His new approach, so diametrically opposed to the psychoanalytic tenets of that day, was remarkably effective. His reputation spread and he began to receive referrals, especially from general practitioners. Friends, too, sent relatives or acquaintances. His clientele consisted mainly of affluent business men and their families and members of high society.

Some of his colleagues became quite jealous. It wasn't pleasant for them to have patients leave their couches to go to the eccentric Viennese and be cured.

He tried to tell them that they could effect the same cures if they would use his techniques, and he eagerly offered to teach them all he knew. But in the recondite psychoanalytic atmosphere of that day, they could not believe that a method of straightforward questioning, coupled with authoritative statements of fact and simple rules for living, could accomplish results where Freudian methods had failed.

"It's your personality that cures them, Low. It's that Viennese manner of yours," they told him, dismissing the whole subject.

Had it not been for the solid backing of Dr. Singer, his novel psychotherapeutic approach at the Psychiatric Institute would likely have had short shrift.

EIGHT

In the spring of 1936 a young medical student named Joe Janis failed his course in surgery at the tough medical school of the University of Illinois. It meant that he would have to take the course over again. But to young Joe it seemed like the end of the world.

Joe's parents had come from Lithuania and spoke broken English. They'd never been to school a day in their lives. It was this lack of theirs which had made Joe, from his earliest days, feel so humiliated that he overlooked their good qualities, such as their love for him and their desire to help him in every way they could. Each mispronounced word they uttered made him miserable. He had become first impatient and then downright angry with them when they failed to learn to speak the new language properly.

He was always out of sorts with his brother and sister too. It seemed they also were completely indifferent to improving their lives. He was constantly urging them to make more of themselves. Desperately he wanted to be proud of them, of himself. For of course he held the same rigid, unrealistic standards for himself too.

He wanted to excel in every field and actually believed he could. Once he'd even made up his mind that he could become another Paderewski if only he tried hard enough. He'd taken piano lessons, though he had obviously no talent along that line, and had practiced long arduous hours in pursuit of his fanciful goal.

Throughout high school he had worked diligently to achieve

scholastic honors and in this he had been successful. He had been
among the top ten of his class of four hundred when he'd graduated from high school in Chicago. He had even given the
graduation address before going on, laden with honors, to the
University of Illinois.

Now he had flunked a test, an important test. What was wrong
with him? He reproached himself for his failure, and somber
thoughts of his complete worthlessness began to nag at him until
his thinking became confused. He lost all his energy and grew
so sluggish it became an effort for him to accomplish the simplest
things. It was as though he were continually pushing his way
through water. In his desperation he even toyed with the idea of
suicide. But he was fortunately too practical a man to entertain
the thought seriously.

Finally the surgical instructor at school noticed his condition
and suggested that he see Dr. Low. His first visit was a brief one,
but enough to impress Joe with the Viennese doctor who sat
facing him. Here was a man who exuded self-confidence. He was
the first person Joe had ever met who was able to convince him
just by his bearing that he knew a little more about any subject
under discussion than Joe himself did. And that wasn't easy, because Joe regarded himself as an intellectual with the answers to
everything.

"What struck you immediately was that he was every bit the
doctor," Joe was to recall in later days. "He had the bearing, the
nobility you associate with this profession. He lived and died by
his dignity. It was a precious thing to him."

When, after examining him, the doctor said, "It seems to me
you need treatment. Are you willing to come to the hospital?"
Joe agreed at once. His condition was so severe that he was to stay
in the hospital for several months.

He was given a few shock treatments to jolt him out of his black
depression. After the very first treatment he experienced the light-
hearted freedom which the shock therapy was bringing to so many
sufferers. Suddenly he could revel in such simple pleasures as
sunlight, the singing of birds, colors, tastes, feelings. It was such
a joyful experience that he made up his mind never to fall ill
again if he could help it.

After the shock treatments Dr. Low began giving him psychotherapy. There was no beating around the bush, no drawn-out

delving into the world of the unconscious. This doctor used the classical rational approach which had long since gone out of style. He cut through to Joe's problem with the lucidity that was his particular genius. He not only had the ability to diagnose, but he could also convey his insights to his patients.

Only a few sessions with the doctor brought the impact of what Joe had been doing to himself plainly home to him. His trouble was a consuming drive for power. He craved the triumph of being a superman, of excelling in everything. His persistent depressions were the result of the unrealistic goal of perfection he had set for himself. Since fulfillment was impossible, his goal was causing him frustrations and tensions that burned up energy, frayed his nervous system, and left him sluggish and confused.

But the doctor never let any of his patients rest on insight alone. He told Joe that to cure himself of his depressions he would have to build up a whole new set of habits. It wouldn't be easy but he could do it if he made up his mind to work at it.

The doctor was a firm believer in the free will of every individual. It wasn't an intellectual conception, it was a vital part of him, as natural as breathing. A person had the choice of changing his habits and bringing himself back to mental health, if he would only exercise his free will.

It was the doctor's compelling personality that gave Joe the incentive to work on himself. But it was Joe himself who did the work, and he was well equipped for it. In his vain striving for perfection he had at least acquired the habit of application. Now he concentrated on getting well.

He learned to lower his sights to a more realistic view of himself. He admitted his tendency to dream of great accomplishments but acknowledged that such dreams were common to mankind. Instead of trying to bring his impossible dreams to fruition and getting disgusted with himself when he failed, he learned to regard them with humor.

When he felt tensions mounting, he trained himself to examine his thoughts carefully. Such examination was called "spotting" by Dr. Low. It meant turning the spotlight on one's mental activities to discover the unrealistic thinking that had slipped in and was creating the turmoil. Once spotted, it could be corrected by exchanging it for a more realistic appraisal.

Joe's constant practice to keep his goals within normal limits was strengthening his nervous system, which was no longer being keyed up by impossible demands. Gradually the energy he had lost became available to him again. He was better able to tackle his problems realistically.

And one day he walked out of the hospital, not yet completely cured, but convinced that that would come with practice. He had a tool to work with—the concept of averageness. So long as he accepted the realistic belief of being average—a man among other men—he had no need to fear that his tensions would mount to another breakdown. In the autumn he would resume his medical education.

2.

As Joe was leaving the hospital another very ill man was entering it. He was not without prestige in the entertainment world, for he was Harlan Tarbell, one of the country's foremost magicians. Harlan's life was made up of continual tours, each involving a procession of one-night stands across the country. Since it was before the day of commercial air flights, he had to travel at night by train. At each stop there were welcoming committees, interviews, luncheons, dinners, and parties in addition to his performances.

For four years Harlan kept up the strenuous pace, traveling from Maine to California, from Florida to Canada. May of 1936 found him in Denver, Colorado, fighting down fatigue as he prepared for his one-night show there. The fatigue worried him and he found time in his crowded schedule to visit a doctor. The doctor, who had a health home, told him he was working too hard and should spend a month at his place.

In August, when Harlan's tour was over, he came back and entered the doctor's establishment. The doctor's regimen was a faddish one. He separated the magician from his wife, held him incommunicado, and put him on a strict fast. On the eighteenth day of his fast Harlan experienced an unnerving psychic experience. He pleaded desperately with the doctor for food, but the doctor was adamant. Harlan wasn't even allowed to contact his wife and the fast continued. On the twenty-ninth day he had another experience so terrifying that he almost died from shock.

By the time Mrs. Tarbell learned of her husband's predicament and rescued him, his body could no longer tolerate food. He tried to get back into his profession with the hope that work would jog him out of the deep depression which had settled upon him. For a while he was able to manage a couple of engagements a week. But work did little to lift his spirits. He still was unable to eat and he scarcely slept at all. At last he became so nervous that he could not perform.

He had always been a sociable man. Now he could no longer enjoy the company of others. The psychic experiences he had undergone haunted him. And presently he refused the company even of his close friends. He spent his days sitting at home staring into space or walking aimlessly around in a starved half-dazed condition.

At last in January of 1937 his distraught wife brought him to the University of Illinois Research Hospital. He was now down to seventy-nine pounds and every movement was a torture to him.

Even Dr. Low didn't see much hope for the emaciated skeleton of a man who sat before him. But he cleared away the intervening red tape and within two weeks made it possible for Harlan to be admitted to the Psychiatric Institute, where he began his long uphill climb back to health. He was given insulin in small quantities to crack the hold his depression had on him, and force-fed to start up his sluggish digestive system. Gradually his strength returned and he began to learn all over again how to perform the routine chores of living.

He learned to eat when he didn't feel like eating. He learned to conquer his fears and inertias by forcing himself out of the sanctuary of his room and ward, a step at a time. He was able to do it, not by trying to reorganize his scattered thoughts, but simply by commanding his muscles to do the acts he set for them.

"Use your muscles." This was the tool prescribed to get him back on his feet again. Dr. Low had discovered that far from having to be always controlled by the brain, the muscles could take over and control the brain when it was paralyzed with inertia and fear. They could perform and reeducate it until it was able to resume command again. Using the muscles was coupled with another tool: "Do the thing you fear to do." The doctor explained to Harlan that doing the thing you fear, when that fear is caused only by nervous symptoms and not by a realistic danger, is the most effective way of removing the tension from a situation.

Presently, by using these tools, Harlan was able to force himself to walk as far as the hospital gate. Next he went out on short shopping trips for doctors and nurses. Finally he began going downtown to have dinner with the old friends he had blocked out of his life for so many months.

In September of 1937, he was released from the hospital on probation. Like Joe, he was improved but not completely cured. That full cure would have to come in the outside world. Dr. Low, who recognized the tenacity of habits, didn't believe in keeping his patients in the hospital any longer than was absolutely necessary. He knew that once the security of hospital routines got into their blood nothing could force them to stay in the world permanently. They would always come back.

Harlan's weight was now normal, his frightening psychic experiences were placed in their proper perspective, but he hadn't conquered all his fears. They were primarily professional ones now. He wondered if his old skills were lost to him forever. When the theatrical Shubert family who were good friends of his, offered him the Selwyn theater for a Sunday matinee, he hesitated. But there was the tool at hand which Dr. Low had given him: "Do the thing you fear to do." So he accepted their offer, and to show their complete confidence in him, they provided him with the necessary stage hands and orchestra.

For Harlan that Sunday matinee was the turning point. All the tricks and maneuvers he had thought he had forgotten or was too clumsy to perform came back to him. Even the old humor, with which he had spiced his former shows, was ready at hand. The successful Sunday matinee was proof that Harlan had fully recovered. He ordered his New York manager to book the season for him.

3.

Joe and Harlan were only two of many patients from all walks of life who were being jolted back to normalcy by shock treatments and then strengthened by Dr. Low's unique psychotherapy methods for a fresh bout with the outside world. All patients were discharged on probation and were expected to return to the hospital at stated intervals during the first months of their discharge to be examined and given additional therapy in case of threatened relapse.

The doctors would have preferred keeping closer contact with their patients even after the probation period was over. But in the old days this had never been possible. When the spontaneously cured patients had come to the end of their probationary period, they had severed all connections with the hospital, which to them was a place of shame. Even their relatives had refused to answer solicitous questions when the hospital staff contacted them.

Now a phenomenon was occurring where the shock-treated patients were concerned. In the spring of 1937 many of those whose probationary period was over began coming back to the Psychiatric Institute on their own initiative. To them the hospital was not a place to be avoided, but a refuge where they had been cured and could be assured a sympathic hearing. Their grievances were many. One after the other they described the humiliations that the stigma attached to their disease was causing them.

Although they had been declared fully cured by their physicians, they complained that the outside world still regarded them as suspect. Family, friends, community, and potential employers all seemed to believe that "once a mental patient, always one." And to avoid ostracism they had to keep their illness a dark secret from everyone. The isolation, the loneliness, the complete lack of sympathy for their problem was often strong enough to cause a patient to relapse.

Finally that fall some of these discharged patients formed a delegation and came to Dr. Low, appealing to him to help them find some solution to the stigma which was ruining their lives. In answer to their pleas he set up a conference with them for November 7 in the old room where, during their stay at the hospital, the patients had gathered for group psychotherapy.

Thirty patients showed up that night, one of them coming from as far away as Pittsburgh. Many were accompanied by their relatives. Dr. Low and his staff and the nurses on the ward made a total of fifty. The small room was overcrowded and the ventilation was bad. The seats were uncomfortable and there weren't enough of them to go around. Many people had to find places on table tops and window sills, but their spirit was electric. Dr. Low beamed at them all like a proud father.

Here in the crowded room they began to speak openly of their illness and suffering. "Why should there be a distinction between people who are sick above the neck and those sick below the neck?" one patient asked. He was referring to the fact that though the cause of mental illness had been proved to be a breakdown in the nervous system, stigma was still attached to those who suffered from it, while no one was blamed for having digestive or circulatory troubles. The patients reached the conclusion that such discrimination could only be the result of misinformation about the illness itself. Once the public realized that this disease also was physiological in origin, it would surely stop condemning innocent sufferers, and the stigma could be eradicated.

By the time the meeting broke up the group had decided to form an organization, headed by Dr. Low, which would serve three purposes. It would provide the patients with a congenial atmosphere in which they could freely express themselves, giving them some relief from the unbearable isolation they were experiencing now. It would enable Dr. Low and his staff to keep a much closer check on the discharged patients than had previously been possible. And it would become a potent force in the battle to eradicate public ignorance about mental illness.

That meeting in that small crowded room was the beginning of the nationwide organization which was later to be known as Recovery, Inc.

Fanny Low, just before leaving Europe.

Fanny and Theresa Low at Coney Island in 1926.

Selma's home in Chicago, where Dr. Low lived on first arrival from East.

Mrs. Mae Low.

Marilyn (right) and Phyllis Low at the piano.

Dr. Low seated with his two daughters, Marilyn (left) and Phyllis.

Dr. Low relaxing at home with pipe and book.

Dr. Jerry Freund's Fairview Hospital in the 1940's and early 1950's when Dr. Low brought his patients there at the time when he was excluded from the principal Chicago hospitals.

Dr. Low with his daughters, Phyllis (left) and Marilyn, at their new home in Evanston, summer of 1949.

Annette Brocken on a visit to Brighton, Michigan, 1955.

Mrs. Low and her daughter, Phyllis Cameron, on the last occasion that Mrs. Low visited Recovery Headquarters, October 30, 1969.

Mrs. Low and her son-in-law, David Cameron, on the last occasion that she visited Headquarters, October 30, 1969. Photo by "Bobby" Coke.

Phyllis Cameron (right) and Marilyn Schmitt admiring portrait of their father, Dr. Abraham A. Low, at Recovery Headquarters, 197 Photo by "Bobby" Coke.

Phyllis Low Cameron holding plaque for Dr. Abraham A. Low Volunteer of the Year Award established in 1971 by the Mental Health Association of Greater Chicago.

Phil Crane, National Director of Leader Training.

Mrs. Treasure Rice, President of Recovery, Inc., May, 1963—May, 1969
May; 1970—May, 1971

NINE

By 1938 the organization was well launched. Harlan Tarbell was named president and an Executive Committee was appointed which would operate under the direction of Dr. Low. Meetings were set up for the first Sunday of every month and membership was to be composed of three sections: regular members (made up of former patients and resident physicians at the institute), associate members (relatives of the patients), contributing members (all those interested in the organization).

A name was selected which was descriptive though lengthy. It was: Association of the Former Patients of the Psychiatric Institute of the University of Illinois and the Department of Public Welfare. In subsequent months that name, appearing on envelopes containing literature from organization headquarters at the Institute, was to generate a flood of anguished complaints. The revealing title had brought suffering and fear to the recipients of the telltale mail, and in some instances actual hardship. One former patient was even asked to move from the rooming house where he lived, the landlord explaining he didn't wish to have any "crazy" tenants there. So a new name had to be chosen— one that revealed everything and at the same time nothing. After much deliberation "Recovery" was selected. From then on it alone appeared on the envelopes of all communications addressed to former patients.

Recovery hadn't been long in existence before its members began to realize that they were missing the psychotherapy classes which they had attended at the hospital. Finally a group of them asked Dr. Low to hold similar classes for them. He was touched and pleased. Despite his busy schedule he set aside the second Thursday of every month for an informal study group to be conducted for the former patients along the same lines as the hospital psychotherapy classes. In the relaxed atmosphere patients could discuss their problems and receive instruction from the doctor.

There were three valuable services which the new organization could provide the staff of the Psychiatric Institute. First, since Recovery meetings were being held in the hospital, the doctors and nurses could keep close check on those discharged patients who attended them. Second, the improved patients still at the hospital could also attend Recovery meetings and become familiar with the organization before they left.

The third service was organized under Miss Beatrice Wade, director of Curriculum in Occupational Therapy at the Psychiatric Institute, and Dr. Low's firm friend through the years. It was the Membership Committee and it was made up of volunteers from among discharged patients who attended Recovery meetings faithfully. These members visited patients with poor attendance records, and while trying to persuade them to return to the meetings took note of any behavioral peculiarities and reported them to the medical staff at the Institute. This enabled the physicians to keep track even of their most refractory former patients.

Another committee was presently formed by members and their relatives. It was called the Employment Committee and its purpose was to find work for those who were jobless. Then a third committee, the Program Committee, was organized to provide entertainment for Recovery members.

2.

In July of 1938 Dr. Low opened a new forum for his ideas and concepts with a bimonthly magazine which was called *Lost and Found,* the title referring to the patients' health which had been lost and was now found. The magazine was to be the first of a long line which, under different names and with only a few years break, was to be published up until the present.

Dr. Low hoped that the magazine would call the attention of his colleagues to the work he was doing and the new methods he was employing in the treatment of his patients. He put in long, loving hours every month editing the little magazine, to which he was almost the sole contributor in those early days. He filled it primarily with material from his psychotherapy classes and his lectures against the stigma. But a few anonymous first-hand accounts by patients and relatives were also included, together with newsworthy items concerning Recovery. During the course of the year the little journal hailed triumphantly the establishment of sister organizations, first at Peoria, then at Alton, Kankakee, and Chicago state hospitals.

"Other cities will follow the example set. . . . Other states will fall in line with Illinois. Soon the Former Patients will be on their march throughout the country. They know their goal: the elimination of the Stigma," wrote Dr. Low enthusiastically.

He had never lost sight of that goal. One of the first moves he made in that direction was aimed at reforming the antiquated commitment law of the State of Illinois. Its very wording was one of the chief humiliations felt by his patients. Such expressions as "apprehended as a lunatic," "arrested by the Sheriff," and "delivered to the asylum" gave the impression of a criminal rather than an ill person. And the court record which followed the commitment order also seemed to bear this out.

Fortunately for the movement, Dr. Singer was thoroughly in agreement with Dr. Low in his determination to change the law. In fact it had been Dr. Singer's work in earlier years which had already been successful in modifying the Illinois statute to make it less harsh than those of many other states.

Since further reforms, however, would entail a thorough study of the commitment laws of all the states, Dr. Singer appointed a panel of five psychiatrists, of whom Dr. Low was one, to collect the voluminous material. Once it was gathered, a lawyer's help had to be obtained to draft the new law—but not just any lawyer. Dr. Low, who knew so well the power of words to hurt or heal, didn't want a cold, legal document, no matter how efficient it might be in content. He wanted something, in his words, "written with spirit and love," "specialist knowledge" combined with "warm humanity." And he wanted it at no cost to Recovery members or their relatives, for it was the heart of the Depression and most of them were poverty-stricken.

Finally he appealed for help to his good friend Professor Leon

Green, dean of Northwestern University Law School. Professor Green, who had a close relative under Dr. Low's care, responded by appointing a young graduate student, Joe Nellis, to do the necessary abstracting and compiling from all the material that had been gathered.

Once Nellis had completed the first draft of the statute, a battery of professors versed in constitutional and criminal law would work it into final shape. Then it would be Recovery's job to publicize it, to present it to the state legislature, and lobby for its passage.

3.

At the same time that he commenced his campaign against the antiquated law, Dr. Low also gave his full attention to another source of stigma. He, more than anyone, was painfully aware of the part ignorant relatives played in the relapses of his patients. And so he inaugurated a series of lectures for those who still had relatives in the hospital. In his own colorful language these lectures were for the express purpose of "disinfecting the stigma-infested haunts" of the home environment. He was given a lecture hall at the university for the purpose. And here the relatives gathered twice monthly on Sundays, bringing with them the more recovered of the hospital patients.

Such training courses for relatives have become far more common today. But in that year of 1938 they were so novel a procedure that some of the relatives felt they were being imposed upon. They bitterly resented the loss of their Sunday holiday, but no excuses were accepted by the adamant doctor. They had to be there.

Mae might have wished, too, for these Sundays alone with her husband, but she knew that wasn't possible. If she wanted to be with him it had to be at his place of work. So she and Phyllis began to attend the relatives' meetings also.

The lively little girl would sit quietly while her father was lecturing. But after the meeting was over she would go racing up and down the hall outside the lecture room, her long dark hair flying around her shoulders. Her mischievous laughter echoed in the old corridor as her mother went chasing after her. She was a welcome spot of brightness in the drab lives of the patients. As they watched her they laughed, too, somehow participating in the gaiety of her freedom.

Although he had so little time to spend with his child, Abraham kept close watch over her upbringing. There was one thing he insisted upon: the little girl shouldn't be treated as a child prodigy. Once when Mae was teaching her the names of the presidents of the United States, he said bluntly, "Don't fill her mind with that rubbish. Go back to your nursery rhymes and your nonsense stories. We don't want a precocious child. We want a healthy, normal one."

He loved her just the way she was, but he had never really given up his dream of a son. And when that fall Mae became pregnant, he once more began speaking wistfully of the little boy they would surely have this time.

All this was changed one cold, rainy night when he returned bone-weary to the family apartment, wet through, his shoes soaked. He found Phyllis waiting solicitously for him in the front hall, one of his slippers grasped firmly in each hand. She would not let him remove either hat or coat until he had taken off his shoes and put on the dry slippers. For a long while that evening Abraham remained silent and thoughtful. Finally he said to Mae, "You know, a son would never have done that for me."

After that night Mae never heard him mention his desire for a boy again. And when on May 24 of the following year blonde little Marilyn arrived, he showed pleasure rather than disappointment. Regardless of Old World standards, he had come deeply to appreciate daughters.

4.

Beginning in August of 1938, Recovery had begun soliciting contributions from among its members to help defray the costs of winning public support for the reform of the Illinois Commitment Law. Everyone responded with such generosity that Dr. Low was troubled by it. In some cases, knowing that those who pressed dollar bills upon him were in straitened circumstances, he tried to refuse. But such was the gratitude of the donors that they wouldn't hear of taking their money back.

By the end of the year the treasury boasted three hundred dollars. And in the spring of 1939 Recovery launched its campaign. It began when the moderator of a popular radio program offered to do a series of shows presenting the problem of the stigma as it affected the patients' individual lives. Several volunteers agreed to appear on the show anonymously and describe their experiences.

They performed with conviction but the program turned out to be a great disappointment. Though it was beamed into thousands of homes, only a few letters of appreciation or inquiry came to Dr. Low's desk afterwards. The public had simply not responded.

The next step in the campaign was a series of lectures given by Dr. Low. Each one of them was followed by a discussion period during which the former patients and their relatives bravely stood up and described their experiences. Only the public still wasn't there to witness it, to hear what they had to say. The Recovery members themselves supplied the bulk of the audience.

Dr. Low was more disheartened than he cared to admit. How was the public to be educated, he asked himself, if its interest in the plight of the former patient couldn't even be roused enough to come and take a look? Perhaps the printed word was the answer. If an article on Recovery and what it was doing and attempting to do could appear in a national magazine, it would attract the attention of thousands.

He was elated when Dr. Paul de Kruif, the popular medical writer, took an interest in the little organization, asked for an interview with one of the members, and promised to write about it. Another opportunity for getting the message to the country at large seemed to present itself in the person of a young newspaperman by the name of Greer Williams, who had attended a couple of Recovery meetings and had then started talking with the doctor. Dr. Low was impressed by the young man's enthusiasm, and as usual when he had such an audience he used Williams as a sounding board for his ideas. Relaxed and at ease as he always was in such situations, the doctor made no attempt to curb the free flow of his opinions, often delivered in the colorful language which had so fascinated his audiences of earlier years. Williams, sensing an exciting story, finally suggested that he write an article on Recovery.

5.

With two articles promised him, Dr. Low then examined another possibility: bringing Recovery to the attention of his colleagues in the psychiatric profession. The convention of the American Psychiatric Association was being held in Chicago that May, and Dr. Low had been asked to read a paper on Recovery before it. To spotlight that paper, why not have Recovery call a convention of its own at the same time, bringing in delegates from its sister associations and setting up an exhibit at the Psychiatric convention headquarters?

All went as planned, but the results were again disappointing to Dr. Low. He was unable to describe all the functions of Recovery in the bare twenty minutes allotted him. It was only as he began to read his brief paper aloud that he realized unhappily that it was not only dull but uninformative.

However, he felt that his failure to get Recovery across should have been more than compensated for by the young women who managed the Recovery booth. They did an effective job of showing how they were eradicating stigma in their own lives by giving their full names, answering questions, and describing their illnesses. All in all, they acted like any other normal young women, a far cry from the usual secretive, cowed manner of the former mental patient.

Many psychiatrists stopped at their booth to hear what they had to say and all of them seemed quite interested. But only one of them, apparently, felt it worthwhile to visit the Recovery headquarters at the Institute and see what was going on. That one man was Dr. Meduna, the famous inventor of the Metrazol treatment. He showed up before an audience of former patients and spoke to them. What impressed him most about these Recoveryites was the warmth and sense of companionship and closeness among them, which he recognized as a great therapeutic power.

As for Dr. Meduna himself, he made his way without difficulty into the affections of those who heard him. "Why he is so plain!

I just felt he is my brother," one of them said, voicing the opinion of all. And they rushed up afterwards to shake his hand and thank him in person for restoring them to the outside world. Their affection and gratitude touched his heart so deeply that Dr. Low, in writing of the event for his journal, said whimsically, "Recovery and Dr. Meduna seemed to have found one another."

6.

In July of 1939 the two long-awaited articles came out. Dr. Paul de Kruif's entitled "Men Against Insanity," was printed in *The Country Gentleman* and was gratefully and enthusiastically acknowledged by Dr. Low.

It went differently with the other article by Williams, which came out in the *Forum*. Even its title had a sensational ring to it: "The Revolt of the Ex-Insane." And the rest of the article followed suit, decrying psychoanalysis as a form of cure.

Dr. Low was never one to mince words where his opinion of the psychoanalytic method was concerned. But he was as shocked as anyone to see his opinions so colorfully set forth in a popular magazine, where they were more likely to discredit than to further his advanced ideas. True, his name was never mentioned in the article. He was simply referred to as "the director." But the Psychiatric Institute and Recovery were both identified.

In that era when psychoanalysis was a chauvinistic theory and its practitioners too sensitive to public criticism to have developed any sense of humor, the article fell like a bombshell. To them Dr. Low had now become no less than a traitor to his profession.

The extent of the feeling against him was revealed when one by one the resident physicians and interns came back from their vacations with stories of the shocked reactions of the professionals across the country. They themselves, embarrassed and put on the defensive, asked Dr. Low scathingly how he could have permitted the terrible blot to be registered against the Institute.

He entered the fall a chastened man with his mind made up. The article had come about because he had been trying to educate the public, and it was not the public after all whom he had to win. If he wanted to get Recovery into the hospitals across the country, it was the cooperation of the psychiatrists that he needed. From now on he would do everything in his power not to alienate them. He would be the soul of restraint.

But by this time it was too late. Already distrustful of his novel approach to patients, of his expressed disapproval of the psychoanalytic method, the psychiatrists as a group felt uneasy about him. And the article seemed to justify their apprehensions. The wedge it drove between him and them, instead of closing, only grew with the years.

7.

That November Recovery reached its second year of existence and the Program Committee arranged an anniversary party to commemorate the event. It was held on November 24, 1939, in the International House of the University of Chicago, and it was a gay affair with card games, raffles, refreshments, music, and dancing.

On the surface it looked like any ordinary party. But to Dr. Low, strolling among the guests, stopping to chat a little with each in turn, catching snatches of the conversation going on all around him, it was a miracle that brought tears to his eyes.

Most of the founders were present. There was slender, agile Harlan Tarbell with his skillful hands and humorous patter. Throughout the year he'd been giving shows for Recovery members and the patients in the Psychiatric Institute. With that bravery peculiar to him, he'd been fighting the stigma by joking about his own mental illness from platforms across the country.

There, too, was Joe Janis, back in medical school again. Dr. Low was well acquainted with Joe's straitened circumstances. He'd been through the same experiences in his own youth. He'd benefited then from the generosity of his brothers. Now he was able to pass along their goodness by slipping Joe five dollars or so for spending money every week. He was to be as proud as a father when the following July the young man graduated from medical school and, despite stiff competition, obtained an internship at the Cook County Hospital.

In a very vital sense all these people were Dr. Low's children.

What a long way they had come with him from that first frail beginning. Everywhere he looked inside Recovery he could see nothing but growth and promise. In contrast, everywhere outside he seemed to encounter obstruction and failure.

He had dreamed of sister associations springing up in every state of the Union. Instead, even the associations which had already been established were dying. Those in Kankakee and Peoria were gone. Only the one at the Chicago State Hospital, where Dr. Harry H. Garner was clinical director, was still functioning.

So little a dent had been made on public opinion in the age-old problem of the stigma that the Program Committee had had difficulty renting a hall for the party. Several owners had turned them down for fear that equipment would be damaged by the "destructiveness" of former patients.

But the worst blow of all was the cold silence the new organization was receiving from the psychiatric profession. Although a couple of health magazines had accepted and published two articles on Recovery, the official psychiatric publications had given it no more than brief notices. Even when Dr. Low had submitted a paper on Recovery, it had been returned to him with the suggestion that he outline the objectives and activities in a six-hundred-word paragraph—as though anything vital could be said about Recovery in so brief a space. He'd already had experience with that when he'd given his truncated speech at the convention.

The superintendent of one midwestern state hospital had shown enough interest to send a staff physician to Chicago to study Recovery methods with the idea of starting a sister group in his own hospital. The physician had attended a Sunday meeting and a group psychotherapy class. He had sat in on the Program and Employment Committee sessions and had studied every phase of the organization's plan. When he took his leave, he had said, "How can we ever hope to accomplish what you have achieved? Frankly, I feel it is beyond our capacity."

This was the fault pinpointed, Dr. Low told himself. No one could believe that the patients themselves were really capable of doing what the Recovery members in Chicago were doing. It seemed impossible for his colleagues to accept his penetrating statement: "It may safely be assumed that self-guidance is an effective attitude to the sense of isolation and an adequate check on the danger of relapses." It was a day when no one believed a patient was capable of self-guidance at all.

All around him he felt the vacuum of silence. It seemed to him that he was a man among sleepers, trying hopelessly to rouse them. He was convinced that without such an awakening which would bring their active cooperation, Recovery was doomed. What possibly could be accomplished for the thousands upon thousands of sufferers by one small isolated spot of brightness in one state hospital? That was the only future that, beaten and disillusioned, he could see for Recovery as the old year ran out.

With that tremendous weariness of soul, he sought out Dr. Singer and to him he confided his troubles: the staggering weight of his thankless, profitless work, the wall of indifference that closed him in, the cul-de-sac in which he found himself. And he wondered out loud if it was really worth while going on.

Dr. Singer listened gravely. In his early days he, too, had fought equally scarring battles against the inertia of the times for reform in mental hospitals. His star had been steadily rising of late. Already president of the American Neurological Association, he had just the past December been elected president of the Illinois Psychiatric Society. But he had not forgotten the past and he understood the sense of failure and near despair he saw now in the face of the younger man. Carefully he chose his words, words that would burn themselves into Dr. Low's heart.

"Pioneering means hardship in the beginning and accomplishment in the end," the older man said slowly.

Then in a rare moment of candor, foreign to him, he went back into his own life to describe the thankless pioneering he himself had done in the field of mental illness. He told of the obstacles he had found in his attempts to better the treatment of the suffering patients, of the resistance he had met to so many of his plans. Never before had he talked to Dr. Low so frankly of his early struggles. It was as though in speaking of them now, he was handing on a sacred trust.

"It had to be done and it was done," he concluded simply. "You'll have the same experience."

Dr. Low was to remember those words to the end of his life. He was to take them as his motto: "It had to be done and it was done." And he, too, was to pass them on to Recovery as a principle by which to live.

TEN

Annette Tobin was an attractive young school teacher, but her health was far from good. She had developed colitis, and whenever she was troubled it would express itself in this agonizing form of intestinal disorder. Annette was sure she had some serious organic ailment. She began going from hospital to hospital, searching for a diagnosis of what was causing it, a diagnosis that would lead to a cure. Finally she went to the famous Mayo Clinic for a thorough checkup. "Just nerves" was the diagnosis. Rest was prescribed along with mild doses of phenobarbital. For a while this helped a little, but not for long.

The colitis quickly came back, along with other strange and frightening symptoms. She couldn't sleep or eat. Every mouthful had to be forced down. As time went by she began to develop a sense of unreality. She knew she was touching things, yet she could feel nothing. It was as though she were no longer able to make connections with the everyday world.

Annette was in love with Clem Brocken, a good-natured architectural draftsman. He persuaded her that marriage might settle her nerves. Annette agreed and they were married. Two days later she found herself sicker than ever. She had to take a leave of absence from her teaching and enter General Hospital in West Chicago.

A gastrointestinal specialist was called and he brought in another doctor for consultation. They suggested exploratory surgery, but Annette, a very intelligent woman, wasn't impressed. A doubt was awakening in her. The Mayo Clinic had diagnosed

88

her trouble as nervous in origin. She asked to see a psychiatrist and was referred to Dr. Irene T. Mead. Aften ten sessions with Annette, Dr. Mead confirmed her suspicions and suggested that she either enter the Chicago State Hospital or the Psychiatric Institute of the Illinois Research Hospital, where a new experiment was being conducted in group therapy by a Dr. Abraham Low.

Since Dr. Mead favored the Psychiatric Institute because she felt that Annette would profit from Dr. Low's new therapy, Annette chose this hospital and Clem took her there. By this time Annette, who is a tall, large-boned woman, weighed only ninety-nine pounds and looked like a skeleton. She was not only weak from emaciation, but the sense of unreality persisted.

For almost two months the hospital concentrated on building up Annette's health and helping her regain her lost weight. For this she was given small injections of insulin before each meal. During that early period she encountered Dr. Low only briefly when he was making the rounds of the hospital with his staff. He would stop and look at her and say, "Let's see, this is Annette," and pass on.

Annette couldn't judge the man very well from these brief encounters, but she formed a very vivid impression of him at the first psychotherapy class she was allowed to attend, and that impression was a negative one. She felt a distinct aversion toward this little doctor with the Prussian manner. He'd sit at the table in front of the class and call up one or two of the patients to join him there. He'd ask them questions and discuss their problems. And if he thought they weren't cooperating, he'd be quite blunt about his disapproval.

It was this that Annette resented. She didn't think it was right to subject these sensitive, ill people to such bluntness. After all, being both sensitive and ill meant that you deserved more understanding than the ordinary human being. Herself, for instance: she had always been an extremely sensitive person; she had indeed taken a certain pride in it.

At Annette's second session an out-patient, who was coming back for the psychotherapy classes, got angry and voiced all the criticisms Annette had been thinking. The doctor didn't snap back. He didn't try to soothe her either. He simply said calmly,

"If the engine of your car breaks down, you seek an expert who knows what to do for it, and you don't tell the expert what he should do. It's the same thing here. I am the expert. You're here because I know more about this than you do."

Annette's eyes were opened. The feeling of antagonism vanished, and in its place came a fervent desire to absorb all the doctor had to give.

His cool authoritative manner, his firm conviction that he could cure, encouraged her. If she followed his orders, she told herself, she would get well. And she noticed that the out-patient had been impressed too. Despite her tirade, she was back the next time.

Annette noticed other peculiarities about the doctor's form of therapy besides his blunt manner. He never went deeply into the past. When someone would ask him, "Now, do you know what in my life caused this symptom?" he would brush it aside with the reply, "Who can say?" Yet despite his novel approach he had a way of cutting through the problems to the trouble spot in the personality that was creating them. Bit by bit, as Annette attended the classes, certain aspects about herself which she'd never known before were revealed to her.

Her sensitivity, for instance. She began to realize that her attitude was, "I am the most sensitive patient in this hospital. I am the exceptional one he is not going to be able to do anything with." He gave such an attitude short shrift because, he explained, it wasn't netting her anything but a little pride. If she would acknowledge that as a human being she could only be a good average at best, that the only exceptional people in the world were possibly saints, she would be able to accept herself as she was. It was her effort to acquire perfection that was engendering the tensions which were causing her symptoms.

Then there was the matter of her temper. Annette had always thought she was in good control of that. After all, she never did blow up at people. But now she began to understand that actually she had a large share of uncontrolled temper and that she was allowing it to burn and boil inside her. The doctor defined temper as being of two kinds: angry temper, which is directed at others, and fearful temper, which is directed at oneself.

Most surprising of all to Annette was the revelation that the long forbearing silences which she maintained when anyone offended her were actually not control of temper. They were sulking, a form of silent angry temper which was just as capable of causing the tensions that led to colitis and her other symptoms as violent explosions would have been.

Month by month, as Annette learned to spot this temper in herself and her intense craving for exceptionality, she began improving. Her colitis became less agonizing. Her sense of unreality started to fade and her appetite began to return. As she improved she began to take an active interest in the other ward patients. One girl especially appealed to her. Her name was Rosalie T. and the two quickly became good friends.

Rosalie's illness had begun with a severe psychoneurosis. It had caused her so much suffering that one day she had jumped from a height with the intention of ending it all. The only result was that she had broken her leg. Rosalie's leg had healed, but her illness had intensified. To escape her problems and the pressure of responsibilities at home she was making the familiar "flight into disease."

Finally, when her depression reached the point of desperation, she had come to the Institute, where she had begged for the magical cure of shock therapy she had heard so much about. But a careful examination showed that Rosalie had no need of such treatments and she was given intensive psychotherapy instead.

2.

That year of 1940, which found Annette and Rosalie on the ward of the Research Hospital, was a year of festivities in the little Recovery organization. The anniversary party had proved such a success that the Program Committee had begun planning a party or a picnic every month.

At that stage of his experimentation with Recovery, Dr. Low felt that the parties were a good thing because they provided social activities for those patients who, because of stigma, felt isolated in the outside world. Even the patients at the hospital who were about to be discharged were allowed to go to the parties in the care of nurses or relatives. And Rosalie and, later, Annette were among those who went.

Finally Rosalie was discharged from the hospital, and eventually Annette, too, was well enough to spend weekends at home. Clem took a furnished apartment in the neighborhood and picked Annette up on Saturday and brought her back Sunday.

One Saturday afteroon they stopped at the market to do some shopping. Clem went to buy the groceries while Annette went into the nearby bakery. She expected to meet Clem outside afterwards. But when she left the bakery, he wasn't there. She waited awhile and he still didn't show up. At last she decided that he'd misunderstood her and gone home. In later years Annette was to wonder whether it hadn't all been a scheme arranged between Dr. Low and Clem to reawaken her self-reliance, but all she felt at that moment was a touch of the old panic.

"Here I am by myself—what am I going to do?" the thought flashed through her head. Then she remembered some of the tools she'd learned in the psychotherapy classes. "Move your muscles" was one. You could always do that, no matter how many fearful thoughts were confusing your brain. "Distressing but not dangerous," was another. It meant that no matter how frightening your symptoms might be, you could still operate if you realized they weren't dangerous. So she made her way home without too much trouble, and she knew then that she was going to be cured eventually.

At last, six months after she had entered the hospital, Annette was well enough to be discharged. Often enough before at the psychotherapy classes in the hospital she had heard the doctor asking the patients who were preparing to leave, "Now, what are you going to do to insure your health?"

The patient would reply, sometimes grudgingly, "I suppose I have to go to Recovery."

To which the doctor would answer dryly, "That would be a good idea."

But Annette showed no reluctance when she gave her answer. She meant to do everything possible to maintain her health. She joined Recovery at once and became one of its most ardent supporters.

By this time another interesting development had been taking place in the little organization. Social clubs had begun forming within it. When Annette left the hospital there were a number of such clubs: the Fortnightly Club, the Companion Club, the Merrie Followers, and several Senior Clubs for the older members and the relatives. Rosalie had already joined the Companion Club, and now Annette and Clem joined one of the Senior Clubs.

The club members held social get-togethers in one another's homes or had theater parties or picnics or similar outings. In order to keep check on his patients, Dr. Low would occasionally visit the various club affairs. Subsequently, however, he was to de-emphasize all Recovery social clubs because he found that they tended to isolate his patients from the world instead of helping them face it.

3.

The Low family had now moved to a large second-story apartment on Pearson Street on the famous Chicago Gold Coast. This was a social milieu and invitations were plentiful, but the Lows turned them all down, restricting themselves to visits with old friends such as the Bisnos and the Nemkovs who lived nearby, with Mae's mother and sister, and with various members of the Low family who might be passing through town.

Phyllis and Marilyn were always included when guests came to the house. And when their parents went visiting the girls usually accompanied them. They were expected to behave properly on such occasions, but they didn't always do so. And more than one acquaintance was to hear their father saying in mock despair, as they shamelessly interrupted conversations, "Here I am a psychiatrist and I'm supposed to be handling people, and I can't even handle my own children."

Once a week as a treat the family would go out to an expensive restaurant for dinner together. They all loved those nights on the town, Abraham in particular, who enjoyed dining out as much as his wife and little daughters. But he also took the occasion to bring a few basic lessons home to them. As they learned to read the menu, they began selecting the highest quality dishes—a shrimp cocktail, salad, a steak—only to hear their father caution them at times, "Oh, no, that's too expensive. Now we'll go down the line."

It wasn't that he begrudged them the meals—his purpose was to make them aware of the cost of living. Part of their lesson was that whatever they ordered they were expected to eat. Sometimes they'd sit for a long while staring at the plate full of food they'd asked for in a rash moment.

Aside from these few excursions, the family social life was channeled almost entirely into Recovery activities—that little organization which both Dr. and Mrs. Low were beginning to refer to as their third child. They attended Recovery parties. And if there were daytime picnics they took Phyllis and Marilyn along to play with the children of the Recovery members.

Once a month, on a Saturday afternoon, Dr. Low held a meeting at his home with the chairmen and the secretaries of the various committees. Any other patients who wished to come were welcome too, and Annette and Rosalie and a few others were frequent visitors. They would be greeted by Mrs. Low at the door and get a glimpse of the two merry little Low girls before the children were whisked out of the room.

Then business would get underway. Many subjects were dealt with—from Recovery policies to social activities and even to establishing a transporation fund for patients who weren't coming to meetings because they lacked carfare. After the business Mrs. Low would serve coffee and refreshments and there would be a pleasant social interlude, with Dr. Low leaning back in his chair, tranquilly puffing on his pipe and taking it all in with his warm, indulgent smile. A day in the Low home was a treat his guests looked forward to all month.

4.

That year of 1940 Dr. Low was to make another discovery about this growing creation of his, the Recovery Association. All along he had been aiming against the stigma in the outside world as the chief source of his patients' relapses. And there was stigma there, often black and ugly. But the greatest stigma, he was beginning to realize, lay deep in the patients themselves.

As they learned to conquer it through having a sense of belonging in Recovery and through training in the group psychotherapy classes, they were able to build up their own self-respect and their resistance to outside reactions. Not only were they preventing relapses in themselves, but they were also finding the courage to go out and get well-paying jobs on their own initiative. The services of the Employment Committee were no longer needed and it was disbanded.

Another strange thing had begun to happen concerning the outside world which had been so indifferent all through 1939 when the little band of Recoveryites had put forth every effort to impress it. This year Recovery had forgotten the public and concentrated on its own activities and the public had begun showing an interest. Reporters had come to interview members about their clubs and parties and they were responding by boldly giving out interviews with full names and front-view pictures. Letters of commendation were coming in by the score.

By this time Dr. Low was learning to curb his impatience toward his colleagues who still would not join him in investigating this stimulating movement of patients toward self-help. Over and over he reminded himself that they weren't exactly to blame for their conservatism. After all, Recovery was still very young—not yet three years old. How could you prove anything, really, in three short years? But surely when all the facts were in, other professionals would become as excited as he and would come to learn the techniques that were transforming terrified, beaten human beings into zestful men and women again.

ELEVEN

That summer of 1940 a somber event occurred which was to change the whole course of Recovery. On August 29, Dr. Singer, who had gone to his summer home in New Mexico, died of an embolism after a car accident. When the news reached Dr. Low, he was filled with shock and grief. The loss of Dr. Singer would leave a wide gap in the Psychiatric Department of the university where he had spent so many years of devoted service.

From the first, Dr. Singer had been a firm friend of Recovery and all that it promised in the way of after-care for the discharged patients. He had always found time to help along the new project and he had placed the resources of the Psychiatric Institute at its service. Office space, supplies, stenographic and secretarial work had all been freely provided.

It was his full support that had made possible the sister associations at Peoria, Kankakee, Alton, and Chicago. And he had not accepted discouragement when one by one the first three had failed. He had also taken an active part in the preparation of the new commitment law. Having been elected president of the Illinois Psychiatric Society in December of 1938 he had used his powerful position to get the Society to endorse the reform statute. At the time of his death he was president elect of the American Psychiatric Association. In that important office he would have been in a position to bring Recovery to the attention of psychiatrists across the country. Now that he was gone, Recovery had lost its most influential friend.

Upon Dr. Singer's death, Dr. Low became acting alienist and acting director of the Psychiatric Institute. To all his own work he had to add Dr. Singer's manifold chores. He also had to fend off alone now the mounting criticism of Recovery which some of the staff members of the Illinois College of Medicine were expressing.

The complaint of the critics was that the College of Medicine was a research institution, and that Recovery was just another of the projects that had been initiated there. It had obviously been completed to everyone's satisfaction, because Dr. Low had already published a paper on it. So it should now be concluded.

Dr. Low was called before the Board of Trustees of the medical school to present the case for Recovery. He explained that the experiment, far from being concluded, had actually only just begun, that there were many facets yet to be explored.

He told them of his dream: after-care associations established in all state hospitals across the nation. These associations, he pointed out, would save taxpayers millions of dollars by preventing thousands of patients from suffering relapses.

But it was on the sick that he dwelt most fervently—the welfare of that multitude of patients too poor to afford expensive psychiatric help, who were returning again and again to the hospitals without much hope for the future. It was for these ill ones who had so often touched him to tears, to whom he had dedicated his life and talents, that he pleaded that day before the Board. They could be helped, he insisted, by the simple self-help, after-care techniques which he was in the process of developing in Recovery.

He won his point with the Board. One of the members, Oscar Mayer of the meat-packing industry, was especially impressed by the latent seeds of promise in the young organization. But they all voted that the novel experiments should continue.

2.

In October of 1940 Dr. Low launched one of the new experiments which he had mentioned to the Board. For a long while he had been aware of the steady stream of patients suffering from chronic ailments who came to the dispensary for treatment. Many of these patients had been returning year after year without seeming to improve. If these "functional" ailments were emotional in origin, psychotherapy classes should help them.

He requested the departments of medicine at the Research and Educational Hospital to send their chronic patients to the class he would arrange for them. Only a few came at first. But as the weeks went by, more and more began to show up.

In working with them Dr. Low became increasingly aware of another phenomenon he hadn't expected to find among these patients. None of them had a court record or had been committed to a hospital; yet they seemed to suffer more keenly from the sense of stigma than the committed patients. Why?

In probing he discovered that it was just because they hadn't broken down with any diagnosable illness, because they looked well and the doctors said they were well. Their deep fatigues that often prevented them from getting out of bed, their head pressures, heart palpitations, and terrifying panics had been diagnosed as "just nerves." If all they had was "just nerves," or "imaginary" aches and pains, then why didn't they show enough spunk to "snap out of it"?

Dr. Low, far in advance of his time, was becoming increasingly aware that the illness of the psychoneurotic, like that of the mental patient, had a physiological basis also. It sprang from an inborn weakness of the nervous system. It was this faulty system that caused distressing symptoms. They were the same symptoms experienced by everyone. He had proved this by a constant, vigilant survey of his own body responses, in which he had detected the echo of almost every symptom the psychoneurotic patients had described to him. The difference lay only in degree. The psychoneurotic's symptoms were so intense that they were often bizarre manifestations that filled him with terror. The terror in turn intensified the symptoms by causing tension. Symptoms fed fear and fear fed symptoms until a vicious cycle was created which immobilized the patient. The mocking attitude of relatives and friends, who were prone to interpret his continuous, very real suffering as laziness and a fundamental lack of character, contributed to his agony by filling him with self-loathing.

Dr. Low felt certain that the psychoneurotics as well as the mental patients could profit by becoming members of Recovery.

The problem was how to get them to attend Recovery meetings. It wasn't going to be easy. Since their main terror was that of going insane, they were afraid even of coming in contact with former mental patients. Yet, Dr. Low realized, it was only by conquering this fear that they could eliminate their main source of tension—the fear of the permanent handicap. Always the philosophy was simple: "If you want to be cured, do the thing you fear to do."

Strategy was needed to coax the psychoneurotic to face his terrors, and casting around as to the best way to go about it, Dr. Low settled on Annette Brocken, the former school teacher who was now well on the way to being cured. How she had changed since she had been admitted to the hospital! He remembered her then, tall and gaunt, with a face drawn from suffering and fear. Who would recognize that former wraith in the vibrant, attractive young woman who still attended psychotherapy classes, who never missed a Recovery meeting, who came to the committee gatherings at his home almost every month?

Dr. Low possessed an uncanny knack of getting to the inner core of each patient's personality, of estimating the potential qualities which that person possessed, and of making use of those qualities when the need arose. In Annette he saw the unique stamp of leadership and authority, both attributes of a good school teacher. She also had a firm grasp of Recovery methods and aims. She had the presence needed to impress the psychoneurotics in his new class and to allay their fears about hospitalized patients. He asked her if she would attend these new classes and act as an ambassador for Recovery.

As he had expected, Annette reacted enthusiastically. Since at the time of her illness she had obtained a two-year leave of absence from her teaching, she had plenty of leisure. And she was so devoted to Recovery that she was ready to do all in her power to further it.

In December she attended her first psychotherapy class among the psychoneurotics. The next week, at Dr. Low's suggestion, she took along Rosalie T. Every week the two girls went to the class for the clinic patients and talked about Recovery, and especially about the parties and the social clubs which Recovery members were enjoying. Finally they were able to persuade two of the braver patients to come to a meeting. They found it a harrowing experience. Just listening to the former mental patients discussing their experiences sent them into a panic, and it took some persuasion to get them to go again. But at last Annette and Rosalie were successful.

The second time the two patients went, they found it wasn't so bad as they'd at first thought. And after several meetings they began helping Annette and Rosalie round up other prospective members. When they had ten or twelve, they were all welcomed into the Recovery Association as the Dispensary Group. It was the first group devoted to self-help to be established for nervous patients who had never suffered a breakdown or been hospitalized. Recovery had made another long step into the uncharted land it was exploring.

3.

Despite his extra burden of work following Dr. Singer's death, Abraham still found time for those few precious moments which he shared with his family when he returned home at night. He loved especially to roughhouse with his two little daughters and at times there was such pandemonium in the living room that Mae would remonstrate, "If you don't stop that, they're going to grow up to be tomboys."

He always agreed with her—theoretically. But the next evening would find him back on the floor again romping with the girls, a pastime that proved not to be without its hazards. One day with Marilyn in his arms, he crashed against a delicate French chair that was Mae's particular pride. Off snapped a leg and the chair toppled over. Mae rushed in to see the shambles and began to scold him sharply. Then all at once she became aware of the contrite expression on his face and couldn't say another word.

Although Abraham loved that evening romp with his children, he wasn't what one might call an indulgent father. One evening Estelle Nemkov answered her doorbell and found him standing there with a box of skates in his hand. Estelle had bought them for Phyllis so that she could skate with her own little daughter.

"What's the matter, don't they fit?" she asked him, concerned.

"I don't know," he replied. "I haven't allowed her to try them on. I'm returning them to you. I hope you'll understand, but I don't want you to bring gifts to my child."

"But why?" Estelle asked, puzzled.

"Because it deprives her of the joy of wanting," he explained. "When my daughter says she wants skates, I will let her want them for some time, and then I will get them for her. Don't you realize that by giving her something even before she asks for it, you're depriving her of the greatest pleasure of childhood—the pleasure of wanting and hoping?"

Dr. Low was just as common-sense about calling in the pediatrician for minor illnesses. "Pediatricians are for sick children," he would tell his wife when she reported some minor ailment. "Don't bother him or me. Call your mother."

Mrs. Willett knew all the old-fashioned remedies and once, at least, when Marilyn had a bad case of croup, one of hers seemed to prove more efficacious than the pediatrician's. When Mae told her husband about it, he looked at her over the bowl of his pipe, a twinkle in his eyes. "Well, it didn't hurt her," he conceded.

He was never a man to decry the psychological power of folk medicines, for he was a far greater believer in the curative power of nature if left to herself than in all the drugs of the pharmaceutical houses. His children were never given so much as a nose spray when they had colds. An aspirin for comfort and a stay in bed with plenty of liquid was still the old-fashioned cure he prescribed.

When later the girls went to school, the uniqueness of their situation became quite evident even to them. "Our father's a doctor," they'd say, half-bragging, half-complaining because they felt left out of things, "and here we're the only kids in our group who haven't been given any antibiotics."

Dr. Low practiced the same health disciplines on himself. He seldom took even an aspirin. And in later years he liked to boast to his patients that by merely adopting the right frame of mind he had prevented himself from catching a cold for more than five years.

Today this realization of the power of the mind over physical health is far more widely understood by the profession than it was in the Thirties. The high percentage of psychosomatic ill-

nesses has been attested to by such notable clinics as the Mayo
Brothers'. And many modern-day doctors place the common cold
high on the list of ailments caused by emotional disturbances.
But in that day the idea was revolutionary and even smacked of
quackery.

4.

Meanwhile the months were going by and no appointment was
made to the position held by Dr. Singer. It was a choice plum
so far as personal advancement was concerned. As director of the
Department of Psychiatry at the University of Illinois Medical
School, Dr. Singer had mounted first to the presidency of the
Illinois Psychiatric Society and then to that of the American
Psychiatric Association. The way of glory and prestige lay simi-
larly open to Dr. Low.

But no one knew better than his shrewd sister Theresa how
important the use of politics was in securing such a position. And
since she was well-acquainted with an influential politician in the
city who knew about her brother and was eager to be of help,
she hurried to Chicago from New York to offer her services.

But Abraham didn't think it was necessary to see the man
because he was sure politics wouldn't enter into the picture. Why
should it? After all, he had been Dr. Singer's associate, working
closely with him over the years. He was therefore the logical
choice to fill Dr. Singer's place.

Dr. Low's friends, like his sister, realized that no such logic
prevailed in politics. They knew that he was very highly regarded
as a brilliant researcher and that he had powerful friends whose
help he could solicit. But they were also aware of the opposition
in high places to this unique and already somewhat controversial
figure. Since most of the controversy was over Recovery, wouldn't
it be worth it to him to drop it? they asked him. After all, it had
been a mere experiment.

Recovery, the child of his creative genius, deeply loved by him,
fought for by him so often with a bluntness of approach that was
offensive to those who had never experienced the driving power
of such extraordinary dedication! How could he in conscience

discard it for his own personal aggrandizement when it promised so much aid to so many countless human beings?

Such was the nature of this unique, dynamic man. In the words of Dr. Joe Janis, today a psychiatrist himself ". . . a man who lived his life by principles that were more important to him than anything else, more than life itself. And he would sacrifice his personal comfort and income and reputation and the esteem of his colleagues rather than to compromise what he thought was the right thing to do for his patients."

TWELVE

Phil Crane came of a fine middle-class family. His father was examiner on the Board of Education in Chicago, the second highest position in the Education Department.

Phil never could understand why he seemed so completely different from his mother and father, brother and two sisters. None of them were troubled with the sensitivity he felt. It seemed to him that he was always at loggerheads with his mother, a woman of strong character and initiative. He reacted intensely to her reprimands, which the other children accepted as normal. Sometimes he would brood for two days at a time over whether he or his mother had been right. And presently he began to wonder in his childish way if he really belonged with this family of his.

When he was nine years old, Phil began having trouble writing at the blackboard in school. He would be seized with self-consciousness, his hand would tense up, and he would have to tell the teacher, "I can't do it."

But he managed to pass with good grades and became an energetic and ambitious high school student, working summers and holidays in a clothing store to earn his pocket money. Of course he planned to enter a university, as had his brother and one sister. They had attended the University of Illinois, but he chose the University of Michigan, from which his father had graduated Phi Beta Kappa.

His father had been a member of one of the best fraternities on campus, and Phil fully expected to join it. But he was unable to establish normal social relationships with his classmates. They

104

felt he was too cocky and superior, and the fraternity didn't even offer him a bid. This blow to his expectations reactivated Phil's childhood suspicion that he didn't belong with his family. He speculated that perhaps the fraternity boys had rejected him because they had seen beneath his mask and had recognized the truth—he wasn't his father's son.

But father's son or not, Phil was determined to show the fraternity what they had missed in him. He took an active part in the school's extracurricular activities, working on its theatrical productions and helping put out the college magazine. By his senior year he had worked himself up to the editorship. Despite the extra hours he was spending on all these activities, he managed to graduate with good grades.

From the University of Michigan, Phil entered the University of Chicago Law School. Again by concentrating all his efforts he was able to complete law school, pass the Illinois Bar examinations, and become a member of the Illinois Bar. But to attain these goals he had had to push himself relentlessly. The strain on his nervous system showed in his increasing irritability and restlessness. He began to have difficulty eating and was sure he was suffering from a weak digestive system. At night he couldn't sleep. Or if he did, he would wake up at three o'clock in the morning, the victim of black depressions.

Though Phil was now fully equipped to start practicing law, his increasing irritability prevented him from launching into that profession. Instead he went through a succession of jobs which he obtained through his family's influential friends. But he couldn't hold them because he was unable to adjust to his co-workers. Finally his mother got work for him as a home-delivery agent at the Chicago *Sun-Times*. For four years Phil worked at this job and was able to handle things satisfactorily. In 1939 he married and it looked to the family as though he was going to settle down.

By the end of 1940 Phil's fine record at the *Sun-Times* earned him a promotion, and from then on he had to work with others. Again he couldn't make friendly contact with them. His tensions built up. His sleeplessness and stomach upsets increased in severity. And once more the old suspicion came back that he was a stranger among his own family. He thought at first he might be an American Indian, or perhaps an Oriental. As the delusion deepened, he became convinced he was an Afro-American, although he never told others of it. He talked instead in a fervent, rather incoherent way of black men and their problems and his own deep sympathy for them. And he began to wander around the black community for hours at a time.

He was now acting so erratically at home that Phil's wife, at her wits' end, told his family. His father was beginning to realize that Phil was seriously ill, but his mother couldn't accept the thought of mental illness in the family. His brother and sisters, too, felt the weight of the same stigma. But as time went by it became obvious to everyone that he was worsening. He lost his promotion and went back to his old job, but he couldn't hold that one either. So he quit altogether.

Now completely driven by his delusion, he felt he ought to be living in a black neighborhood. So one wintry night he set out to find his real home. The temperature was in the twenties and he lost his coat somewhere, but that didn't matter to him. He walked about fifteen miles through the dark, violent slum area. But his only fear was that he would meet with a policeman who would take him to jail. When at last he stumbled back to his sister's place, he was almost frozen and he couldn't remember exactly where he had been or what he had done. He certainly hadn't touched a drop of alcohol. He had never had any problem that way. But some of his money was gone.

In the succeeding weeks one bizarre action followed another in Phil's life. Only he never saw them as bizarre, because he wasn't aware of his confused state, which was so obvious to others. Then one day in his sister's home he built a fire in the kitchen sink. He watched the flames leap upward, not even aware that he could set the house afire. His sister felt she could no longer keep him and called the police.

When they arrived Phil was overcome with panic. He was sure they had come to lock him up. He was not a violent man but he met the police with stubborn resistance and an eloquent tongue. His arguments made no difference. The police were gentle but firm.

They took him to the Cook County Mental Health Clinic first. For a period of three weeks Phil was examined by some thirty to forty psychiatrists. They all came to the same conclusion. Thirty-year-old Phil would have to be hospitalized.

Accepting the fact of her son's mental illness at last, Phil's mother signed the commitment papers and Phil was taken to the ward of the Psychiatric Institute. About three days after his arrival, he met Dr. Low for the first time. The doctor, accompanied by two members of his staff, was passing through the ward. Suddenly he turned and walked forcefully toward Phil, drawing himself up short in front of the young man and looking penetratingly at him, his face stern.

Then turning to the members of his staff he said in that authoritative voice which was to become so familiar to Phil in the years ahead, "This man, Phil Crane, will not admit that he is mentally ill, but all the psychiatrists who examined him at Cook County say without question that he is. Now why is he so stubborn?"

Phil didn't know that in addressing his staff members rather than himself, the doctor was practicing a new technique in interviewing patients. He had discovered that they seemed to respond far better when he talked about them to others than when he accosted them directly.

Phil became more and more uneasy as the doctor discussed him. The thing that troubled him most was the fear that this stern, authoritative man with the penetrating eyes was about to send him to prison. He was glad when the doctor moved on. But suddenly Dr. Low turned around. His face softened. He put his hand on Phil's shoulder and the stern face relaxed in a sympathetic smile.

"This man is very good-natured," he said, still addressing his staff.

Phil's panic began to ebb. In its place came a sense of encouragement, a glimmer of hope. He didn't know what was wrong with him, since he didn't recognize his delusions, or how things were going to be changed. But in a sudden spurt of courage he was sure that there was hope somehow for him and that this doctor with his hand on his shoulder was encouraging him to do his part.

2.

Phil needed all the courage he could get in the months ahead. The road back to health wasn't an easy one. Therapy consisted of shock treatments. But Phil wouldn't go willingly to the therapy room. They had to drag him there each time. His case was so severe that he had to undergo sixty shock treatments during his stay at the hospital. And he saw Dr. Low every day for seven months. It was only little by little that the delusions began to fade and Phil was able to attend the group psychotherapy classes.

Dr. Low had been keeping a close eye on Phil. With his unerring ability he was able to see, beneath the surface of this young man who now had such difficulty in relating to people, a real talent for fellowship and understanding.

Just as soon as Phil's confusion began to clear up, Dr. Low put that talent to use. He had long been aware of the dreary vacant hours that hung heavily on his patients, especially between late afternoon and the nine o'clock curfew. Before the era of shock treatments the passage of time had been a matter of indifference to them. Now they were bored and restless. They needed meaningful activity. A ward newspaper for the patients—written, edited, printed, and distributed by them—would be a fine answer to the problem. It was a unique experiment in those days, but Dr. Low was always trying something new. And of course he couldn't find anyone better to run his projected paper than this good-natured young man who had been editor of a college magazine.

Phil accepted the responsibility with enthusiasm. Soon he had organized a staff of five of the less severe patients. One did the typing. Another stenciled the paper, a third folded it, and a fourth distributed it to the patients on the ward. A fifth raised money, from visiting relatives and friends, to pay for the paper and the costs of mimeographing it. Phil's task was to act as newsgatherer. But Dr. Low made it plain to him that the newsgathering itself wasn't the important part of his job. "It isn't what you write," he told him, "but it is a question of what you can get the others to tell you. Get them to talk, Phil."

So out of the odds and ends of what the patients told him, Phil put his little paper together. There were five standard-size pages to it, and it was called *The Retriever,* because it was a paper for patients all retrieving their health. The first edition printed a saucy little poem to introduce the paper. Entitled "Our Policy" it ran:

> *Blessings on thee, little sheet.*
> *May your life be long and sweet.*

Foreign news we find a bore.
Domestic news we just ignore.
Of Lindy, F.D. not a hoot;
Our news is bound by Institute.
So we launch thee, little rag.
And may our interest never lag.

There were other activities on the ward to keep the patients amused. Every Monday evening there was a party to which Recovery members came to mingle with the ward patients and talk to them about the organization and especially to encourage them to become members once they had been discharged. Every Friday there was an afternoon tea for relatives and friends.

Dr. Low again made use of Phil at these parties and teas by appointing him chief greeter. Phil's task was to talk to the withdrawn or stuporous patients, to try to draw them out, to encourage them to dance. The doctor's confidence in him made Phil feel important. He was needed.

About this time Phil also joined a small study group made up of some of the members on his *Retriever* newspaper staff. This little group, which was inaugurated by Dr. Low, met weekly at the Psychiatric Institute. It was led by two Recovery members, who came to conduct discussions on Recovery techniques, using for their texts the patient and doctor interviews in the *Lost and Found* magazines. Dr. Low hoped that through this study the patients would become inculcated with the principles of self-help before they were discharged.

Phil enjoyed the interesting discussions. He became particularly fond of Joe Janis, one of the two men who led the study group. Joe and Phil became warm friends, and eventually Phil was invited by Joe to become a member of the Fortnightly Club. At last he felt he truly belonged.

3.

That spring of 1941, while Phil was making his way back to health, Recovery was finally preparing for its big campaign to get the new commitment law passed. For almost four years it had been doing all it could to awaken public sympathy to its cause.

Almost every issue of *Lost and Found* had contained stories by relatives and friends describing their unhappy experiences with the old law. Beatrice Wade had taken time out of her busy days to prepare several pamphlets describing Recovery and its battle, and these had been distributed widely. Recovery members had been contacting newspapers, too, fearlessly exposing themselves to the public as former mental patients. And the growing friendliness of the response they were receiving was giving them a feeling of enthusiastic confidence—a confidence Dr. Low himself didn't completely share.

He had been very pleased with the reform statute which Professor Green and his associates had drawn up. But that statute hadn't met with the approval of the Illinois Society for Mental Hygiene, an organization made up almost entirely of lay citizens. And since Dr. Low knew his law couldn't be passed without their cooperation and that of the Illinois Psychiatric Society, he had to wait patiently while the Society for Mental Hygiene took over. It had put together its own bill and presented it to the legislature just the past January. The result had been a dismal failure. It was only then that the Society had decided to cooperate with Recovery.

Finally they'd all agreed on a bill, not as strong as Dr. Low would have liked to see it, but at least a big improvement over the old one. So in the interests of solidarity he accepted the compromise.

The problem now was to get the statute passed. There was a different atmosphere in the capital since the reform-minded Governor Horner, who had brought in Dr. Singer, had left office. Governor Dwight H. Green was now in the Capitol at Springfield. And his apparent lack of interest in health issues was such that by the end of his tenure, according to the well-known biographer Kenneth S. Davis, "the Illinois mental-health program was among the worst in the forty-eight states."

It was this indifference that the Society for Mental Hygiene had run up against in their ill-fated venture. Still smarting from their experience, they warned Dr. Low that their bill had lost because of the complete apathy to the issue among the legislators and some active opposition among high administration officials.

This was the situation that Recovery faced. But its members refused to accept the Society's gloomy prognosis. At a Sunday meeting in April an appeal was made to all those who knew any legislators to pressure them into activity. Then there were the letters. Members, relatives, and friends all wrote. Thousands of letters poured into Springfield.

Still nothing happened. The bill seemed permanently stuck in Committee. Finally Beatrice Wade appealed to a cousin of hers who worked in the office of the late Jack Malloy, editor of the *Chicago American*, a Hearst chain newspaper. Would he, Miss Wade asked, appeal to Mr. Malloy for help in getting the bill out? Jack Malloy was sympathetic for he knew the anguish of a break-down in his own family. He got on the phone to Springfield at once. Could the Governor do him a favor and get that bill out of Committee? he asked.

"Why, Jack, of course, anything for you," the Governor responded.

True to his word, he spoke to the Committee chairman. And almost immediately afterwards the statute was voted favorably out of Committee and became House Bill 631, An Act to Revise the Law in Relation to the Case of Mentally Ill Persons.

A month and a half went by and then came the triumphant announcement: June 12, 1941, House Bill 631 had passed the House of Representatives 122 to 1. Twelve days later on June 24, there was another jubilant report: Bill 631 had passed the Senate unanimously.

It now needed only Governor Green's signature to make it law. There surely couldn't be any question about that because it was his intervention that had got it out of Committee in the first place. That meant that on January 1, 1941, after forty-eight years, the old humiliating law would go out of existence. The Recovery Association had won a tremendous victory. And it was the former patients, relatives, and friends of the Recovery Association that had accomplished this miracle. Through their zeal and numbers they had proved to be stronger than the most powerful opposition. Dr. Low never stopped being astounded by the vitality and capability of the little organization.

4.

That Friday the ward turned its weekly afternoon party into a victory tea. Relatives, Recovery members, friends, all gathered to celebrate. The good feeling of warmth and accomplishment was in the air. Phil felt it too. He was exuberant on more than one count. His delusions were gone. The doctor had promised him he would be released soon.

Phil had already had his taste of the outside world. In the company of Joe Janis he'd been attending the parties of the Fortnightly Club. Then a few days after the victory tea, Dr. Low asked him to take part in a demonstration he was going to put on at the Chicago State Hospital before an audience made up of patients and their relatives and some professionals. The doctor held such demonstrations from time to time to illustrate his techniques, and he usually brought one or more of his improved patients along with him to make a few remarks of their own.

Now it was Phil's turn to talk. He felt a surge of pride. He was nervous too. There were so many people in the room. To be sure they all heard what he had to say, he shouted into the microphone. And although he hadn't given the best performance in the world, the audience seemed to think he had. Afterwards they came crowding up around him to tell him how much they admired his forthrightness. He'd not shown any fear of the stigma as so many others did, they marveled. He had frankly admitted to being a patient. That was real courage. Dr. Low praised him too. It was the final accolade of Phil's hospital stay.

Then on his last day he heard the doctor gravely warning him that he was still only partially cured, that he must come back to Recovery meetings and group psychotherapy if he didn't want the old delusions to return. Of course he would, Phil promised glibly. He wanted to keep on the good side of this doctor, who was a world-famous psychiatrist, and was therefore not a man to be trifled with.

Seven months after he'd been committed Phil was outside the hospital walls again. His wife had sued for divorce on grounds of non-support, so he went home to live with his mother. His old job was waiting for him at the *Sun-Times*.

And he was well. He knew it, could feel it right through to his bones, even though his record said it was just a partial cure and the Army turned him down because of that. The only trouble was his stigmatized past kept nagging at him. If he could just wipe it completely out of his memory, then everything would be all right again.

He told himself that it was the hospital stay that was at the root of his stigmatization. He hadn't really needed to go here, he'd just been railroaded in by his family. Regardless of what he had promised the doctor, he made up his mind to stay away from the Psychiatric Institute, and that included Recovery, too, since it met there.

THIRTEEN

At seventeen Ann Landis had had her first breakdown and her mother had taken her to a psychiatrist. She had recovered more or less spontaneously, though she still retained the timidity and self-consciousness that sprang from a deep mistrust of herself. However, she had married and borne two children, a boy and a girl.

She was twenty-nine when her illness struck her again. It happened in the kitchen. Ann had always prided herself on being able to make delicious brownies. Now a tray of cake was cooling and ready to be cut, and her five-year-old son was begging for some.

She lifted her hand with the knife in it, when suddenly World War II, which was going on at the time, seemed to be vividly present in her own kitchen. All at once, beyond a shadow of a doubt, she was sure that she was about to betray some of her government's secret plans to the Nazis, who were then goose-stepping over Europe. She had only to move her hand or arm in a certain way and the code would be broken.

Quickly she put the knife down. The little boy who had been waiting hungrily began to cry. And Ann came to her senses. Resolutely she picked up the knife again and cut the brownie cake for him.

For the moment the incident was forgotten. But later Ann began to fret about the strange thought that had occurred to her so unexpectedly. Why had it come? What did it mean? Through the long night hours she mulled the question over and over, all her energies draining out into that one obsessive thought. A leadening fatigue began to weigh her down and she could no longer concentrate on even the simplest household chores.

Then fear became her daily incubus. She feared going to sleep and not waking up. She became especially terrified of meeting people. When her children brought their friends home from school, she would hide from them. When her own parents came to call, she would go into her bedroom and kneel by her bed, praying for strength to meet them.

Finally a religious obsession struck Ann full force. A Baptist, she had been practicing her religion faithfully. Now she was sure that God was commanding her to save the whole world. If she didn't start working at it, her own soul would be damned. So Ann began proselyting with fanatical zeal.

Ann's husband, John Landis, like so many other relatives, didn't realize that Ann's abnormal behavior was a sign of illness. He thought she was guilty only of nonsensical behavior and that by criticizing her sternly for it, he could "bring her back to her senses." Ann accepted his criticisms as just and also began criticizing herself for behaving as she did. The more she condemned herself, the worse her state became.

Finally, under the delusion that Jesus Christ had ordered her to commit suicide, she drained a bottle of iodine. Fortunately she swallowed too much and threw it up. But now John became thoroughly alarmed and took her to their family doctor. He suggested that Ann see Dr. Low, so she went with her husband for a consultation.

After Ann had been examined, Dr. Low took John aside. His wife was seriously ill, he said. She had to come or be brought regularly to the group psychotherapy classes at the Illinois State Research Hospital. Only under these conditions would he accept her as a patient.

Now that John understood that Ann was sick, he dropped all criticism and promised to cooperate with Dr. Low in every detail. One thing Dr. Low was very careful about was not to run up his patients' bills, and he was especially solicitous of those who were in modest circumstances. Instead of sending Ann to the hospital for a series of shock treatments, he gave a simple prescription for home hydrotherapy, which was to be religiously followed. He suggested that John engage a woman to do the treatments, but there was not much money in the Landis family then. And since John was a newspaper pressman, working from four o'clock in the afternoon until midnight, and had the daytime off, he decided to take care of it himself.

Every morning and afternoon he wrapped Ann in a sheet dipped in water in which Epsom salts had been dissolved. Over the sheet he wrapped a woolen blanket. Ann had to stay in this cocoon one hour in the morning and another in the afternoon. After each session John rigorously massaged her arms and legs.

Along with this treatment Ann was given a little private counseling for a while. And of course she went regularly with her husband to the Thursday group psychotherapy classes at the university. Those classes became the highlight of her whole week. Presently she found the courage to attend them alone. She also attended the Recovery Association meetings which were now being held every other Sunday.

She was learning a great deal about herself. She discovered that just because thoughts and ideas came to her she didn't have to believe in them. It was her belief in their danger that was causing her trouble. Belief in danger, she was taught by Dr. Low, always causes fear, and fear creates tension.

She also learned from him that the deep fatigue she was feeling, the panics and obsessive thoughts, were "distressing but not dangerous." She learned to "command her muscles" to do what had to be done despite all her symptoms—tremors, palpitations, stuttering, painful blushing. Even Dr. Low freely admitted his own propensity to blush in his early years and said that in new situations he still did so. It was just an average symptom, nothing to be alarmed about.

Ann learned, too, the technique of motionless sitting to be practiced when she felt her tension mounting. She learned to recognize the presence of tension by the symptoms it brought on: pains in the back, head pressures, palpitations, tremors, preoccupation, and inability to concentrate. Then Ann would find a comfortable chair, sit down, and go quietly through her body, checking and relaxing every muscle. She would look straight before her, focusing steadily on a single point and controlling even her blinking. During this time she would counteract the disturbing thoughts that flitted through her brain by telling herself "distressing but not dangerous." Sometimes Ann would practice motionless sitting for as long as ten minutes at a time. And she would give herself credit for this effort toward mental health. Dr. Low called this self-endorsement, which meant self-praise for one's efforts, an attitude which if adopted would bring relaxation in contrast to self-blame which causes tension.

Gradually, as the months went by, her delusions disappeared. She began to feel a sense of freedom and well-being she hadn't experienced for years. And she knew it was the psychotherapy classes and Recovery that were curing her. She and her husband were to become as devoted to the doctor who had helped them, and to the little Association in which Ann felt such security, as had Annette Brocken, with whom she became good friends.

2.

At the group psychotherapy classes Ann often saw a young man with an expression of dazed bewilderment on his face. His name, she learned, was Frank Rochford. In 1926 Frank had graduated from the University of Chicago with high expectations. He had majored in the Romance languages and had planned to teach in this field. But he hadn't been able to find any position available and had become a bookkeeper. He'd held that position for five years and had acquitted himself well.

Then in 1931, when he was twenty-six years old, he had found himself beginning to lose sleep. It was the sleeplessness, he was sure, that was leading to the enervating fatigue from which he began to suffer. He could scarcely get to his job in the morning. He was no longer able to engage in outside activities and, one by one, began to sever his social contacts. This gave him more time to rest. But all the rest in the world didn't seem to help. The fatigue only grew worse. Finally it became so overpowering that he had to give up his job.

Many people would have considered Frank's move a rash one, for this was during the Depression years and jobs were hard to find. But Frank couldn't see that that made much difference in his case. He couldn't have worked anyway. He took a room near his mother's home and lived there by himself on his meager savings. By careful planning it was possible to exist on five or six dollars a week. But that didn't leave enough for medical help. Frank did go through a couple of clinics, but he didn't learn anything from them except that there was nothing "organically" wrong with him. How could there not be, he wondered, when he was always so tired?

For two years Frank drifted in this tide of inertia. During the whole time he didn't experience any emotions at all—neither the lows of depression nor the heights of excitement. His was a gray world. And it wouldn't have helped him to learn that his ailment would one day be diagnosed as a "combination of a neurasthenic-obsessive psychoneurosis."

After two years of living this drab life in his little room, Frank moved back into the family home because his sister, who stayed with their mother, had become quite ill. When his sister died, he continued living there. Frank's mother, who was in reality his aunt, was a domineering woman with a strong sense of possessiveness toward her adopted son. The relationship between mother and son did not provide a healthy atmosphere for Frank.

Finally in 1937, his savings gone, he knew he would have to find a job of some kind. Bookkeeping was out of the question, but he managed to get part-time work as a service station attendant. It was below his training and capabilities but it had its advantages. The work seemed to be less of a strain on him than the book-keeping job had been. And the station was near his home, so that he could still get in his quota of rest. All the same he found it very difficult to drag himself to work every day. And he was haunted by the fear that the time would come when complete inertia would overtake him and he would have to give up entirely.

Then in 1941 a former schoolmate, who had been having problems of his own, told Frank of a certain high school principal who had charge of emotionally disturbed students. The principal had helped him and might be able to help Frank also, his friend said. Frank went to see the man and was told about the psychotherapy classes Dr. Low was conducting at the Research Hospital. Frank was thirty-six then and had been suffering for ten long years. The psychotherapy classes sounded rather offbeat to him.

Whoever heard of counseling a roomful of people at once? But he was suffering so much that he was ready to try anything.

He began attending classes, but he wasn't impressed by them. It was the people he met there, people like Ann Landis and Annette Brocken and Joe Janis, who kept him coming back. They were all so enthusiastic about how much they'd been helped that he felt there must be something in it. And in April he became a member of Recovery, as much for the fellowship he found there as for anything else.

3.

That summer of 1941 Dr. Low was to get his first bitter lesson in politics. He was to learn that even after the stunning victory of the Recovery forces in pushing the reform statute through the legislature, they could still lose their battle by a simple legal ruse. On the last day possible, just before the legislature adjourned, Governor Green vetoed the statute. He had delayed his action long enough to prevent the legislators from overriding his veto. His excuse was that the state attorney general had declared the law unconstitutional, a strange explanation in view of the fact it had been drawn up by Professor Green, dean of Northwestern Law School, one of the foremost legal institutions in the nation. Insiders said that the Governor had been pressured into the veto by judges in downstate Illinois who had seen the lucrative court fees slipping from their grasp, and by psychiatrists who felt that the new procedures, though so much more humane for the patients, would prove too time-consuming for themselves.

Bravely in the *Lost and Found,* Dr. Low promised that the fight against the stigmatizing law wasn't over, that it would be taken up again the following year. But then the second blow fell —the blow that took away even the forum from which such a campaign could be mounted, together with the base for Recovery itself.

It had been decided to separate the Department of Psychiatry at the University of Illinois Medical School from the office of state alienist. Dr. Low was bypassed and Dr. Francis J. Gerty was appointed head of the Department of Psychiatry with Dr. Low retaining his position of assistant director of the Psychiatric Institute. Dr. H. R. Hoffman, an ardent psychoanalyst and neighbor of Governor Green, was named state alienist.

Now the climate, which had never been friendly to Recovery, became out-and-out inimical. Dr. Hoffman especially didn't like the way the organization was being managed, and as state alienist he could close all state hospitals to Recovery groups. Even in the Psychiatric Institute Dr. Low could see no future for it. His greatest fear was that its direction would be taken from him and placed in the hands of others who already were clamoring to change it to suit their own ideas.

The first steps of the campaign to separate him from Recovery had already been taken. His reputation was being attacked. Finally, according to his widow, Mae Low, Dr. Hoffman openly leveled the accusation of monetary culpability against him. Since the Psychiatric Institute could accept only a small number of those who applied for admittance, suggested the new state alienist, Dr. Low's choice of patients was based solely on the bribes he received from relatives. This slander against his ethics was too much for Dr. Low, who threatened suit unless the vicious canard was retracted. Dr. Hoffman did so, but the shadowy campaign of vilification continued unabated. Under the circumstances Dr. Low could see no alternative but to liquidate the little organization immediately. He planned to offer such a motion at the next executive committee meeting of the Recovery Association, which would take place in the fall.

Meanwhile he had to make some explanation to the Recovery members of what he was planning to do. His summer vacation was starting, but he delayed leaving town long enough to attend the Recovery meeting that Sunday, July 13, 1941. There he made his dreary announcement—since professional recognition was apparently not to be achieved in the near future, the only course that he could see open to him was to resign the presidency of Recovery and to request its liquidation.

The announcement stirred up an outcry of indignation and despair from the packed room. The sense of loss, the old prison sense of fear and isolation fell like a heavy blow on many of them. With the sounds of grief and fear ringing in his ears, Dr. Low set off with his family for the little resort town of Fish Creek,

Wisconsin, feeling very much like the murderer of his own child. A poignant letter from the Wisconsin woods to Beatrice Wade, who from the very beginning had been a devoted Recovery volunteer, reveals the background of his long, discouraging struggle to get recognition for the organization, and the anguish of his final drastic decision.

". . . You know that recent changes had their effect on Recovery. Many of our arrangements are now subject to criticism, and some procedures have already been objected to. I expect more of this in the near future. If I add that vicious gossip has been spread about my personal integrity with regard to Recovery, you will realize that I have ample reason for believing that the fate of the organization is in the balance.

"We were never liked. We were, I understand, too active. The dislike turned into positive suspicion when, in 1939, we dared issue our preliminary draft for a new commitment statute. Ever since, I was isolated and avoided. The further developments you know. Nevertheless, I carried on and never thought of giving up. If I do that now, you will realize that the reasons must be compelling.

"My reasons are simple. If we do not liquidate we will be forced out of existence, not by violence but by gentle strategy. The action will of course be aimed at me, not at Recovery. The misfortune is, however, that Recovery is in no position to continue without my guidance. The techniques without which Recovery cannot exist (group psychotherapy, group instruction, and study classes) are not known to anybody but me. I have tried to persuade some influential men to let me hold a course for our physicians with a view to teaching these techniques. But I was unsuccessful in the past. That I shall be more successful in the near future cannot be assured. It would take many months of intensive training to teach physicians how to apply Recovery methods. At any rate, at present Recovery cannot continue its complex functions without my leadership. In other words, if the decision is that I have to go, Recovery will have to go too. This is my view of the situation. The executive committee may decide otherwise, and if it does so, I shall certainly cooperate. Perhaps a way will be found to continue the organization after I resign the presidency.

"Of course, there is the possibility that support will develop and that the drastic decision will be reversed. For the present, I am rather pessimistic about the possibility of quick support. But I hope my gloomy outlook will be challenged by subsequent events.

"I do not have to tell you that I reached the decision after much inner struggle. One does not like to murder one's own child, and if a man decides to do such a thing he does it in order to forestall something worse than murder, for instance, death preceded by prolonged agony. You know better than anybody else that Recovery was my child. I prized it as the most valuable of my creations. All of this I do not have to tell you. You know it and you will understand that if I suggest that its life be ended, the decision is forced on me by circumstances which I cannot control.

"Again support may develop. If it does not I have the consolation that our work was not futile, that a way was shown how to relieve misery and that the way will some day be followed by others. Fortunately, the techniques have been deposited in *Lost and Found* and can be revived any time it is desired."

Then, ever mindful of the confusion and apprehension that the uncertain status of Recovery might be causing his beloved patients, he appealed to Beatrice Wade for help: "In the meantime, there may be alarm among the members, and I am certain that if you have the opportunity you will try to reassure them. For the present, no final decision has been made and my pessimism may yet turn into a guarded hopefulness."

His poignant letter concludes on a lyric note. "In spite of all these new developments I have managed to keep my spirit and to enjoy the beauty of a scenery which in its naturalness makes one forget strategy, clever tactics, and ruthless rivalry."

FOURTEEN

Dr. Francis J. Gerty, an amiable man, had been head of the Department of Psychiatry at Loyola University in Chicago and director of the Psychopathic Division of County Hospital before becoming head of the Department of Psychiatry at the University of Illinois Medical School. A man of eclectic nature, he felt that all schools of thought should be equally represented in the department which he now headed. So, though during Dr. Singer's lifetime, clinical psychiatry had been in the ascendancy there, Dr. Gerty began bringing in numbers of psychoanalysts to balance things out. Foremost among them was the well-known Dr. Franz Alexander, long associated with the Institute for Psychoanalysis in Chicago.

Dr. Gerty must have been sorely disturbed by the little Recovery Association which, in his reconstructed department, stood out like a sore thumb. Nothing could raise the hackles of his psychoanalytic associates more than that organization and its director. This placed Dr. Gerty in a precarious position. Any overt move he might make against Recovery would set its militant members buzzing about his ears like angry hornets.

And there was the problem of Dr. Low himself. Dr. Gerty had the highest respect for him as a brilliant researcher. Moreover, he had been so long on the university staff and had acquired so many admirers among the Board of Trustees that it might be most impolitic to lose him now. But Dr. Low had complicated matters with his blunt manner and forthright declarations against corruption and ineptitude, which had offended some of his colleagues. And now they were looking at the assertive Recovery Association

123

and Dr. Low's encouragement to former patients to manage their own affairs as the last straw.

The members were a maverick group. The very day Dr. Low returned from his Wisconsin vacation in August, a delegation led by Joe Janis was waiting to greet him and present him with a list of ninety new members. They had recruited these members during his absence to show their firm faith in the future of the Association.

Actually they had done more than this. They had organized committees which had met with representatives of the Research Hospital and the State Department of Public Welfare to demand the continuation of the after-care project. They carried enough weight, both in numbers and influence, to cause the department heads to appeal to Dr. Low to reconsider his decision to liquidate the organization. And Dr. Conrad Sommer, chief medical officer of the Department of Public Welfare, promised that he would give full support in helping him organize Recovery in state hospitals.

How many of the promises were mere lip service was proved as the days passed into weeks and no final decision nor any concrete move was made. While Recovery waited, group psychotherapy classes were terminated and all the other activities were broken off.

In a letter to Miss Wade, who had left Chicago and was now teaching at the University of Michigan, Dr. Low wrote concerning the events of that trying time. Dated October 1, 1941, the letter reads in part: ". . . You know that Dr. Sommer was or seemed eager to enlist Recovery's cooperation. But things dragged and a decision did not materialize. In the meantime, Recovery was left to shift for itself without active leadership on my part. Finally, I told Dr. Sommer that I was ready for action and that if the Department of Public Welfare did not know its course yet, Recovery would make its own decision. He then suggested a conference with Dr. Gerty which took place September 16. On this occasion both Dr. G. and Dr. S. suggested that the best solution would be for Recovery to move downtown. I immediately accepted and was happy to be given a chance to make the move at the suggestion of others. In other words, the decision was by mutual agreement. . . ."

Dr. Low was frankly relieved at getting Recovery away from the Institute. Now, whether Recovery could survive the drastic move or not, its integrity would at least be preserved—an integrity that would enable him to resurrect it at some future date when the climate might be more favorable for its growth. As for the present, the next step was to find a home for the small organization in the cold, indifferent world into which it had been so summarily thrust. The Recovery treasury contained a mere two thousand dollars, but the dedication of the members more than made up for their straitened circumstances. They showed themselves far more capable of practical accomplishment than even Dr. Low had ever given them credit for. One member took charge of renting a three-room office in the De Paul University Building on East Lake Street. The largest of the three rooms would seat from thirty to forty people and could be used both as a classroom and a conference room.

On September 30 the Curtis Hall of the Fine Arts Building was obtained as a meeting place for the public group psychotherapy classes which Dr. Low planned to hold every Wednesday. Former patients and their relatives would be interviewed at these classes, to be given free as an educational service for the public. Collections only would be taken. But since the hall could seat at least 360 persons, the classes, if successful, would both pay for its rental and help defray the expenses of the little Association, now completely on its own.

At the same time Dr. Low tendered his resignation to the University of Illinois Medical School, where he had been prominent for so many years. So far as teaching was concerned, he felt that his value there was over. Under Dr. Singer there had been a singleness of purpose, but now the old sense of solidarity was gone. Duality seemed to permeate everything.

The sense of discord was not only in Dr. Low's own mind. Over and over again he had been made painfully aware of the confusion among the students due to the wide variance between the psychoanalytic and the clinical psychiatric viewpoints. Where before they had accepted his authority, now they questioned his every statement in the light of contradictory pronouncements by other doctors. If this was happening to him, he knew it must be happening in the classrooms of his colleagues with whom he might not agree in principle, but whose authority as teachers he thoroughly respected.

However, the chief reason for his leaving the post he had held so long was Recovery, which he would never desert so long as it had a chance to live. In the same letter of October 1, he explained to Miss Wade: "Since a reorganization of this kind will require my full attention, I offered my resignation as assistant director but was only granted a three-months' leave of absence. The University even offered me an absence with pay but I declined. It is better to be rather independent.

"Everything seemed thus well settled until yesterday I received a telephone call from Dr. Gerty asking me to meet him at a luncheon engagement, as the agreement needs some modification. He mentioned over the phone that he felt uncomfortable at the fact that I should discontinue my teaching and that I should be dropped from the payroll. This indicates that certain people got together and decided it was unwise to let Recovery be on its own. We shall have a conference tomorrow, Thursday, and see what are the proposals. Generally speaking, I feel that the present arrangement is satisfactory but if either the University or the Department or both have suitable suggestions, I think we should accommodate them. Recovery is a public trust and should endeavor to maintain contacts with the educational and welfare organizations. At any rate, the men will not find us intractable. I was happy to note that our membership, although somewhat bitter, is not bellicose. I try my best to alleviate their feelings and to create a spirit of cooperation. We have been mistreated, but Recovery must learn to control its temper."

2.

One of the casualties of that trying time was Ann Landis. She had returned from a vacation in Wisconsin to find the group psychotherapy classes terminated and Recovery in a turmoil. A sense of insecurity began to haunt her. She felt neglected, forgotten. Presently the old delusions and obsessions began coming back. They became so strong that Dr. Low prescribed shock treatments this time, but since he knew that the family couldn't afford to send Ann to a private rest home, he arranged for her to be brought to the psychiatric ward at the university on an outpatient basis. And after a series of six shock treatments Ann was again free of her confusion.

It was surprising to Dr. Low that not more of his patients were breaking under the strain of readjustment during those first two months. Recovery had always been sheltered in the Institute. Now it was learning the facts of life in the hard, competitive world of Chicago's Loop.

First, there was the matter of furnishings for the new offices. Recovery members had expected to pick up some secondhand things for about two to three hundred dollars. But with World War II still going on and Pearl Harbor less than four months away, prices had skyrocketed and even a few bare essentials would have drained Recovery reserves. The members were in a panic until, fortunately, Harry Zieve, a long-time friend of Recovery, came to the rescue and obtained the necessary furnishings for a nominal sum of $127. This astonishing reprieve buoyed everyone's flagging spirits. The first hurdle was passed.

Another problem was assistants to take care of all the work which formerly had been performed by an efficient hospital staff. Now most of it would have to be done by volunteers, but Dr. Low felt that two paid employees at least would be necessary. He hired a handicapped former patient to act as receptionist at thirty dollars a month, and a former patient to serve as executive secretary at forty dollars a month. Both these modest stipends came from his own pocket. And apologizing for the paucity of the sums, he promised that should Recovery prove successful in its new home, wages would be raised to "full-time compensation."

As might have been expected when an office is run by amateurs, the efficiency which the Recovery Association had enjoyed while in the hospital was now lacking. Many things that before had been accomplished quickly and smoothly went at a crawl. And many chores that should have been done were neglected. Dr. Low dreamed of the day that Recovery could afford a professionally trained office secretary, preferably a former patient.

3.

There were many in psychiatric circles who expected that Recovery would die once it was removed from the shelter of the Psychiatric Institute. But this showed no sign of happening. Instead Recovery members, from their new precarious perch, continued their vociferous clamor to establish Associations in state hospitals. They deluged the Department of Public Welfare and the doctors in charge of the hospitals until finally their demands bore fruit.

In October the Department of Public Welfare called a meeting in Springfield, Illinois, where Dr. Low was invited to present the basic issues of Recovery. He outlined the development and work of the Association and felt the reception was both friendly and sympathetic, but no decisive action was taken. Instead it was agreed to call another meeting in December.

But December slipped by and 1942 came in and no meeting was called. The Recovery members didn't intend to take such a snub quietly. In their assertiveness they were unlike any other former patients the doctors had ever seen. They were always behaving in totally unpredictable ways. Now on January 1, they called a mass meeting at Curtis Hall. Before a packed room of interested well-wishers they voiced their vehement objections to the way they were being ignored. Because of the cavalier treatment they were receiving, they said, Recovery was being barred from the state hospitals. They had no other choice but to vote to liquidate the little organization which had done them so much good.

Smarting under the adverse publicity, the Department of Public Welfare immediately sent its representatives to contact Recovery and ask it to reconsider. Four days later, on January 13, Dr. Low met with the director of the Department, who presented him with a plan for introducing Recovery techniques into the state hospitals of Illinois.

The first hospital to make the experiment was to be Chicago State, which had always been friendly territory, although now Dr. Garner, the former clinical director, was no longer there. Of course everything couldn't be done at once. Some experimentation would be necessary to adapt the techniques to the larger hospital which contained some 4,500 beds in contrast to the two-ward, sixty-bed capacity of the Psychiatric Institute. But everything augured well, for Dr. Low seemed to have the full cooperation of the Department of Public Welfare, Dr. Gerty, and the doctors at the hospital.

There was one chance he didn't want to take in this new venture, however, and that was the loss of Recovery's independence, which he meant to guard at all costs. So he wrote in the *Recovery News* which had succeeded *Lost and Found:* "Recovery's spirit is that of SELF-HELP. When we asked the Department of Public Welfare to assist us in our work, we merely asked for an opportunity to demonstrate our ability to practice self-help. We did not ask for money or resources of any kind. We are determined to ask for nothing of the sort in the future. We shall see to it that our work shall not be a tax on the state treasury. . . . No grants, subventions, or contributions will be requested of or accepted from the state institutions."

Of course Dr. Low realized that such independence had to be paid for and he made an appeal to the little group to provide the necessary funds: "Our needs will be far greater than they were at the Illinois Research Hospital. We shall have to maintain our downtown office with two salaried employees. Moreover, we will be obliged to enlarge the resources of the Transportation Fund in order to enable our indigent members to attend our meetings and parties. . . . We are certain that our members will not forget this most precious piece of self-help practiced in and through Recovery."

4.

In a letter to Beatrice Wade dated March 19, 1942, Dr. Low expressed buoyant optimism over the psychotherapy classes he had started at the Chicago State Hospital: ". . . we had our first well-conducted class Tuesday, March 17, in the Diagnostic Building, with about seventy patients attending, all of them prospective candidates for parole. The effect was sparkling. If you know how little I am inclined to be carried away with preliminary success,

you will understand what I mean if I say that the group psychotherapy class was a signal achievement. It cemented all the workers into a unified group. I anticipate splendid cooperation although
some hitches are bound to occur yet."

However, the forces against Recovery were not to be so easily
cajoled into cooperation as Dr. Low had at first believed. Less
than a month after the beginning of the classes, there was a
dwindling in the number of patients attending, and the staff was
beginning to bring these patients in late. Then it became quite
obvious that the patients who were coming were not on the verge
of parole but were still so ill that they couldn't respond to the
group psychotherapy techniques. Their unresponsiveness, Dr. Low
realized, would be used as proof that Recovery wasn't really
working.

It was a subtle form of sabotage and finally he appealed for
help to the ward doctor who had proved most loyal to him. As
he describes in his letter: "I asked Dr. McCorry whether she could
not induce the physicians to take a hand, and her reply was that
she could not get cooperation. She authorized me to use her statement at will. When I had her information I told Dr. Gerty that
I intended to discontinue the class. He left the decision to my
discretion."

So Dr. Gerty discreetly washed his hands of the whole trouble-
some project. But Dr. Low and his Recovery members were not
ready to give up the battle yet. The relatives got busy and contacted the Department of Public Health, and when they got no
satisfaction there, they wired the Governor to express their alarm
over the treatment Dr. Low and Recovery were receiving and to
request an interview. When the telegram was ignored, the Governor was deluged with letters insisting that he meet with Dr.
Low. Should the meeting take place Dr. Low hoped to convince
the Governor to appoint a subcommittee to make a careful study
of Recovery. He was sure such a study would reveal the organization's true value and the state government would give it official
endorsement. From there it would be possible to make the movement nationwide.

"This may sound unreasonable," he admitted in a letter to
Miss Wade. "But I cannot afford to be fed promises year after
year. Recovery will either be very great or not at all. . . . The

spirit of the members is that of true indignation. They feel they have been tricked, and I have been gravely insulted."

He concludes his summation of the situation with the unquenchable crusading spirit of his nature, and his incurable optimism. ". . . If the members succeed I shall of course resume the work. If they fail (which I think is almost impossible) I shall withdraw completely and work for the Recovery idea without a Recovery organization. That can be done too."

And he adds, somewhat nostalgically, looking back over the long years in which Recovery had absorbed most of his time and interest, "In addition it will be about time to look after my family and my private affairs. So you see, I am not disheartened by any means."

5.

By midsummer Dr. Low was to learn once more the wide gap between public demand and political conscience. In reply to the flood of letters that came to his desk, Governor Green did indeed call a conference which was attended by his representatives, the Department of Public Welfare, and psychiatrists from the University of Illinois. But Dr. Low's dream of establishing Recovery on a nationwide, or even a statewide basis, was rejected. His request for a thorough investigation of Recovery techniques and their value to patients was turned down by all the doctors to whom he had sent letters of appeal.

Now he could see only a dead end for Recovery. The Association had been developed as an adjunct to state hospitals, to be implemented and supervised by psychiatrists. Without their cooperation, it had lost its reason for existence.

Once more the Recovery members gathered in Curtis Hall and heard their doctor's wishes, and this time they mournfully acceded to them. Recovery was finally and utterly dissolved. It was the end of a way of life that had meant salvation for most of those in the big hall that day. They left the meeting stunned, and many of them were in tears.

FIFTEEN

When Dr. Low wrote Beatrice Wade that he was going to carry on Recovery techniques without the organization itself, he was referring to the private psychotherapy classes which he began conducting early in 1942 at his office on Michigan Avenue. These classes were run along the same lines as the ones at the hospital, with doctor-patient interviews.

Dr. Low had approached the venture with uncertainty, not sure that he would have an audience for this form of group therapy, so unique in those days. In the hospital he'd been assured of an audience because patients had been brought by attendants. But there was no one to force his private patients to come. Yet he was astonished to find them there filling the room every Thursday. His fees were nominal—$2.50 a session per person, and an even lower rate if more than one member of the family wished to attend, since he wanted to make it particularly attractive to relatives.

His private consultation fees were as nominal as those for his group therapy classes. He charged $15.00 for the initial complete examination—in later years he was to raise it to $30.00—and never more than $5.00 for an office visit. He wasn't unaware of how contrary such low fees were to normal American policy, for he once told a patient, with a wry smile at his extreme statement, that the main thing in life in the United States was to make money.

2.

Though Dr. Low's methods were decried in psychoanalytic circles, he was highly respected by many others in the medical profession.

132

A few private psychiatrists were already referring some of their patients to him, the first crack in the wall toward recognition of his techniques. And as the knowledge of his successful therapy continued to spread in medical circles, many more general practitioners, some from outside Chicago, started sending him their psychoneurotic patients. One of these patients was Harriette Weech, who came to Dr. Low in the early fall of 1942.

Harriette lived with her parents on a farm in the Illinois countryside. She'd been born with a weak heart and as usual in such cases her mother had pampered her. As Harriette grew older she took care never to make any unnecessary exertion. But despite all her precautions she began to develop daily headaches that by the afternoon became almost unbearable.

She took all kinds of medicine but nothing seemed to help, so she went through the Iowa City Clinic only to have her ailment diagnosed as "migraine due to tenseness." Finally, by 1939, two or three years after the onset of the headaches, the attractive young school teacher had to give up her job and resign herself to a life of semi-invalidism.

Her doctor suggested that since she'd quit work maybe a trip and a change of scenery would do her good, so she decided to pay her aunts in Idaho a visit. All the aunts were very sympathetic to their stricken niece. They tried to interest her in doing things— attending night school, taking art lessons, going on fishing trips. Nothing helped.

Harriette was sinking into a deeper and deeper depression. Sure there was no hope for her, she began to think of suicide. Then after two years in Idaho, she returned to her home and went again to her doctor. This time he told her, "I think I have someone who can help you, Dr. Abraham Low in Chicago."

He seemed so sure about Dr. Low that in the early fall of 1942 Harriette went to Chicago for a consultation with him. By this time she had become so confused that she couldn't even make her way about the big city by herself, so her sister Alice accompanied her and they took a room at the Rita Club, a Catholic organization.

At first Harriette herself didn't feel much confidence about this new doctor. How could he do anything for her when no one else had been able to? But in her very first consultation with him he gave her so much confidence that she came away thinking, "He *is* going to help me, I know it. If I just do what he tells me, I'll get well."

Harriette began seeing Dr. Low three times a week. Each consultation lasted about half an hour. During that time Harriette began learning things about herself which astonished her. She'd been thinking her headaches were due to something organic, her heart maybe. Dr. Low told her it was purely and simply her tense muscles that were causing her headaches.

Instead of resting all day long, what she had to do was to move those muscles. He prescribed three walks a day, two or three blocks at a time, morning, noon, and night—six blocks in all. It sounded easy, but it wasn't. Harriette hadn't moved her muscles for so long that she was weak. She had to will herself to take each step, and at each step, fear of endangering her heart almost paralyzed her. She was afraid she might collapse.

Sometimes she'd indulge herself and forget the walks. And each time she did she got a severe reprimand from Dr. Low. Sometimes his voice was so stern that she would go away crying. They were tears of anger. How could he treat her in this way when he knew she was an invalid? She never talked back, though she would nurse her grievances in silence for a day or two at a time. But she always returned to him.

To her he was the grandfather image, which, as she explains, was even more authoritative than the father image. He stood so straight and always appeared so confident that he inspired confidence in her. That was why, in the end, she obeyed him.

Early in his counseling Dr. Low warned Harriette to expect the inevitable setback. He cautioned all his patients about it so that when one came along they wouldn't give up hope. No matter how severe a setback might be, he told them, it would be only temporary if they just wouldn't work it up into a vicious cycle.

Harriette, like every other patient, had her share of these setbacks—periods so low in vitality that she wanted nothing more than to stretch out limply on a bed as in the earlier days. But she forced herself to use her muscles.

To keep going was the important thing, Dr. Low told her. So, obeying his orders, Harriette got a part-time job at the switchboard of a girls' club. Three months later she was handling a full-time job at the Methodist Publishing House. It didn't require much thinking, and since her headaches were less intense, she was able to hold the job easily.

After two more months Harriette passed a Civil Service Examination and was accepted as a children's librarian at the Chicago Public Library. By this time the old thoughts of suicide had faded, and hope and a new vitality had taken their place.

3.

At the psychotherapy classes Harriette struck up a pleasant friendship with Frank Rochford. Frank had given up his work at the service station and was back at bookkeeping again. When Recovery had left the Psychiatric Institute, he had consulted with a private psychiatrist for a while. But then Dr. Low started his group psychotherapy classes and Frank dropped the psychiatrist and started attending them instead.

He was attracted to Harriette at once. He liked to chat with her at the classes. And sometimes he went over to see her at Recovery headquarters, which was still open even though Recovery had been officially liquidated. This was because of Annette Brocken, who had decided to keep things going as long as the money lasted. Still on her leave of absence, she was spending long hours at the office straightening out the files and records. There were always volunteers to help her out: Ann Landis and Rosalie T., and now Harriette and Frank.

Occasionally Dr. Low would come over for a cup of coffee, a pot of which was always kept warm. While he was there he would advise his old patients on individual problems and sometimes talk to the group as a whole. He did this as a courtesy because he didn't expect it to hold together much longer. After all, it is the nature of groups to split up and disperse once they have lost their purpose.

As for himself, he had other plans to occupy his time. Now that the United States was in the war, too, he knew that the psychiatric wards of the Army hospitals would be overcrowded and doctors would be scarce. The condition might provide him with an opportunity to introduce his revolutionary group psychotherapy techniques. He decided to apply for a commission after the first of the year.

In October he broke the news to Annette. Instead of accepting it with resignation as he had hoped, Annette was horrified. This was something she'd never even imagined—to lose not only Recovery, but the group psychotherapy classes and Dr. Low himself!

In that time of crisis Annette, with the decisive vigor of her personality, made a sharp appraisal of Recovery. Let the Fortnightly Club and the Companion Club and all other clubs organized for purely social activities go. Let everything go but the one essential —training. She importuned Dr. Low at least to teach the little group how to study and discuss *Lost and Found* so that they would have something to use after he'd gone.

He shook his head. Impossible, he told her. You couldn't train a lay group to carry on without the supervision of a psychiatrist. Nothing like that had ever been done before.

But Annette was a determined young woman who wouldn't take even that decisive refusal for an answer. She'd received too much help from Recovery to relinquish it without a fight. She approached the dues-paying members and asked if they would chip in to keep Recovery going. She'd hold expenses down by using her own home for the Recovery office. And they could meet in the Lake Shore Field House for their training sessions. It was so close to Dr. Low's home that he'd have to pass it coming and going.

When everything was set, she buttonholed Dr. Low and told him they'd arranged things to his convenience, even to the meeting hour which would be held every Saturday at 2 P.M. Surely he could drop in for a little while to work with them on a study format.

As Annette had expected, he couldn't turn them down because he never could refuse a patient. Finally he agreed that so long as he was in town, he'd meet with them on Saturday and conduct the panels as he always had. Jubilantly Annette sent out cards to the old-timers—Ann Landis, Frank, and Harriette—asking them to be on her first panel. Thirty or forty others also gathered in the Field House that afternoon, eagerly awaiting Dr. Low.

He arrived punctually, formally interviewed a patient as in the past, and gave an impromptu lecture on a topic which had been suggested by the interview. For the first few weeks the meetings were held in this old conventional way, always followed by refreshments either at the Field House or in a nearby restaurant. This modest form of socializing was designed to take the place of the elaborate get-togethers of the now defunct clubs.

Things might have gone on like this indefinitely, but one memorable afternoon Dr. Low phoned to say he was going to be delayed for perhaps forty-five minutes to an hour. Annette heard the news in consternation. What could she do to keep things going for forty-five whole minutes? she asked herself. She decided on a talk session. But the group was too large to allow everyone to have his say, so she selected a panel of four with herself acting as moderator.

Annette and the panel members began discussing the problems that had brought them to Recovery, their hospitalizations, the effect of stigma in their lives, the daily frustrations they were still experiencing, and the self-help tools they were using to overcome them. In the midst of this rather chaotic discussion, the doctor walked in.

Annette looked at him gratefully, ready to turn the floor over to him. But he waved her aside. There was a gleam in his eyes, an eagerness in his voice. "No, no," he told her, "I want you to go on."

So the group continued while Dr. Low listened intently. This was something he had never expected possible: patients proving that they actually could help themselves and each other without the strict supervision of a psychiatrist. The proof was before him.

Of course things had to be worked out. In the months ahead he and Annette and the others experimented on a format. At first they held a loose discussion period such as the one he'd walked in on, and this would be followed by a lecture from Dr. Low. But as time went by he began to realize how easy it was for members to stray from the Recovery techniques and Method. He himself could restrain such tendencies when he was there, but after he was gone there would be no one to bring them back into line.

To counteract this danger he inaugurated a preliminary reading of various passages in the *Lost and Found* magazines. These articles contained all the necessary techniques so that by reading them the patients would be constantly indoctrinated in the true Recovery Method. At the same time the passages which were read would take the place of his presence there, constituting the authority which would serve as the basis for the discussions which would follow the reading.

Another rule, which Dr. Low formulated after listening to a few panels, prohibited patients from diagnosing their ills or those of others and giving medical advice. As a doctor he saw how harmful such a practice could be when followed by an uninformed layman. One of the most important rules, however, didn't spring from his observation of panels but from an experience at home

One day he dropped in unexpectedly at lunchtime to find Marilyn squalling in the bathtub and Mae on the telephone. Though he didn't say anything, Mae could see the disapproval on his face. She dropped the phone and ran to get the child.

"Who was on the phone?" he asked her when she came back.

"A patient," she answered.

He picked up the phone and found the patient still on the line. He chatted for a few minutes and then hung up and turned to Mae. "How long did she keep you on it?" he asked.

Mae admitted it had been at least half an hour. Further probing revealed that this had been happening frequently. Whenever patients who were suffering symptoms couldn't find the doctor at his office, they'd phone his home and pour out all their woes to Mae instead. Mae didn't have the heart to discourage them, even though they were taking up much of her day. She thought it was her duty as the doctor's wife to sympathize and try to raise their spirits.

Abraham listened to her story, his face growing thoughtful. "I suppose patients are experiencing this with one another too," he said when she had finished.

At the next Recovery meeting he made inquiries and learned it was true.

"You're not helping the other person," he told them bluntly. "You're just giving him a chance to work himself up even more. The thing to do is not to let him unburden himself of this endless tale of woe. Stop him and ask for a bare report and then give what encouragement you can."

In accord with his twosome principle, he called it "complaining versus reporting," pure sabotage. So was inaugurated the five-minute telephone call which is still enforced today among Recovery members when, in desperation, they phone each other for help.

4.

As the fall progressed Annette came up with another idea. In addition to the Saturday afternoon panel meetings, why couldn't they also have home panel groups around the city so that more people could be reached? Dr. Low thought that was a good idea so he began his first Leader Training Course. It was held at night in Annette's cramped apartment, and sixteen or seventeen Recovery members showed up faithfully once a week to receive their instruction from Dr. Low. People were packed in like sardines and since there weren't enough chairs to go around, they perched on waste baskets turned upside down and on cushions strewn on the floor. But that kind of discomfort didn't bother them. They were as eager as Annette to keep Recovery going.

By December of 1942 the new project was introduced in a circular issued by Annette Brocken. In addition to the Saturday afternoon panels there were to be home meetings during the week. These home meetings were eventually to be located all over Cook County. They were to meet every Wednesday night. Two or more recovered patients who had received adequate training were to be assigned to each group. They were to conduct the meetings as they were being conducted at the Field House, with readings from *Lost and Found* and discussions, after which there would be a social gathering with refreshments.

The circular then went on to say that two such groups were functioning already and a third was being formed. "Note that the emphasis is now on instruction, not on recreation and entertainment," stressed the circular. "Note also the importance placed on utter frankness in discussing our experiences of mental disease and adjustment."

Dr. Low was to express his wonder at this new turn of events in a letter to Miss Wade, dated December 20, 1942. It reads: "You thought perhaps I had forgotten you. The fact is I am as busy as ever and a trifle more than usual. I am gradually winding up business as I am going to ask for a commission after New Year's.

"You will receive a circular letter next week telling you about a new Recovery project. So you see, the thing lives on no matter how much I tried to liquidate it."

Then after explaining the new format of self-help and how it was arrived at the day Annette made history by leading a makeshift panel, he continued, wonderingly, "Now they felt they were able in a manner to teach and decided to establish a service in which recovered patients would take care of non-recovered patients, both profiting by teaching or being taught. . . . It is a big success already and has placed the principle of self-help on an uncompromising level."

And, still marveling at the ever widening area of self-help the patients were opening for themselves, he went on: "By the way, some of them actually develop mastery in interpreting *Lost and Found*. Membership is growing at a gratifying rate without office or correspondence. From present indications, this project ought to have a far better future than its previous Recovery predecessor. The motto is: We do not want merely to improve; we want to be cured and to keep cured."

He added somewhat sadly the thought that he should be taking his departure just when the dream he had believed lost was about to be developed in a new and wonderful direction: "It is unfortunate that I should have to leave at this juncture but nothing can be done about that. Annette Brocken has firm leadership of the project." And since at that time he was still convinced that Recovery would fare best under expert psychiatric guidance, he concluded wistfully, "It is a tragedy that the men in authority do not take steps to get the Recovery issue under their wing. Unfortunately, I have not been able to convince my colleagues that this Recovery issue cannot be easily disposed of. Today I know that the members are determined not to give up. . . ."

So ended the old year in an upsurge of vitality for Recovery. And no one was more surprised at the turn of events than Dr. Low himself.

"He never lost interest in us," Annette says today, looking back.

"But he might not have continued working with the patients and instead devoted himself to writing if it hadn't been for that afternoon when he came in late. He got a lot of material after that and then he wrote our textbook, *Mental Health Through Will-Training.*"

SIXTEEN

Fortunately for Recovery, Dr. Low's application for a commission in the Medical Corps was rejected because of his age and his foreign birth. So he was free to develop the Association along the new lines. In the months ahead, he and Annette Brocken worked out the format of the home groups in greater detail. Each one was to be held down to fifteen members, which was about as many as could be comfortably accommodated in a private home. The members of each group would take turns holding the weekly meeting in their homes. But there would be only one authorized leader to a group and he would be thoroughly trained by Dr. Low. This leader would act as the authority for the members in his group. If he didn't know the answers to their questions he was to appeal to Dr. Low, to whom he would also report on the problems of his group members. This was Dr. Low's famous "chain of command" system, and through it he was able to keep a far closer supervision over his patients than would otherwise have been possible.

Even after a leader's training was over, Dr. Low didn't leave anything to chance. Periodically he would visit the different home panels to be sure everything was being run properly. It was always a red-letter day when he came—for everyone but the leader, who often complained of "butterflies in the stomach" at having to perform before his critical eyes.

The Recovery format was now established, but it was still in a state of fluidity. Though the techniques and tools for self-help had been fully developed during Dr. Low's tenure at the Psychiatric Institute, he was still searching for the most effective way of presenting them through the panel. He was constantly making changes, and it would take a number of years of trial and error before he finally would be satisfied.

Meanwhile, constant experimentation was being carried on as a joint venture between himself and Recovery members. Whenever a pertinent point was brought out during a panel discussion, it would be discussed over coffee later. Someone would come up with an innovation and it would be tried out. Occasionally it would work and be adopted. More often it would be discarded.

2.

Dr. Low's lectures on Saturday afternoon continued to be the highlight of Recovery activities. In these lectures, as in his private dealings with his patients, he continued to be as authoritarian as ever. Yet his authoritarianism was not that of an official to mere underlings. It was rather that of a leader who, within the context of his medical knowledge and experience, led by virtue of his own personal experience and his painstaking experimentation on himself.

His humility was extraordinary in that day when the profession believed that the relationship between patient and psychiatrist should be that of a child to the awe-inspiring father image. Dr. Low was not afraid of revealing himself to his patients as a human being, with shortcomings like theirs which also required correcting. In his various lectures he was to admit frankly:

"As a human being be sure I share all your imbecilities and your stupidities and I'm just as dumb as you are in many things. And everybody is. But I take my smartness and my dumbness not too seriously. . . . I have an egregious sense of importance. . . . It always comes up. I always feel, 'I am the smartest, the finest, the most vital person there is,' but I don't believe it . . . sometimes I lie down and daydream and then I have all kinds of fantasies how important I will be some day. Well, it will be about time if it should materialize. I'm not just getting younger, you know. And then all of a sudden after a minute or two I remind myself, 'Well, that's all nonsense, why should I dream about greatness and

glamor and fame and fortune and so forth?' and then I stop because it appears ridiculous to me. I have applied a sense of
humor. . . ."

And: "I remember many of the evil things I have done, not all.
What do I do then? Why do I not sink in the ground with shame?
It was an average past. Why should I blame myself for an average
past?"

And: "But look what goes on in me. What a wretched person I
am. I have worked for many years and heaven knows how many
mistakes I make when I work. I make a great many mistakes . . .
I know about black spots in my life. Nobody else knows about
them. I could work myself up about the dusky part. It all comes to
this matter: averageness. Everybody is average."

And: "I felt insecure, but did not become discouraged. I do not
say life is not worth living any more. I keep up my courage. I
have air hunger frequently. I have frequently awakened at night
with pain."

And: "Everybody develops habits. When I was a boy, I was awful. I was a nail biter. I bit my nails. That went on for years and
years. What did I get out of it? Nothing. Nothing but annoyance,
embarrassment, a sense of shame! Tremendous incentive to stop
it! It looked ugly. Could I make up my mind to stop it and it
stopped? It took years and years. It was a habit."

And: "I remember once I went to a physician when I was a
youngster, and I told him I sweated at night. I told him I felt palpitations. I told him I felt feverish, and I felt fatigued, tired all
the time. Maybe I told him I thought I had tuberculosis. I was
pretty dumb and, of course, the great trouble was I must have
read an article about it."

And: ". . . It [the impulse] always comes by Fate. I get such impulses, much more dreadful impulses. But my nerves have been
steeled and trained to develop resistance, and when dreadful and
mischievous and lascivious and blasphemous impulses reach my
brain, I look away and wait and they will depart. And they depart
in no time because my resistance has been strengthened and Fate
is not strong enough to break my resistance once it is strengthened
through training."

More than once he was to admit frankly that he had at one time
been a nervous patient himself and to express wondering grati-

tude for his own escape from the torments of such an illness. He had, he said, been one of those, so few in number and so fortunate, who had experienced a spontaneous cure.

So he established himself as the leader who knew the way because he had been there himself and felt no stigma about admitting it. It was this sense of camaraderie, coupled with uncompromising authority, which so drew his patients to him.

As time went by, Dr. Low discovered that those of his patients who attended the Recovery meetings made the quickest improvement. There was still something almost miraculous to him about the way patients responded to one another, finding both the encouragement and the companionship that gave them the incentive to make the long hard fight back to health. He began to urge more and more of his private patients to go to Recovery. His chief problem was with the big business men and society women among his clientele. Although they gladly and generously contributed to Recovery, it was almost impossible to get them to come to the meetings. Their wealth and social status gave them too much a sense of exceptionality and stigmatization to admit their illness so openly.

The patients of average means, the patients who could not afford to remain ill for long periods of time, were the ones who profited most. They began coming in such numbers that Recovery presently had too many people to fit into the little Field House, and it moved into larger quarters in the old Republic Building. The new room was much too expensive for Recovery's slender resources, so to help pay for it Dr. Low transferred his private group psychotherapy classes from the reception room in his office to the new location.

3.

Though Recovery now was no longer associated with any state institutions, the antagonism which it had engendered, instead of dying out, seemed only to be increasing. The growing hostility was apparently in direct ratio to the success of the organization and was aimed chiefly against Dr. Low.

So threatening was the attitude of some professionals that it began to affect his wife as well as himself. Day by day Mae suffered agonies, fearful every time her husband came home it would be to announce the ultimate blow had fallen: the revocation of his license to practice. There were already rumors abroad that this was about to take place. She was so anxious for her family's welfare that at first she tried to dissuade her husband from continuing his lonely battle against such seemingly insurmountable odds. Wouldn't it be wiser, she asked him, just to practice his profession quietly and forget about Recovery?

But he would have none of it. Recovery promised too much for humanity to be given up without a struggle, at whatever cost. And finally Mae, caught up too in that spirit of sacrifice, stopped trying to change his mind.

The threat to rescind Dr. Low's license never materialized, but other punitive measures were taken against him. All state hospitals were abruptly barred to him, and one by one most of the private hospitals followed suit. Finally his patients were admitted only at Parkway Sanitarium and St. Joseph's, where the nuns who ran the hospital had such a high regard for his capability and integrity that they refused to be intimidated.

Then Parkway Sanitarium declined and St. Joseph's closed its psychiatric ward. Fortunately, a new sanitarium, Fairview, was emerging as an up-to-date private sanitarium. Dr. Low had given much valuable aid to Dr. Jerry Freund, the founder, during the early beginnings of the sanitarium, and now Dr. Freund's full cooperation could be counted on. Except for this, Dr. Low would have been hard pressed getting much needed hospital treatment for his more severely ill patients.

4.

It was about this time that Dr. Low heard that Joe Janis had become seriously interested in marriage. Joe was now situated at Memorial State Hospital in Elmhurst. But he was also giving his off-hours to his old mentor, making housecalls for him at night and on Saturdays and Sundays—work that he was to continue doing for ten more years.

Joe had fallen in love with a beautiful young widow, Mary

Corcoran, who was a nurse at Elmhurst. As he had become serious about her, he had told her all about his stay in the Psychiatric
Institute. So when he proposed, it was natural for her to go to
Dr. Low to ask him if marriage was permissible. Dr. Low assured
her not only that it was, but that it would be a fine thing for them
both. Unknown to Mary, Joe had gone to Dr. Low with the same
question and had been encouraged too. So in February of 1944
they were married. It was Joe's first marriage and Mary's second.
Her first husband had been dead for a number of years.

It was only after their marriage that Mary's troubles started,
though she'd always had a nervous disposition. She began suffering from strong guilt feelings at the nagging thought that she had
been unfaithful to her dead husband by remarrying, and she
vented her sense of betrayal by lashing out at Joe in temperamental outbursts.

Joe recognized her problem as emotional and he knew the
remedy—the private psychotherapy classes, which were now being
held every Tuesday, and Recovery on Saturday. The trouble was
Mary didn't want to go. She'd try all kinds of ruses. She'd pretend
she was ill. By putting her thermometer on a hot electric pad and
then placing it in her mouth, she could come up with a very convincing 103-degree fever—convincing that is to anyone but a
doctor. Joe knew what was going on but confined himself to re-
marking that he had never seen such a high fever with such a
normal pulse.

Being a determined man, he wouldn't let up on his relentless
pressure to get Mary to Recovery. Sometimes he would manage
to bring her to the very door of the meeting room before she gave
him the slip. More often he was able to get her inside, but then
Mary would just sit through the panel in sullen silence. She
brought the same uncommunicative silence to her private consultations with Dr. Low.

Joe insisted on those weekly sessions, though Mary was of the
opinion that this man's theories were just a lot of nonsense. Still,
she had to recognize his kindness. He never tried to force her to
talk nor did he say much to her. He usually dismissed her after
about ten minutes because there wasn't any rapport between them.

But he never gave up with her and he was always there when
she needed him. During those early years her very life was being

jeopardized by her obsessions of guilt. And it sometimes seemed to her that she could absolve herself only by committing suicide. She would take sleeping pills, and there were several nights when her condition was so serious that Dr. Low had to be called. Each time he stayed with her till morning, patiently pulling her back from the death she was so assiduously courting.

For some five years Mary held out against her husband and Dr. Low and Recovery. Then suddenly one day something clicked and she really began seeing sense in the Method and working to master use of the tools. Dr. Low said that she had just absorbed Recovery by osmosis through the group, as had been the case with other patients of his.

Mary didn't know how her cure had happened, but she became very active in Recovery. Eventually she began leading a group of her own, and she worked on her marriage, which had deteriorated to such an extent that it was being threatened by divorce. Today, some twenty-six years later, Mary's marriage is a harmonious one. She leads a full, well-adjusted life and has a wide circle of friends.

5.

Mary's case was one of many similar instances of devotion displayed by this remarkable doctor to his patients. It was one of the things that gave them such confidence in him, for though he never pampered them, they knew he would always be there when they needed him. Where their well-being was concerned, he was prodigal with the sparse leisure time at his disposal. And many Saturday afternoons preceding and following the panel and refreshment time at the Republic Building, he was in his office giving a free consultation to some Recovery member in danger of a relapse.

One Saturday it was Ann Landis. As he delivered his lecture his practiced eye told him something was wrong with her. He could see it in the intense expression of her blue eyes and the tight set of her jaw. After the meeting he made his way to her.

"Ann, what's the trouble?" he asked her.

The kindly concern in his voice drew her out. She told him haltingly that the old religious obsession had come back full force.

She was sure it was her duty to convert all the people in the world. She couldn't get rid of the thought.

"I want to see you at the office within three-quarters of an hour," Dr. Low told her.

When Ann walked into his reception room, there he was waiting for her. He told her to sit down and began to explain to her that she was in a vicious cycle. He drew a circle to illustrate just how she'd been caught up in the cycle and was going hopelessly round and round in it. But Ann hardly heard him. Her powers of concentration were all but lost. Dr. Low became convinced that she would need shock treatments to bring her back to normal.

Just then, however, the telephone rang and he excused himself to answer it. The person on the other end was a member of his own family. And right before Ann's eyes Dr. Low shed his authoritative manner in a most remarkable way and became an altogether different personality—gentle and conciliatory. How surprisingly different he was! Ann listened, fascinated. It was this forgetting of herself that snapped the circuit of her obsessive thoughts. When finally Dr. Low hung up and turned back to her he saw a transformed woman, relaxed and alert. The conversation had not only broken Ann's vicious cycle but had enabled her to understand exactly what a vicious cycle was. It was an understanding so complete and vivid that she never had to have another shock treatment, though at first from time to time she still suffered serious setbacks.

The setbacks were heralded by an inability to concentrate on her work and Ann realized that when that happened she should phone Dr. Low at once for a private consultation. Over and over together they would review the Recovery tools until they became second nature to Ann. She learned not to attach danger to her periods of confusion but to cultivate the patience to wait them out. In that way she wouldn't work herself up into a vicious cycle. She learned to command her muscles to continue with her household chores even though her mind was confused, and she practiced motionless sitting. Eventually she learned how to recognize a delusion when it first came and to dismiss it immediately. And she was well on her way to a complete cure. Today she is beautiful and vibrant with health.

SEVENTEEN

Two years before her illness struck, Gertrude Beres, a young housewife, had been working as a clerk in a five-and-ten-cent store. Everything had begun with a deep depression accompanied by long spells of crying. Thinking she was just overly tired, she quit work. But the depression continued and was followed by terrifying symptoms—palpitations, air hunger when she would have to gasp and struggle for breath, and a sense of unreality. Most unnerving of all was her fear that she would lose control and harm her mother, her husband, or herself. She became so terrified of this impulse that she wouldn't touch a knife or leave the house alone or stay in it alone.

One day a friend told her about Dr. Low and Recovery. Gertrude decided to see this doctor and made an appointment with him, but she had to get her sister to accompany her because she couldn't leave the house by herself. When the two young women entered the consultation room, Dr. Low astonished Gertrude by looking from her to her sister and asking, "Which of you is the patient?" Gertrude had been sure her suffering was written plainly on her face.

She spilled out all her symptoms to the doctor and when she came to the end of them, he said simply, "You will get well." And Gertrude believed him. After a few private consultations she joined Recovery. The people she met at the Saturday panels gave her a sense of security. They were so friendly that Gertrude quickly made new friends. And they all assured her that they had once felt the way she did but that now they were getting well.

At Dr. Low's suggestion Gertrude began going to a home group every week, though she had to travel there by bus or streetcar. And she began practicing the Recovery Method. She forced herself to handle knives in the presence of her mother in order to conquer her fear of her impulses. She made herself move her muscles to go out when she felt like staying home, and control them when she felt like running away and hiding. She learned to call her "crying spells" a "crying habit," because a "spell" connotes incurability while a "habit" can be changed. And then she practiced eliminating her crying habit.

Gertrude seemed to be making progress until about a month later she suffered the inevitable setback. "I'm getting worse instead of better," she told Dr. Low in despair. "Now I have everyone else's fears as well as my own."

He smiled at her.

"You would have developed them anyway," he told her. "At least here in Recovery you will learn how to handle them."

2.

One day in 1944 another young woman named Caroline Philipp walked into Dr. Low's office with her husband, Raymond. Caroline had been an essentially healthy person when she married Raymond, though she had a nervous disposition and a tendency to be a perfectionist. But about two years after her marriage she had a miscarriage, and because she so much wanted a child, she began consulting with doctors about her condition. Finally she was given an operation, but it proved to be a failure and other physical difficulties developed which required additional operations. Within the course of two years Caroline had three more major ones. She developed a deep depression and a tendency to go into hysterics.

One of the doctors who was treating her made matters worse by telling her bluntly that she wasn't fit for marriage and should have remained single. Night after night Caroline would lie awake worrying about the doctor's words and wondering whether she would be able to perform properly as a wife.

The more she worried, the more upset she became. Her head

felt as though it were constantly in a vice that was being tightened hour by hour for hours. The excruciating pressure would block out conversations so that though she heard what was being said she couldn't remember it afterwards. She began to wonder if she had a brain tumor or some other serious illness, and kept visiting the office of the family physician to be reassured. He wanted her to see a psychiatrist but Caroline refused. She was afraid she'd be stigmatized just by being seen in his office.

Meanwhile things were going from bad to worse. Caroline no longer dared to go out for fear she would burst into tears, though for a while she was able to entertain at home. Then one evening she walked into the living room to greet some guests and felt something like an explosion suddenly blow up in her head. That frightened her so much she stopped inviting friends over and talked with them only by phone. But finally the day came when, in the middle of a phone conversation, she felt as though she had fallen off her chair. One side of her head went completely numb, and she was sure she was having a stroke. So she stopped answering the phone. By this time the outer world had become so fuzzy that even when she was with people, she never felt in touch with them.

3.

In 1944, nine years after her suffering began, Caroline experienced the most horrifying sensation of all. She was lying stretched out in bed when it suddenly seemed to her that her ams and legs were no longer attached to her body. It was just as though she was here and they were lying over there at a distance. She was separating from herself.

In terror, Caroline pulled herself together and rushed again to her physician. This time he told her, "There is one doctor who, I believe, can help you, a Dr. Abraham A. Low. I've been following his work for some time and he has marked success with his patients. He's a nerve specialist."

Though Caroline would have nothing to do with psychiatrists, she agreed to go with her husband to see the nerve specialist. He turned out to be a solicitous and gracious man whose piercing blue eyes were filled with sympathy as he asked her to sit down. He took her personal history himself and Caroline was soon launched into all her symptoms—symptoms which she was sure would show the hopelessness of her case. But when she came to the most terrifying of them all, that of feeling disconnected from her legs and arms, he stopped her.

"That's a sense of unreality," he dismissed the whole subject. "I've had many patients sit here and tell me the same thing."

Caroline stared at him. She'd asked the butcher, the grocer, the neighbors, her friends, anyone who would listen, about such symptoms. And they'd all told her they'd never heard of them and if she didn't get rid of them soon, she'd certainly land in a mental hospital. And here was this doctor treating them as though they were a common thing.

Next Dr. Low took her into the examining room where he gave her all the routine neurological tests. Caroline didn't know that they were for the purpose of establishing her sanity, but all at once she saw a psychiatric diploma on his wall. Panic and shame and anger surged through her. She'd been trapped by her doctor.

She scarcely listened to Dr. Low, who was telling her about an organization named Recovery and suggesting that she meet a couple of Recovery girls in his outer office. But Caroline didn't want to meet anyone. She burst into tears and refused. Dr. Low didn't urge her. He turned to her husband and said, "Mr. Philipp, Mrs. Philipp is very ill. But if she does what I tell her, I will see that she gets well." Then he patted Caroline on the shoulder and made another appointment for her.

As soon as Caroline got home, she phoned and canceled the appointment. For a month she stayed away. But the symptoms kept growing more terrifying and at the same time she kept remembering the kindly doctor who had patted her on the shoulder and promised to make her well. Finally she phoned her own doctor and told him she wanted to return to Dr. Low.

"I don't know whether he'll take you after what you did," her doctor chided her. "But I'll phone and ask him."

Nobody was more relieved than Caroline when she found herself again in Dr. Low's office. He asked her how she felt and with that encouragement Caroline launched once more into a description of all her sensations. She began with the head pressure and started working down, symptom after symptom, rather enjoying herself. She had only reached her shoulders when she was stopped short by the doctor, who put up his hand.

"Stop, stop," he ordered bluntly, "I've heard enough."

Caroline was mad enough to burst into tears again, but he didn't give her a chance for that. Her symptoms, he told her, were too common to be discussed and he wasn't particularly interested even in what had started them, though he rather suspected it was the succession of operations, coupled with her weak nervous system. The job ahead of her was to build up that system. And there was a Method for doing it, tools she could use. She would learn all about them at the Recovery meetings. She was to start attending them, as well as Ann Landis' home group. Dr. Low asked Raymond to go with her at first. He always liked to have the relatives attend some meetings, at least, so they would be able to see how to cooperate with the patients at home.

4.

Caroline's first experience at the home group was an alarming one. Others far sicker than herself were there. Some even laughed out loud for no reason at all. Caroline, who had a habit of murmuring to herself now and then, was sure that exposure to these people would make her even worse. At her next consultation with Dr. Low, she told him flatly that she couldn't go any more.

He merely sat back in his chair and looked at her calmly. "Well, that is up to you, Mrs. Philipp," he told her. "But this is my treatment. If you want to come to me, you must go."

Unlike many psychiatrists, Dr. Low never acceded to a patient's fear of picking up symptoms from other patients. He had found that a psychoneurotic patient was prone to develop new symptoms anyway—through such chance happenings as reading a newspaper, seeing a street accident, or attending a social gathering, and that it was virtually impossible to protect him from his own suggestibility. The better solution, he felt, was to help him build up an immunity to it. A Recovery meeting was the best place to do this because there the patient would not only be exposed to suggestible situations but would also learn how to control his reaction to them by practicing the Method. Again and again patients attending Recovery had proved the truth of this theory by eventually becoming immune to all forms of crippling suggestibility.

Though Caroline didn't want to keep going back to Recovery meetings, she obeyed because this doctor was so sure of himself that he gave her confidence too. Then presently, Dr. Low had a long candid talk with Raymond. He told Raymond that he had been a good, kind husband—too kind in fact, because he had pampered his wife and made her even more of an emotional cripple than she already was. Now he had to help her get well by no longer commiserating with her when she complained of feeling terrible. Instead, he was to remind her: "Use Recovery." Raymond was eager to cooperate, and he and Caroline began to work together at home for her health.

After a while Dr. Low told Raymond he was not to accompany Caroline to the meetings any more. She had to learn to go alone. It was an agonizing experience for Caroline. Sometimes she was so preoccupied she would forget to pay the bus fare. At other times she'd get off at the wrong corner and be filled with despair. "I can't function the way I used to. I'll never be well again," she would tell herself. Then she would remember that Dr. Low had told her she must move her muscles even though her mind wasn't functioning properly, and she would do so and eventually find her way again.

Presently, as she went to meetings and practiced the Method, she began to get a more objective view of things. Though she still had the symptom of murmuring to herself, she was realizing that it came from preoccupation, not from losing her mind, and that took the feeling of danger out of it. Then she found she was beginning to read and remember what she read. She was quite satisfied with her progress.

But Dr. Low never let a patient be content with mere improvement. And next he was asking her to take notes for him at the Saturday panel meetings. Caroline hadn't worked since her marriage. And now she told him belligerently, "If I take them, I won't be able to read them." But Dr. Low insisted. Other girls were taking notes too, which he used to see if he was getting through to his audience. But his chief objective was to make his patients feel respected by asking them to do something important for him. Self-respect was something they all badly needed, because they'd been looking on themselves as failures for so long. However, the notes were also to serve a purpose he had not then planned. They were to preserve for the future many of Dr. Low's lectures and his doctor-to-patient interviews that would otherwise have been lost.

5.

By this time Recovery had grown so rapidly that even the old Republic Building was becoming too cramped for meetings. In May of 1945 it moved its offices to the YMCA building at 185 North Wabash. Volunteers were needed to answer the phone in the new office and Dr. Low asked Caroline to be one of them.

Once more Caroline demurred and once more she was overruled. She began spending a half-day in the office three times a week. Dr. Low would drop by almost every day to see how she was getting along and he'd phone her a couple of times from his office. Then presently he began giving her a little dictation over the phone. The first time he asked her to take something down for him, Caroline started to say, "I can't." But she was learning now to spot her negative response to everything, so she said instead, "I'll do it." Each time she gave that kind of answer some more of her lost confidence would return to her. But it was still hard for her to accept the doctor's diagnosis that she was getting better.

One time she did a brief typing job for him and he said encouragingly, "Just look at the nice work!"

"Yes," Caroline answered, "but I am a complete mess." And she put her head down on the typewriter and sobbed like a two-year-old.

That summer of 1945 Caroline attended her first Recovery beach party. Dr. Low, as usual immaculate in his conservative business suit and tie, was there with his family. Even at a picnic he never dressed informally, but he always thoroughly enjoyed himself. He would stroll from group to group, spending a few minutes talking to each person. They were all so different here, where their object was just having fun. Here he wouldn't even let them bring up their problems.

When Dr. Low found Caroline he brought her over to meet his family and then he asked her to take Phyllis and Marilyn around and introduce them to the other patients.

"You want *me* to, Dr. Low?" Caroline asked in a tremulous voice. She had such a low estimate of herself that she couldn't believe this astute psychiatrist, who knew all her shortcomings, would trust his little girls to her.

"Yes, Caroline, take them around," he reiterated. So Caroline went off with Marilyn and Phyllis while Dr. Low watched her, smiling, knowing how much that simple little gesture would do to bolster her self-confidence.

6.

About two months after the beach party, Dr. Low phoned Caroline at home one day and asked her to meet him at his office. When she went there, Caroline learned they were going to the public library. She was terrified. "I can't, I can't," she wailed.

But Dr. Low wouldn't take no for an answer. So Caroline, notebook in hand, went with him to the library. As they walked down the street, she thought to herself, "Why, this eminent psychiatrist isn't ashamed at all of being seen with me! He doesn't think I'm such a mess." Caroline was grateful then that her inner confusion wasn't expressed in her outer looks. That was one thing Dr. Low had complimented her about—he was always looking for something to praise in a patient, and with Caroline it was her neatness. She'd never let her appearance go as some patients did.

When they got to the library, Dr. Low asked the librarian to get the *Index of State Libraries* for them. When she did, he took it to a table, opened the book, and said, "I want you to copy this page for me, Caroline."

The perspiration was pouring off Caroline. She was ready to fly out the door. But when she looked at Dr. Low, she saw his face set in stern lines and knew she dared not run. So she began. But she hadn't gone far before she started sobbing, "Dr. Low, I can't go on, I just can't."

"You can," he told her firmly, and Caroline realized by the tone of his voice that there was no other way out. So she forced herself to finish copying the names.

When they left the library she was shaking, but Dr. Low didn't seem to notice. "Caroline," he said, "you go again tomorrow, by yourself. You take the book and copy for five minutes and then you come to my office immediately afterwards."

All Caroline's pleas couldn't get her out of it. She had to go back to the library alone the next day and copy more names. She was able to fight back the hysteria while she worked, but as soon as she entered Dr. Low's office the tears came pouring down her cheeks. He let her cry unchecked, though for the past months he had been training her to control what he called her "crying habit" with a firm, "That is enough, Caroline. Try to curb it."

Now as she quieted down he asked, "You were terribly upset?"

"Yes," Caroline assured him, hoping for sympathy, but he gave her none. "Tomorrow you go again," he told her. "And this time you stay ten minutes. Time yourself."

So Caroline had to repeat the ordeal. But after that third library visit she found to her surprise that she didn't mind it so much after all. Finally the day came when Dr. Low looked at her and said, "It went pretty good today, not so bad. Good, Caroline! Good!" And he was beaming.

Now, instead of just a few phrases over the phone, Dr. Low went on to dictating whole letters to Caroline in the Recovery office. Caroline found him easy to work for. He dictated slowly, and whenever she did a capable piece of work he would always stop to praise her. Every once in a while he would pronounce a word Caroline didn't know and she'd tell him so. "Hmmm," he'd respond and spell it out for her and explain its meaning. "Well, now you've learned a new word," he would say with pleasure.

Caroline found it restful just being around him, and, interestingly, part of that feeling of restfulness came from his pipe. It always lay in evidence, propped against an ashtray on his desk. Sometimes if she was particularly tense and upset, he would lean back and reach for it and begin to puff and say, "Well, how does it go?" And just the sight of him and the pipe would have a relaxing effect on her.

7.

But not everybody found the doctor and his pipe always so restful. There was Frank Rochford, for instance. Frank had been doing well, because of his faithful attendance at Recovery meetings and his practice of the techniques. Although he still suffered periods of lassitude, they were never strong enough to force him to quit his exacting bookkeeping job. And whenever he felt the need of a little personal help he could ask for a consultation with Dr. Low.

One memorable day when he went for one of these consultations, the doctor brought up another subject which didn't have anything to do with Frank's own problem. He wanted to know what Frank's intentions toward Harriette Weech were. Frank bridled. You would think this man was Harriette's father, not her psychiatrist!

But if Frank's feelings showed in his face, Dr. Low took no note of it. He just went right on puffing calmly on his pipe and discussing the relationship. He knew Frank and Harriette had been seeing a lot of each other at Recovery functions, he explained, and that was normal. But just recently he'd heard that Frank was going over to Harriette's house on Sunday mornings and taking her to church. And he knew that though Frank had been baptized a Catholic, he wasn't in the habit of attending Mass. To a man so finely attuned to the nuances of life as was Dr. Low, the whole situation was beginning to look serious.

Frank sat and stared while the doctor talked. He seemed to know just about everything that had been going on between him and Harriette. You were spied on in Recovery! The grapevine passed along all the information it had whenever Dr. Low asked for it. And of course Harriette herself during her consultation periods was obligated to tell him everything she'd been doing.

And now the doctor, without saying anything out-and-out, was delicately laying down an ultimatum in that subtle way of his. Either treat the girl seriously—which Frank knew meant marrying her—or break up with her. Frank couldn't think of a rebuttal to the doctor's presumptuousness, but his temper reached boiling point. When he left he was still seething at the thought of how he had paid his good five dollars for a private consultation and had been forced to spend his time discussing Harriette.

As for marrying the girl, the whole idea was ridiculous and the doctor should have been the first to realize it. Frank couldn't even think of bringing a wife into the house he shared with his domineering mother. She'd hate Harriette for taking him away from her and the friction would probably give Harriette another nervous breakdown.

But after Frank had cooled down, he began to think of the alternative. If he wasn't going to marry Harriette, he'd have to stop seeing her. The more he thought about doing without Harriette's companionship, the more he knew he couldn't. He loved her.

In the fall of 1944, despite his domineering mother, Frank proposed to Hariette and was accepted, and they became formally engaged. The following June, less than three years since they had met, they were married in the Catholic church in Harriette's home town of Woodhull. Dr. Low didn't attend the ceremony but several of the Recovery members did. They celebrated it as an historic occasion, for it was the first wedding of a Recovery couple.

EIGHTEEN

For some four years Phil Crane kept to his resolution to stay away from Recovery, and Joe Janis, who had become his sponsor, was concerned about him. Phil was always to be grateful to the young doctor for his interest. It was because of Joe's urging that he went once to a Sunday afternoon gathering at Dr. Low's home. It had taken a lot of courage for Phil to do that because he was terrified that once the doctor laid eyes on him he would be bundled off to the hospital again.

Instead Dr. Low greeted him with a look of genuine pleasure. He'd been so concerned about Phil that he'd been phoning his mother at regular intervals to see how he was getting along. Now he exclaimed warmly, "Oh, Phil is here!" With that one remark he brushed aside Phil's uncooperative behavior and settled approvingly on the one positive effort his patient had made to conquer his fear and come. Phil, basking in the friendliness, enjoyed himself thoroughly that afternoon.

But a single visit in Dr. Low's home couldn't help Phil. Bit by bit through the years that had followed his discharge in 1941, he had been growing more and more irritable at home. Finally he had moved away to the Northside YMCA. Then he had begun avoiding his family and former friends completely. Finally one day Dr. Low received a phone call from Phil's mother. She told him that her son's delusions were back, that he'd moved from the YMCA to a shabby room in the poor section of town, and was again thinking of himself as an Afro-American. The people at the

Sun-Times told her that he was growing more and more confused and was troubling the other employees with his peculiar ideas.

Dr. Low phoned Phil himself and called him over to the office. After an examination Phil found himself in St. Joseph's Hospital for another series of treatments. But even though he had relapsed, Phil was in far better condition now than the first time. He had to stay in the hospital only three weeks and take fifteen shock treatments. When he came out he went home to live with his mother again. But he wouldn't go back to the Chicago *Sun-Times* because he was ashamed to face his former employers. Instead he found himself a job as a house-to-house salesman of musical instruments. Somehow getting this job through his own merits and not through his family raised his self-esteem.

Phil still didn't want to have anything to do with Recovery, but Dr. Low warned him that if he didn't he would wind up in the hospital again. So Phil compromised. Recovery home meetings were out because they weren't supervised by a professional. But he agreed to go to the regular Saturday afternoon panel and the monthly Wednesday panel and lecture which Dr. Low was now holding. And of course he would go in for office consultations and the private group psychotherapy classes. He'd even condescend to attend Recovery social functions if Dr. Low, the great Viennese psychiatrist, was there to supervise them. His reasoning was elementary. Dr. Low to him meant prestige, and prestige was very important to him in those days because he had no inner sense of self-respect to bolster him.

2.

While Phil was on the ward at St. Joseph's, he met another patient of Dr. Low's with whom he was to establish a warm friendship over the years. His name was A. Ernest Hoffman, known to his family and friends as Ernie. And he came from the little Iowa town of Muscatine, where he had owned a successful undertaking establishment. He had a lovely wife and two fine children and was highly respected in his community.

Ernest was a man who had cared deeply about his clientele. He knew how, in the first flush of grief, those who came to him were tempted to express their love for the dead by lavishing much needed money on expensive coffins and elaborate services. When they were people of modest means, he did his utmost to dissuade them from such costly expenditures. And his genuine warmth and concern during those first bleak hours of loss was a great comfort to them.

But Ernest was a sensitive man and he had to pay a toll for the empathy he felt for those who streamed through his funeral parlor over the years. He began to build up a state of tension which resulted in bloating of the abdomen and acute distress after meals. Like many others before him, Ernest discovered that when he was up in the sky his tensions diminished. He took flying lessons so that he could escape into the air when pressures became acute. He was the first man in Muscatine to get a private pilot's license. That was in 1930. From then on, whenever he could find time in his busy day, he would go for a flight.

Then World War II came along. Pilots were grounded. Gas was rationed. And Ernest found himself deprived of the hobby which had meant so much to him. Without an outlet his tensions increased, and his abdominal distress became steadily worse. Eventually, no matter what he ate, he suffered the agonizing distention. He began to suspect cancer but for many years fear kept him from consulting a doctor.

At last, in 1944, after almost fifteen years of suffering, he found the courage to go to the Mayo Clinic where he was given a thorough examination. The doctor's diagnosis was "diverticulitis of the colon."

Ernest was given some medication to relieve his distress, but the drugs affected his vision and he couldn't see to do his work properly. He began to worry about his eyesight, and since he couldn't believe the diagnosis of the clinic, he still feared he had cancer. This dread of total physical collapse was so strong that in 1945 he felt compelled to sell the business which he had built up over twenty-five years. Now, added to his deep concern about ill-health was a haunting sense of remorse at having failed his family. His daughter was just then entering college. The boy was in junior high school. Both were wonderful children, yet he was letting them down because he wasn't working, he told himself.

His self-accusation was really unjustified, for Ernest had an independent income, but he let it go on nagging him until he became totally preoccupied with gloomy thoughts of failure and disaster. His wife, Viola, seeing the helpless confusion into which her husband was drifting, was becoming frantic. Their family physician didn't know how to advise them. There seemed no place to turn for help until one day relatives passing through town told her about a physician in Chicago named Dr. Abraham Low who had had great success with a member of their own family who had been suffering a similar illness.

Viola didn't wait. She took Ernest to Chicago immediately and asked for an appointment. After a careful examination Dr. Low confronted the worried wife. "Mr. Hoffman will get well," he assured her, "because he has a fine character. He will work at it. But he must go to the hospital now." He saw Viola's worried look and added, "I suppose you'd like to know how long he'll be in the hospital. It'll be about six weeks."

So Ernest went to St. Joseph's Hospital, where he received several shock treatments to break the vicious cycle of his over-powering fear. During the time he was there, Viola attended Recovery meetings where, one day, she met the wife of a doctor who was one of Dr. Low's patients.

"How many times has your husband had a breakdown?" the woman asked.

"This is the first and I do hope the last," Viola answered.

The woman replied, "My husband broke down every year for twenty years. We went from doctor to doctor, and Dr. Low was the first one who was able to help him."

Twenty years of illness before help came! Viola was filled with gratitude that she and Ernest had found the right doctor the first time they looked. She was determined to do everything Dr. Low prescribed to help Ernest get well.

Ernest made rapid progress in the hospital. His confusion and preoccupation cleared up and within five weeks, earlier than Dr. Low had promised Viola, he was dismissed. Now followed the after-care part of the treatment. It was the usual prescription Dr. Low gave his patients. Ernest was to study the "Three Volumes" as they had come to be called. They were three little booklets which contained some of Dr. Low's interviews with patients and his subsequent explanations about the cases. He'd tried to get the books published, but publishing houses had all turned them down with the excuse that the material wasn't of enough general interest. So finally Dr. Low had paid to get the "Three Volumes" and other similar literature mimeographed so that his patients would have the necessary textbook materials.

The other part of the prescription was going to be harder for the Hoffmans. It was weekly Recovery meetings. Muscatine was two hundred miles from Chicago and driving in every week would mean a real sacrifice, but Viola was determined that they should do it, because the doctor had assured her that if Ernest followed his orders he would get well.

Ernest himself was skeptical. He wasn't convinced that Dr. Low was the answer to his problem or that his ailment was primarily a nervous one. It took all Viola's urging to get him to plow through the little books. He just couldn't seem to find anything applicable to himself in the cases which Dr. Low described there. Nonetheless he kept on reading, and once a week he and Viola would drive to Chicago for the Recovery meetings. After a while a strange thing began to happen. Ernest started to see clearly that everything in the volumes really did apply to himself. He lost his skepticism and began working wholeheartedly at getting well.

From that time on, Ernest started making a definite improvement. The distended abdomen and the distress that had caused him so much suffering for so long began to diminish and then disappeared completely. One by one, he began to enjoy again the dishes of which he'd been so fond and which he had had to deny himself for almost twenty years.

How had it happened? He'd dropped his self-diagnosing and had accepted the word of Dr. Low and the Mayo Clinic that his physical illness wasn't anything serious. By dropping his own dismal prognoses, he had released the tension that had been causing the trouble. Dr. Low liked to say in his classes, "If my patients have to diagnose, why don't they diagnose something good for themselves?"

Though Ernest was recovering, he still suffered setbacks. Some of them were caused by well-intentioned friends who, when they met him on the street, would say commiseratingly, "Ernie, you are *going* to be all right." No matter how well he felt, their words made him feel that there was something wrong with him still, and he would go home utterly discouraged. Then, too, there was a lot of stigma toward mental and emotional illnesses in the small town of Muscatine, and Ernest felt it keenly.

Dr. Low had instructed Viola to keep her eye open for setbacks in Ernest, and whenever she saw him slipping into the familiar pattern of preoccupation, she was to ask him to put in a long-distance call to Dr. Low. Sometimes after talking to him Dr. Low would suggest that Ernest come in for a three-day series of treatments on an outpatient basis. During their stay in Chicago, he and Viola would be guests of Frank and Harriette Rochford, with whom they had become close friends. There were many friendships of this type in the close-knit Recovery group.

3.

Frank and Harriette's home was a pleasant place to visit, but it hadn't been so in the beginning. Frank's mother had proved just as difficult as he'd expected her to be. And though she didn't express her resentment toward Harriette in open quarrels, she made the younger woman feel her antagonism keenly. As can be imagined, that kind of life gave rise to many classic examples which Frank and Harriette gave at the Recovery panels.

But Dr. Low didn't leave his newlyweds to work things out completely by themselves. Once again in a memorable conference with Frank, he put before him the necessity of making a choice. Who was more important in his life, Dr. Low asked, his mother or Harriette? When he had answered that question honestly, he had to act on it.

Once the question was asked the answer was simple—Harriette, of course. Harriette would always come first. So Frank went to his mother and told her that for the sake of harmony he and Harriette would have to move. Frank's mother, realizing that he really meant what he said, came up with a counterproposal; she would sell the house to them and go to live with her niece.

So Frank and Harriette bought the house and peace settled upon the Rochford family. It was into this home, now harmonious, that Viola and Ernest were welcomed when they came to Chicago.

4.

On one of these trips, in September of 1946, Ernest presented Dr. Low with an idea he had been discussing for some time with Viola. He had become aware, through his own illness, of others in his neighborhood who were suffering as he was. Couldn't he start a Recovery group in Muscatine to help them?

Dr. Low's first reaction was as incredulous as it had been when Annette had made her proposal to keep Recovery going. He was sure that a group as far away as Muscatine would need an attendant psychiatrist versed in the Method to keep things on the track. However, he didn't close the door on Ernest's idea. He promised to think it over and let Ernest know his decision by letter.

That letter wasn't long in coming. Dated October 3, 1946, it showed that incredulity had given way to restrained excitement. It reads in part: "The idea about a group strikes me, of course, like the fulfillment of a dream. If it could be done, well, that would be a most significant development . . . it would be a splendid piece of organization if a loose group could be formed to meet, let me say, once a week and to read or discuss the books or the *Recovery Journal*. The successive steps would have to be treated as trials with temporary errors and failures and final success. . . ."

Ernest didn't waste any time. Within the next few days, he and Viola had held their first Recovery meeting in Muscatine. The members consisted of several of Dr. Low's patients who lived nearby whom he had recommended to Ernest. That meeting was acknowledged by Dr. Low with cautious enthusiasm in a letter dated October 8, 1946: "You certainly are a fast worker. Well, I am happy that you are. . . . You will do well to consider yourself a pioneer, that means a man who has to proceed step by step. There is no doubt that some of your steps will land you in a blind alley. But that does not matter. If you think of yourself as a pioneer, you will not be disappointed if things prove to be balky."

The letter ended on a note of ebullient optimism: "I am delighted at this development. Whatever else may come out of it, this much is clear: I will have a place to send some of my out-of-town patients who cannot come to Chicago for after-care. This is a great benefit for me and will, I hope, be so for the Recovery issue as such."

Slowly the Muscatine Recovery Group grew as Dr. Low continued to recommend it to other patients in the vicinity. Before long several were driving seventy-five to eighty miles to the Hoffman home for the Saturday afternoon meetings. Ernest was never left to founder. In the midst of his busy day Dr. Low always found time to shoot off a letter to his "lieutenant," as he liked to call him, sending advice on the problems of various patients, or just notes of encouragement. Most of all he warned Ernest not to take responsibility for failures, because failures, of course, there were. And Ernest with his conscientious nature couldn't help feeling responsible when a severe relapse overtook one or another of his Recovery charges.

By February 6, 1947, Dr. Low had become so thoroughly impressed by the Muscatine experiment that he was writing: "You know, Ernest, I am not given to gush and hysteria. But I must tell you that I am simply thrilled by what you are doing with your group out there. You see, my patients are all worried about what may happen to them should I for some reason cease to direct them. Well, you have shown what can be done without my close and personal supervision. I do not exaggerate if I place so much emphasis on the quality of your accomplishment. There are other considerations. Suppose some of these days the Recovery Association engages in publicity efforts. Well, your group demonstrates that any place, any time, a handful of people can take matters in hand and, with the aid of the *Journal* and the books, manage to practice the self-help system. . . . Well, you go ahead and what you do is of the greatest significance locally, nationally, and internationally, or it will be some day. . . ."

That May a lengthy article appeared in the *Recovery Journal* describing the Muscatine experiment, and the Recovery Board of Directors voted to give the Muscatine group the status of an official branch. In July Dr. Low paid his first visit to the new branch. Ernest and Viola invited him and Mrs. Low to stay with them, but though the Lows sometimes threw their own home open to out-of-town Recoveryites, Dr. Low made it a point never to run the risk of obligating himself to a patient by accepting such invitations. So he asked the Hoffmans to make reservations for them at the local hotel.

The arrival of the Lows was a gala event in Muscatine, coming as it did only nine months after the founding of the little group. Some thirty to forty members, including relatives, were there. And Dr. Low's eyes shone as he looked out over this little band of followers. Once again it had been his patients, these dear ones of his, as he was now referring to them, who had dared attempt what his more sober scientific caution had told him was impossible.

5.

When he returned to his office in Chicago, Dr. Low found an ever-mounting number of letters on his desk. Recovery was getting known around the country, not only from brief notices in out-of-town newspapers, but also because two national magazines, *Hygea* and *Your Life,* had recently published articles about it. Some of the readers of the articles had become so interested that they had written in to join the organization, paying the low yearly membership fee, which included a subscription to the *Recovery Journal.* Now as they read the articles about the Muscatine experiment, these laymen, who lived in such distant places as Washington, D.C., St. Louis, Los Angeles, South Bend and Winnipeg, wrote in wanting to know how they could start Recovery groups in their own cities.

Several psychiatrists were becoming interested also. Dr. Stanley R. Dean of Stamford, Connecticut, sent in an order for books and pamphlets with the intention of establishing a group of his own. And another psychiatrist from Saskatchewan, Canada, came to Chicago for a week to study the Recovery Method so that he could use it in his province.

But most members of the profession, particularly those in the Illinois state institutions who were predominantly psychoanalysts, continued to remain aloof or to react with hostility toward Dr. Low. And in Chicago some professionals were now openly using the epithet "quack" in reference to him.

The most discouraging thing to Dr. Low about the antagonism

directed against him was that it never resulted in a confrontation between himself and his opponents. He would have welcomed such a frank discussion, even an argument about it. Instead he was enveloped in a fog of silence that extended from state to national levels. It was obvious that a doctor in such poor standing at home wasn't going to be given much chance to express his views abroad.

As his widow used to describe it, "I would go to conventions with him and his isolation was very noticeable. He was never asked to discuss a paper or give a paper."

Not that he didn't make the attempt, even against insuperable odds. His sister and brother-in-law, Jack and Theresa Ditesheim, remember one such bitter occasion. He had come East to attend a psychiatric convention and was staying with them in New York. He'd brought along a carefully prepared paper on Recovery. He was, he told them, planning to appeal to the Program Chairman to give him an opportunity to read it, though he didn't expect much success. He tried and failed, and since his purpose in attending the convention had been thwarted, he could see no reason for staying any longer. He returned the next day to Chicago, leaving behind a skeptical sister and brother-in-law. How could a man with a truly great idea be so thoroughly repudiated? they wondered.

"Maybe it is a crazy theory that he has," Jack voiced his doubts aloud to Theresa. Today he explains ruefully, "In my business —Swiss watches—the best watchmakers are always recognized by other members of the profession and I thought the same would hold good in his too. I couldn't understand how all the other psychiatrists could be wrong and he could be right. That didn't seem possible."

Besides his loyal wife, it was mainly those who had received the miracle of health through Recovery who really understood what Dr. Low was doing. And it was to this adopted and ever growing Recovery family that he turned more and more for companionship and appreciation as the years went by—his little band of followers who sometimes, when he faltered, boldly led the way into this strange, wonderful country of the mind they were all exploring together.

NINETEEN

Maxine White of Hopkinsville, Kentucky, contracted encephalitis when she was a child and nearly died. The illness left her with a weakened physical and nervous system, and when she was fifteen she had a breakdown and was taken to Vanderbilt University Hospital in Nashville, Tennessee, for observation and treatment. Within the year Maxine seemed to recover, and when she was sixteen-and-a-half, she married a young postal clerk named H. A. Kennedy. And a year later she bore him a son.

When the boy was seven years old, Maxine's husband died, leaving her to support the child and herself with no skills beyond her own determination. Those were the war years and women with special talents were needed to work on the Army posts, one of which, Fort Campbell, was located just outside Hopkinsville. So Maxine went back to Vanderbilt, this time to take special training in nursing, and after about a year she was able to find work at the Army hospital at Fort Campbell. But she soon left that employment when she was offered a better paying job as hostess at the Army Service Club.

The Army personnel and Maxine's co-workers liked this attractive red-haired young woman who was always so cheerful, so eager to please, and so responsible in her work. They could overlook her sieges of ill-health even though sometimes she was absent for three days at a stretch, immobilized in bed with blinding migraine headaches. Maxine suffered other symptoms too. Often without any apparent reason her heart would start to pound, then to skip beats, and finally to palpitate faster and faster, all the while feeling as though it were ballooning out in her chest. At the climax of this weird experience she would feel her very life beginning to ebb away from her, vein by vein, artery by artery. The horrifying experience would seize her with panic.

"I'm dying. I'm dying. Get me help," she would scream in a strangled voice.

Then someone would rush for the phone, and soon an ambulance would come shrieking up to bear Maxine off to the Army hospital. Here she would undergo a complete examination and the verdict would always be the same: "nerves."

Sometimes the bizarre sensations would strike when Maxine was sitting in some restaurant off the Post. Then, leaving her meal unfinished, she would rush for the door, throwing five or even ten dollars at the cashier as she went by and not waiting for her change. Down the street she would go at breakneck speed until a doctor's sign caught her eye. She would burst into his office and demand that the receptionist get the physician to examine her at once. If she couldn't find a doctor's office, she would rush up to a policeman or just a passer-by screaming, "I'm dying, I'm dying. Get me help. Please get help."

Then the sirens would wail again and Maxine would find herself in another ambulance headed for another hospital where she would be given another thorough examination. One by one she exhausted all the doctors and the hospitals around Hopkinsville.

Occasionally Maxine would have to go out of town. Terrified at the thought of being caught alone in a strange city when one of the attacks struck, she evolved an efficient method of handling the situation. The first thing she'd do after boarding the train was to look for someone who lived in the city for which she was heading. Then she would start up a conversation, during which she would try to ferret out the names and addresses of doctors who lived in the vicinity of the hotel where she planned to stay. With these names in her purse, she would know where to find a physician at once.

Maxine couldn't accept the combined verdicts of all the doctors she saw—"It's just your nerves. It's in your imagination." She was sure that anyone whose imagination could conjure up such bizarre sensations would be crazy. So rather than entertain the thought that she was losing her mind, Maxine convinced herself that she was suffering from some rare heart disease. Eventually the doctors would recognize it and find a cure, she comforted herself. Meanwhile she ought to take measures to preserve her health.

So Maxine began cutting out exercise of all kinds, especially climbing stairs. If she had an appointment with a doctor whose office was above the first floor, she wouldn't go to see him unless there was an elevator to take her up. And if she was accompanying someone who had to go upstairs, she'd stay below until he returned, though she might have to wait two or three hours. Of course dancing and all other social activities were completely eliminated.

But for all Maxine's care her terrifying seizures only grew more frequent and horrifying. She didn't realize that by concentrating on them she was increasing her tension and therefore her symptoms. In 1943, she returned again to Vanderbilt for another thorough checkup. The doctors there, as usual, found nothing wrong with her. But one of them who was a good friend suggested that she go to the Mayo Clinic for a second consultation.

Mayo's was a magic word to Maxine. The fees were high, she knew, much out of reach of her modest salary, but it would be worth it to find out what was wrong with her. So Maxine went through another thorough examination at the Mayo Clinic. The diagnosis that came back was "hyperventilation," a grand-sounding word, but it just meant a nervous condition brought on by inhaling too rapidly and getting too much oxygen in the blood. The cure Maxine was given was, primarily, to blow into a paper bag when she felt the panic coming on.

Maxine returned to her job disconsolately. Somewhere, somehow, there had to be an answer, she told herself. A person wasn't meant to go on and on suffering like this without relief. She began to do a lot of reading in all the little digest magazines which concerned health to see if she couldn't find the solution to her illness.

One day in 1945 Maxine picked up *Your Life* magazine and read about an organization called Recovery, Inc. That organization, it seemed, was devoted to helping people with "just nerves" regain their health. She liked the common sense approach, the sense of fellowship that jumped out at her from the printed page. Here were people who had suffered as she was suffering, and who were getting well.

Maxine didn't waste any time. She phoned Dr. Low immediately. But he discouraged her from coming to Chicago just then. Housing, he said, was very scarce there because of the war, and unless she had plenty of money, she might get stranded in the big city. So Maxine reluctantly gave up the idea and stuck *Your Life* away in a chest of drawers where she promptly forgot about it.

As time went by Maxine's constant preoccupation with her agonizing symptoms made her so confused that she began having difficulty performing even the simplest jobs. And at last her employers began to realize how ill she really was. When her annual leave with pay came up from the government, they suggested she might be helped at the Langley Porter Clinic in San Francisco. They would send her there if she would agree to being an experimental patient.

So Maxine crossed the continent and went into the hospital and was treated like royalty while the clinic psychiatrists, who were of the psychoanalytic school, began delving into her past. They came to the conclusion that her problems stemmed from traumatic experiences she must have suffered in childhood. Maxine was unable to dredge up anything of importance there, but she was gradually gaining the impression, from little things said and questions asked, that the doctors believed she hated her mother. This she couldn't accept. But she began having a guilty conscience about the psychoanalysts who meant so well and were so interested in her. She felt under obligation to repay them. Perhaps if she could convince them that she really did hate her mother it would, at least in part, give them a feeling of accomplishment. One day she got up enough courage to run out of her room into the hall of the hospital screaming, "I hate my mother. I hate my mother."

The nurses went scurrying for the doctors. The doctors came to hear Maxine scream and they were very pleased. This was a real breakthrough, they told her. She would get well now that she had disgorged her repressions. So, having repaid all the nice people at the hospital, Maxine went home to her mother in Hopkinsville, no better than when she had left. She took a job in a little dress shop in town, but presently she exchanged it for a better paying but more exacting one with Montgomery Ward and Company.

2.

On October 1, 1947, tragedy struck the White family. Maxine's sister, a sufferer from "nerves" like herself, broke under the weight of grief she felt for a son killed in service and committed suicide. Maxine became so overwrought that she couldn't go to the funeral or to work. Continual panics were sweeping over her.

It was at that point that she remembered the *Your Life* magazine which had been lying in her dresser drawer for two long years. She clipped out the piece about Recovery and put it in her purse and hurried to Vanderbilt University Hospital to show it to her doctor friend and ask him what he thought about her going to Chicago for treatment.

He read the piece and shook his head. He'd never heard of either Dr. Low or Recovery, he said, but he gave her two alternatives: "You can go to Chicago to him or you can come here for dynamic psychiatric care with us because the hospital has just opened a psychiatric ward. But you must make your own choice."

It was a grave decision for Maxine. If she chose the new doctor it meant uprooting herself from her home town and going off to a strange city where even her chance of livelihood might be threatened. On the other hand, Vanderbilt was near her home and she knew everybody there. But it didn't take her long to make up her mind, and she chose Chicago.

Her mother and aunt agreed that her decision was the right one. Her aunt promised to come and stay with her mother and help take care of Maxine's son, who was then twelve. Montgomery Ward agreed to transfer her to their store in Chicago so she'd have a job when she arrived there. Everything settled, Maxine set out, this time taking the precaution not to phone Dr. Low for fear he would tell her again not to come. She was checked into a Chicago hotel before she finally contacted him.

"Where are you?" he wanted to know. And when he learned she was in Chicago, he said, "I don't usually have office hours on Saturday, but come over tomorrow about twelve o'clock."

Maxine went trembling, to find the new doctor a kindly man with a decided accent and a gentle smile. He talked to her for a short time, shrewdly appraising her. Then he told her, "We're having a meeting over at the Recovery headquarters at 185 North Wabash. I want you to go to it. And then you can come to my office on Monday."

Maxine went to the Recovery room and the minute she entered it she sensed the same fellowship that she had experienced when she had read the article in *Your Life.* She had the feeling that here at last she would find understanding people. It gave her a genuine sense of security.

On Monday Dr. Low gave Maxine a thorough examination. When she told him about all the doctors she'd seen, he asked her to count them for him. This proved quite a chore for Maxine. Even she hadn't realized how many there were—one hundred and eleven in all. Dr. Low was the one hundred and twelfth! Maxine's record number of physicians stamps her as having been Recovery's classic case of the patient commonly and disdainfully known in professional circles as a "crock." A crock is the disturbed, symptom-led patient who wanders from doctor to doctor, refusing to accept the unanimous diagnosis that the true cause of his complaints is "just nerves."

Before Maxine launched into a description of her manifold symptoms and sensations, she told Dr. Low deprecatingly, "Of course I know that these are all only imaginary." But surprisingly, this unique doctor stopped her short, making it plain that he didn't go along with that "imaginary" business.

"Don't ever let me hear you say that you imagined this," he told her, "because you don't imagine it. You have the sensations. And though they're not caused by organic troubles they're still very real. It's an imbalance in your nervous system."

The imbalance could be corrected, he continued, if she would cooperate with him. Maxine was eager to do that. Three times a week she went to see him for consultation. During these sessions he explained many things to her, things which no one else had thought of, but which were so simple that they were almost obvious, once they were pointed out. It was her belief in danger, Dr. Low explained, that was causing her to keep such a close watch on every symptom she had. And this concentration was increasing her tension, and that in turn was making her symptoms worse. She was causing herself a lot of needless suffering with this vicious cycle she had created.

The belief in danger, he went on, was expressing itself in three ingrained fears, the fears from which most nervous patients suffer. The first was the fear of physical collapse. That was at the root of Maxine's terror every time a strong symptom came. The second was the fear of imminent mental collapse, that the bizarre sensations she was experiencing were the precursors of insanity. And the third was the fear of sustained handicap, a dull certainty that she would always have to go on suffering in this way. This fear developed when either or both of the first two fears continued for any length of time.

Her belief in these three dangers, Dr. Low told her, had become so crystallized that even when the doctors had assured her there was nothing to fear she hadn't been able to believe them. And now it would take more than his own rational explanations to bring the truth home to Maxine—that no matter how distressing her symptoms were, they weren't dangerous.

Maxine would have to work consciously on her will and make her muscles act in spite of her fears until she had proved to her mind that they were groundless. Once she wholeheartedly accepted this belief, she would be cured. With this goal in mind, Dr. Low gave Maxine his first directive, a simple "move your muscles" order. There was to be a Recovery square dance that Saturday night. "I want you to go to it and I want you to dance," he told her.

Maxine hadn't danced or climbed steps or done any unnecessary exercise for seven years. And she was scared. But she went and found Phil Crane acting as master of ceremonies. He had a way about him that made Maxine feel relaxed and easy right from the start. He took her around and introduced her to everyone. And he saw that she had a partner for the first dance. It was only a slow waltz, but it was about as much as Maxine could do to get through it.

When she next went to see Dr. Low, he asked her, "Well, how did it go? Did you do the dance?"

"I did the slow one," Maxine told him.

His face lit up as it always did when his patients followed his directives. But he wasn't content. He pinched her cheek firmly but affectionately. "Now next week you do the fast one," he told her.

While Maxine was learning to order her muscles to exercise, she was also learning how to control them when panics struck. Then she had to try sitting quietly, letting the panic pass without responding to it. To Maxine that seemed almost impossible while her frantic brain was flashing danger signals to her muscles. She failed over and over again and would go racing eight or ten blocks up Michigan Avenue to Dr. Low's office, where, her eyes glazed with terror, she would tell him she was dying of a heart attack. It never occurred to her until later that if she had really been having a heart attack, she wouldn't have been able to run so far or so fast.

3.

Despite her panics, Maxine managed to hold on to her job at Montgomery Ward. She had always been able to handle her work with enough efficiency not to be fired, but she had a propensity for resigning when she felt the pressures becoming too much for her. One day that moment came in Chicago and Maxine quit her work at Montgomery Ward and began looking for another job that she thought would be easier. Eventually she found one, but meanwhile she found herself growing short of cash.

Dr. Low, learning the circumstances, told her she could wait to pay him until she was more financially able. But Maxine had a guilty conscience about that, so one day she went to his consultation room clutching her wedding ring and a few pieces of expensive jewelry she still possessed. She held her hand out to him, palm up, with the jewelry resting on it.

"Dr. Low," she said, "I want you to keep my jewelry as surety until I pay you."

Dr. Low looked from the jewelry to her face and his eyes were warm with sympathy.

"Magzeen," he said—he always pronounced her name that way— "you feel bad because you can't pay me, huh?"

Maxine nodded.

"No, Magzeen," he told her. "Forget it. It's all right." And he pushed her hand away.

4.

Dr. Low often referred to Maxine as one of his most cooperative patients, but she was also his most severe psychoneurotic, and for a long while she seemed to be making little progress against her panics. Then one morning she had her first triumph. She was at breakfast in the hotel coffee shop, just daydreaming, when the familiar bizarre sensations began to flood her.

Fighting down the urge to rush out of the restaurant, she forced herself to sit there and put the food in her mouth, a bite at a time, first a bite of egg, then a bite of toast, another bite of egg, another bite of toast, a sip of coffee. She could hardly swallow as the sensations mounted in intensity, but she remained where she was until she had forced down the last scrap of food. Then she got deliberately to her feet and made herself walk slowly to the cashier, wait for her change, and leave the restaurant, going at a deliberate pace down the street to her job. Presently the sensations began to subside and she was able to work all day.

Despite Maxine's success in controlling her muscles, her belief in danger was still potent. All that day and the following night she kept worrying that the experience would be repeated. And since it had happened before in a restaurant, she began dreading going back into one. Dr. Low called it sabotaging her success.

During those early months Maxine was upset about her slow progress. While others around her were making decided improvement, she seemed to be stuck in an almost constant round of headaches, palpitations, and paralyzing panics. She began to feel guilty about going to Dr. Low time after time, with the same dreary complaints about her condition. One day she decided to give him at least one cheerful account of herself. Just as before she'd put herself out to please the psychiatrists at Langley Porter Clinic, she pulled herself together and walked into Dr. Low's office, a bright smile plastered on her face. Although she was churning inside with tension, she forced herself to take her seat calmly and to sit erect and immobile instead of wriggling, as she usually did.

Dr. Low looked at her searchingly, "How is it today?" he wanted to know.

"Just fine," she lied and her face felt as though it would crack with her smile. But she answered all his questions cheerily, painting for him a picture of blooming health and composure that bore no resemblance to the cringing, tortured personality inside herself.

He listened attentively. Then finally he leaned back in his chair, drawing on his pipe and looking at her with a glint of sympathetic humor in his eyes. "Not so good today, huh?" he commiserated.

He knew his patients too well to be fooled by outer appearances. And Maxine's show of well-being was so entirely out of the realm of probability that it betrayed her true state. All the same he wanted her to know that he understood and appreciated her effort.

Today, explaining part of the secret of Dr. Low's success with his patients, Maxine says, "It was his nature—his tolerance and patience and understanding—that made him so different. You don't always find many doctors who'll go out of their way as he did for a patient."

TWENTY

Though Phil Crane was going to the Recovery panels and social events and had even taken on the editorship of the little *Recovery News,* he still wasn't practicing the Method. And presently Dr. Low began to notice the strange look in his eyes and his rambling conversation. He phoned Phil's mother and learned that Phil was becoming increasingly irritable at home and was talking about going back to the black neighborhood where he belonged. There was no alternative but to hospitalize him again.

During the three weeks Phil was in the hospital, Dr. Low talked sternly to him. "It's not a disgrace to be ill like this, Phil. You're not a criminal. But you must do something about it, because the more you go into a hospital, the harder it is going to be for you to get out again. The question is, do you care to make the effort? Do you care to be well?"

That clear-cut question sliced like the beam of a spotlight through the fog of Phil's thinking. No, of course he didn't want to spend his life in a hospital. Things had become too interesting for him in the outside world. His employer respected him so much as one of his top salesmen that he had even contributed one hundred dollars to help pay the costs of his hospitalization just to get him back to work again. That did a great deal to boost Phil's self-esteem.

For the first time in his life Phil made up his mind to follow the doctor's orders, even though that meant putting in real effort learning how to practice the Method. When he got out of the hospital again, he was told to attend private psychotherapy classes,

181

panels on Saturday afternoons, and home groups as well. He was also asked to arrange his schedule of work so that he could spend his afternoons at Recovery headquarters. Here the doors were kept open all day by volunteers who were on hand to spot for those who dropped in from time to time with their troubles. They could give Phil a lot of help in learning how to spot on himself.

Dr. Low made it plain to Phil, however, that it wasn't enough any more just to attend meetings. He had to start practicing the Method in his everyday life. For instance, he'd been going to work in the morning by bus, though the El was faster by forty-five minutes. But on the El Phil would have to meet his old friends and confess to them that he had been hospitalized again. Now he had to bear the discomfort and face his former companions in order to overcome the sense of stigma in himself.

He also had to work at controlling his quick temper, something he'd never been able to do in the past when something irritated him. He learned that it was possible, once he remembered that the other person was "outer environment." Recovery termed all people and things outside oneself "outer environment" and taught that it was impossible to change that "outer environment" to suit one's own desires. One could only work on "the inner environment," oneself. Keeping the "outer environment" where it belonged—outside—was made possible by not "lowering the bridge of temper."

Of course the initial flare of anger would always come, Phil found out. It was an hereditary trait that every human being possessed. But it wouldn't stay to play havoc with his nervous system if he stopped judging himself right and the other person wrong. Dropping judgment enabled him to voice his opinions calmly, and he found to his surprise that when he did, people were much more likely to listen to what he had to say.

Phil's hardest task was to spot his delusions when they came back to him. Dr. Low gave him a simple formula for doing this. He was to train himself to look outward to the group, and when he found himself differing from them in his belief that he was a black man, he was to accept the overwhelming evidence on faith and drop his belief for theirs. Phil tried hard to do this, but in those early weeks he often failed and was deeply discouraged

about it. Sometimes in his misery he would unburden himself
to Dr. Low.

"I don't see how I can ever get out of it, Doctor," he would
say. "Look at it. None of the others have been as sick as I have.
They don't talk about so much hospitalization."

"It's true," Dr. Low would agree. "But what of it, Phil? You
can get well anyway. In Recovery even those who are completely
incapacitated can get well if they practice. Practice, practice, practice—that *always* does it."

So Phil went on practicing. And presently he began to grow
aware of times when his mind became preoccupied. Dr. Low told
him that so long as he knew he was in that condition he wasn't
in any trouble. But there were several occasions when Phil wasn't
able to spot his preoccupation and couldn't dismiss the delusions
when they started coming back. Then Dr. Low would have to tell
him he must go to the hospital for a shock treatment on an out-
patient basis.

Phil learned that a great deal of his tension vanished when he
accepted the doctor's diagnosis and cooperated with him by going
to the hospital voluntarily instead of having to be taken there as
on previous occasions. As he accepted the fact that his illness was
just like any other and that it wasn't disgraceful to get hospital
treatment for it, he began losing his sense of stigma.

Phil found that there were many positive benefits to using the
Method he hadn't known about before. As he learned to control
his temper, he became an even better salesman, and for the first
time in his life he managed to live peaceably with his mother.
He was able to conquer his insomnia by lying motionless in bed
until sleep came. And when he stopped attaching danger to his
nervous stomach, his digestion improved. By the end of six months
Phil was entirely well, and the cure has been so lasting that from
that day to this he has not been hospitalized or taken another
shock treatment.

Though Phil was still expected to attend the Saturday Recovery
panels and the home groups, Dr. Low excused him from the
private psychotherapy classes. He told Phil that it wasn't necessary
for him to continue going down to Recovery headquarters either,
but he asked if he would do so anyway to help the other volunteers
spot for Recoveryites in need. This would help him perfect his

own spotting techniques and also allow him to return the aid he had so generously received from others.

Phil readily agreed. During the years that followed, he became one of the most familiar faces at Recovery headquarters. The highlight of every afternoon was Dr. Low's visit. He would drop in about three o'clock for a cup of coffee and stay for ten to twenty minutes, showing the spotters how they could improve their techniques. He didn't just give advice—he demonstrated his Method also. He would talk slowly and calmly and lift his coffee cup deliberately to his lips. Just as deliberately he would take a cookie or a piece of cake, raise it in slow motion to his mouth, and chew on it slowly to demonstrate the complete command he had over his muscles. This calm manner, demonstrated by so busy a doctor, communicated a great deal to Phil and the others gathered there. The control of impulses through the muscles was part of the Method, and Dr. Low himself practiced what he told them to practice.

When it came time for him to go, he would rise slowly from the table. "Sorry, now, I have to leave," he would say, enunciating each syllable clearly. Slowly he would walk across the room. Then at the doorway he would often turn around, and say with his arms stretched out to them, "Goodbye, my dear ones."

"Goodbye, my dear ones"—through all the years of his life, Phil will remember the depth of feeling in that voice as it spoke the tender farewell.

2.

One of the persons who helped Phil most with his spotting during those six months of practice wasn't even a patient of Dr. Low's. She was a young woman named Agnes Dumont. Agnes had come from a family of eight children and had felt rejected as a child. She had developed an intense yearning to be loved absolutely by someone. And it seemed to her that her wish was fulfilled when in 1932 she married William Dumont, because he had chosen her out of all the women in the world.

For eight years Agnes was supremely happy. Then her little daughter Cynthia arrived, and suddenly she found she had to

share her husband's love with the child. The old feeling of rejection came back again, and it grew even stronger when her
husband kept cautioning her to take good care of the child. It
seemed to Agnes that he was doubting her ability to do so and
she felt the heavy weight of responsibility settling upon her.

As time went by she became more and more apprehensive about
the little girl until her doubts crystallized into fear that she herself would harm the child. She began to keep a painful distance
between herself and the little girl, often pushing the child away
when she came too close. She didn't dare play with her for fear
that an uncontrollable murderous impulse would take possession
of her unawares. And she began hiding away razor blades, knives,
scissors, and sharp instruments of every kind.

It became almost impossible for Agnes to sleep at night. She
was afraid of dying and at the same time afraid she wouldn't die.
When she discovered that she no longer had any feeling for her
husband and little girl, she was sure she was going insane. There
were physical symptoms too—palpitations, grinding head pressures, blurring of the vision, and always such nausea that she
couldn't eat. Finally she became so exhausted that she could
hardly exert herself to do the smallest chores.

Agnes's husband was sympathetic and took her to doctor after
doctor. But since she didn't dare talk to anyone about her mental
sufferings she concentrated on her physical symptoms. At home
she complained about them so much to her husband that he
started finding pretexts to leave the house at night.

Eventually on the advice of one doctor, Agnes was admitted to
the psychiatric ward of a Chicago hospital. She spent two weeks
there, and the attendant psychiatrists diagnosed her condition as
an anxiety neurosis, and advised her to take treatment for it. So
Agnes began to see a psychoanalyst. She stayed with the psychoanalyst for three months without getting any better. When he told
her that her troubles had been caused by her parents and home
environment she didn't believe him and stopped going to him.

By this time Agnes and her husband had become thoroughly
discouraged. Doctors' bills for her had been so high that all their
savings were gone, and there still was no cure in sight. Then one
day a friend who went to Recovery begged Agnes to attend a
Saturday afternoon panel and hear Dr. Low lecture. After all,

her friend explained, it wouldn't cost her anything. Recovery was free except for voluntary contributions. That sounded good to Agnes so she went to her first meeting, and while she was there she questioned some of the other patients about their problems. They talked freely, describing all the symptoms which she herself was experiencing. Agnes discovered that even her darkest fear—the dread of harming her child—was really quite an average phobia. What impressed her most was the remarkable progress they were all claiming for themselves through the use of Recovery techniques.

Agnes went home with a new hope in her heart. That night when her husband asked her anxiously how things had gone, she answered, "Well, I'll tell you, I don't know how long it's going to take me, but I am going to get well. I think I've played my trump card."

William looked at her and there were two big tears in his eyes. "You know that's the nicest thing you've said in five years," he told her.

3.

Agnes really went in for Recovery. She attended Saturday panels and home meetings. She spent many afternoons at headquarters, helping with volunteer work and getting spotting from the others. They pointed out the habit she had of constantly complaining and told her she should try to stop it because it was only working up her symptoms. So Agnes practiced controlling her speech muscles, especially at home. And she became so successful at it that William was elated and went around telling everybody that Agnes was completely cured after only three weeks in Recovery.

It wasn't true, of course, because Recovery doesn't usually work that fast. But the sight of her happy, relieved husband made Agnes more determined than ever to keep her suffering to herself. And when she did, she found that the old feeling of warmth for him was reawakening.

Agnes was working, too, on her obsessive fear of harming her child. One night the climax came. She was sitting on the couch watching television, when Cynthia came up to her and laid her head on her lap. All at once Agnes was troubled by a sudden terror that she would strangle the child. She began to tremble, her eyes felt blurry and it was difficult for her to see. She put her hands behind her back, but she still didn't feel comfortable. She wanted to push the little girl away from her to safety.

Then she remembered what they'd told her in Recovery, that she wasn't really afraid of harming her daughter, but only of the sensations she was experiencing, that she could prove to herself that it was a fear *idea*, with no reality in it, only by drawing the child to her and cuddling her. Agnes brought her hands out from behind her back. Carefully she cupped the little girl's chin in them and lifted her face up and kissed her. She looked into the trusting eyes and stroked the silky hair.

"Why, this is ridiculous," she said to herself with sudden insight, and a surge of relief swept through her. "You're not going to do harm to this child. How can you when every impulse can be controlled?"

After that Agnes could afford a warm relationship between herself and her daughter. She was also learning how to relax in other relationships, and this made it possible for her to open herself up to people for the first time in her life. She was able to confide to her unsuspecting husband her fears of being pushed into second place by their child. She established a friendly relationship with her mother and learned to be more tolerant of others instead of allowing herself to be irritated by them as before.

4.

Though Agnes wasn't completely cured yet, everything had become so much easier for her that she was filled with gratitude, and one day about six months after she'd come into Recovery, she told Phil Crane, "You know I'm willing to settle right now for the way I feel. If I never get any better, I'm satisfied."

Phil repeated Agnes' statement to Dr. Low. And the next Saturday after the panel the doctor came over and talked to her for the first time. "When I hear a patient say he is satisfied even though he is still having to suffer," he told her, "believe me, I know he will get well. And you will get well."

Agnes was thrilled by his very evident pleasure over her progress. He struck her then as a most amazing kind of doctor. Even though she wasn't his patient and he'd never collected a single fee from her, he seemed to be as interested in her as in any of the others there. Her first opinion of him was never to change, though she got to know him a great deal better in the years ahead. She was to find him not only one of the greatest men in his profession but also one of the kindest and most humble. He was also a very strict taskmaster, as she was soon to discover.

"You're doing a tremendous job," he told her. "I want you to sit on the panel next week and give an example." Agnes didn't dare refuse, so the next Saturday she gave her first example. It dealt, as was the rule at panel meetings, with some aspect of everyday living. In Agnes' case it was a panic. Before her Recovery training, Agnes explained, when such panics had come upon her, usually in the middle of the night, with palpitations, heavy chest pressure, nausea and sweating, she had wakened the whole household, insisted on calling a doctor, and alarmed everyone with her conviction that she was dying.

But just recently when she'd suffered a similar panic, Agnes went on, she had handled it the Recovery way. Fighting off the impulse to waken her husband, she had turned her mind from her symptoms to concentrate on something objective and without emotion. In this instance it was the reflection of the street light on the wall of the bedroom. She began studying the patterns it made until presently she was breathing normally, the palpitations died down, and she fell asleep again.

Dr. Low found this example so apt in depicting the way the Method worked that he wrote an article about it for the *Recovery News,* which had superseded the *Recovery Journal.* After that Agnes sat on the panel often.

Presently Dr. Low was asking her to lead a home group. For the first time Agnes balked. She wasn't ready for that, she told him. But he overrode her fearful objections.

"I'm the medical director around here, and I know whether you're ready or not," he informed her. "You'll take this group— we need you. Recovery needs you."

Put that way, Agnes couldn't refuse any longer. Recovery had been there as a gift for her when she had needed it. She owed it a debt of gratitude.

Agnes had proved something very important to Dr. Low. She had shown him that a patient could come in off the street and be cured by the group and the Method even without psychiatric counseling from him. That meant that patients all over the country could benefit if local groups were established in their communities. It indicated a very exciting new direction for Recovery.

5.

Agnes was just part of the steady growth Recovery had been experiencing. More and more people, some personal patients, others not, but all hungry for help, were flooding to the headquarters on Wabash Avenue. The room became so crowded that once again Recovery had to look for larger quarters. And this meant higher rent. Dr. Low sent out circulars to all his patients, requesting contributions for the purpose. But always solicitous of those Recovery volunteers who were already giving so generously of their time, he was adamantly against their making monetary sacrifices as well. His views are set forth in a letter to Ernest Hoffman, written in February of 1948: ". . . I want you to know that my regular patients who work in Recovery are not expected to contribute more than some sort of token payment. Five dollars will be ample. I tell you that because I am certain that you may be carried away by your sense of generosity. Let me tell you that I should not like that at all. . . . My wealthy patients have been quite responsive . . . So I feel that my workers, i.e., the patients who really do the work in Recovery, Chicago root and Muscatine branch, do not have to worry about the contributions."

By May of that year with, of course, the generous help of Dr. Low himself, five thousand dollars had been raised and the new Recovery office was established at 116 South Michigan Avenue, where it has remained until now.

With Recovery expanding so rapidly, Dr. Low began to feel the need of full-time, paid employees to help with the work. Annette

Brocken was very valuable to him because of her executive mind. She had already served as president and one of the three executive directors, but on a volunteer basis. Now he offered her a salaried position as executive secretary. But Annette's two-year leave of absence was up and she wanted to go back to teaching again, so she didn't accept the position, though she promised she would continue to help out all she could.

Caroline Philipp was also proving herself a valuable worker in the Recovery office. She was the answer to Dr. Low's old dream of a competent secretary, preferably a former patient, and he asked her to take the job of secretary on a salary that admittedly was ridiculously low. But Caroline felt that even that was too much, especially since she knew the money was coming out of Dr. Low's own pocket. She was ready to work for nothing, so grateful was she for her restored health. But he wouldn't hear of that.

A little later when he broached the subject of a raise, there was a hassle again because Caroline didn't think she deserved it. But Dr. Low wouldn't accept her low estimate of herself. "Don't be foolish," he kept telling her in his gruff, emphatic way. So finally Caroline accepted the raise.

However, her attitude toward herself was changing. In a few days she began thinking, "Well, that shows a nice promotion." And in a couple of months she was thinking about the next raise, and this time when it came she didn't put up a battle about it. She still wasn't being paid what other secretaries were getting, but she was content with the arrangement as it stood. Everything considered, it was really the best job she had ever had.

Another patient whom Dr. Low began calling on for help was Maxine Kennedy. During the past months he had watched her gradual return to health, which in his eyes had been phenomenal. Her migraine headaches had become a thing of the past and most of her other terrifying symptoms had diminished or had totally disappeared. By the fall of 1948 she'd been well enough to visit her family in Kentucky and bring her son back with her, placing him in boarding school.

By this time, feeling herself stable enough, she had made an ambitious decision—to complete her training as a nurse. So she had enrolled at Wesley Memorial Hospital and everything had gone along well until one day the students were informed that the subject of the next day's class would be the care of the body after death. Since the dread of death was Maxine's chief fear, she rushed directly to Dr. Low, expecting him as her physician to forbid her to take part in anything so likely to start her illness all over again.

She waited expectantly, but he only looked steadily at her and said, "So? You'll do it." And Maxine did.

It was Maxine's special talents as a nurse that made her so useful now to the doctor. He commissioned her to take his outpatients to the hospital for treatments, wait for them there, and return them to their homes afterwards. He paid her a pittance for her aid, but put the emphasis on service. He had long since discovered that when one patient helped another his own health improved much more rapidly. That was the reason for the cultivation of fellowship, or "group-mindedness" as it is known in Recovery circles.

TWENTY-ONE

The little girl's mother had had a difficult time with this child-birth. She was under heavy sedation when the father knelt beside the bed and said to her, "Wake up, wake up. Don't you hear our little treasure crying?"

Treasure, treasure, treasure, treasure, the word went round and round her mind in her semidelirium. When the doctor came the next day, he asked, "What are you going to name the baby?"

"Treasure," Mrs. Haley answered without reflection, and so the little girl with the unusual name joined the Haley household.

The Haley home was in Bad Axe, Michigan, a little town of some 2,500 people near the equally small town of Broken Rocks. The family owned a general store where groceries and dry goods were sold.

Treasure had a brother four years older than herself, an even-tempered extrovert who got on well with the world. She herself was a sensitive child. And when she was very small, she was in a state of constant apprehension that sometimes bordered on panic. She was afraid of so many things: the Ku Klux Klan, the strange woman down the block who sometimes paraded up and down the street with a broom over her shoulder, the glowing pot-bellied stove in her home which might blow up one night and set the house on fire. In the summer it was perspiration. Where did it come from and why was she sometimes drenched in it, seemingly for no reason at all?

The little girl's fears increased when she started school. Even in kindergarten she was afraid of competing with other children,

192

afraid of being surpassed by them in whatever she attempted. And this sense of being inferior didn't diminish in the higher grades.

One day she reached a crisis when the children in her class were each handed a piece of cardboard, a pair of scissors, and some pins and told to make an airplane. Instead of concentrating on the work itself, Treasure kept watching the other children, trying to do as they were doing. The result was that when presently they had little airplanes to show for their effort, her desk top was strewn with bits and scraps of useless cardboard. Filled with shame and confusion, Treasure could think of only one way of escaping the situation. She raised her hand and told the teacher she was sick and had to go home. The teacher let her go.

Treasure's mother called the illness a "bilious spell." From then on Treasure found she could make use of those bilious spells to go home when the pressures at school grew too great. More and more, blind panic was taking hold of her. Sometimes it would strike in the middle of class. Then she would have to ask to leave the room. She would go to the little girls' lavatory and stand there in the midst of the shiny chrome and tile, wondering in terror what was happening to her.

With the passage of time a new phobia emerged from her generalized fear. She became terrified of eating when people were watching her. A plate of food set before her would fill her with panic. She'd rather say she just wasn't hungry than try to swallow in front of others.

Her mother took the little girl from doctor to doctor in an attempt to find a remedy for her poor appetite, until soon Treasure became terrified of doctors also. By the time she was ten years old, she had begun to fear people of all kinds. Finally, when she could no longer be persuaded even to step through the school gates, her latest doctor suggested she be kept home for a year. Mrs. Haley complied and then devoted her life to making the little girl well. She brought her a special hospital bed and nursed her as though she were an invalid. Because the doctor had prescribed plenty of vitamins and fresh air, she gave her both, taking her on picnics and walks.

When the next school year started, Treasure agreed to attend if her mother would come and sit with her. For the first three days Mrs. Haley shared her daughter's little desk. After that she stopped going. But Treasure didn't need her any more. Miraculously the old panics and terrors had disappeared. She became an outgoing, friendly little girl.

2.

When Treasure was fifteen her father died. She had always loved him dearly and now she grieved for him, but her grief was normal. And presently she was again taking part in all the school plays, operettas, and athletics. She was very popular—a beautiful, spritely young girl who didn't seem to have a care in the world.

Treasure went on to the University of Michigan and did well there, except that sometimes when she was under heavy pressure, a haunting sense of unreality would brush across her mind, reminding her of all the old terrors that had beset her as a child. Then it would disappear and she would forget it again.

Treasure had a good voice and the summer following her first year of college she was hired as a singer for a fifteen-piece band made up of students from the University of Michigan. The semiprofessional little group toured resorts during the summer and when fall came, instead of going back to school, they did a series of one-night stands across the country, in addition to some eight-week engagements in prominent supper clubs in Cleveland and Louisville. The band was so good that it was broadcast over coast-to-coast radio.

After it broke up, Treasure returned to school, this time at Michigan State, but she didn't go more than one term. Her mother, who had exchanged the general store for a dress shop in Bad Axe, had remarried and gone to live in Illinois, leaving the shop to Treasure and her brother. So Treasure went back to Bad Axe to help manage it.

She was about twenty-two when, some twelve years after her childhood breakdown, she had her second one. Up until that time she had led an extroverted life, going to parties and giving them, singing in the Methodist church choir, and attending church socials. She was engaged now to a young intern named Bill Rice with whom she had been going steady since high school. They planned to marry as soon as he became a full-fledged doctor.

It was in Bill's home, while she was visiting with his mother and sisters, that the illness struck again. They were all eating lunch and just chattering away and having a good time, when suddenly a strange feeling overwhelmed Treasure. She couldn't have described it in words but it terrified her. Her heart began to pound. She became hot and flushed and everything started to swim before her eyes. She got up from the table and went out to the kitchen and just stood there as bewildered as she had been long ago, in the little girls' lavatory at school. Finally, after what seemed ages, the feeling left and Treasure returned to her lunch, a glass of water in her hand as an alibi for her sudden departure.

Treasure tried to forget about the incident, but two weeks later at a Methodist church supper the terrifying sensation came again and she could hardly get her meal down. She decided there must be something wrong with her and went to Ford Hospital in Detroit for a complete examination. All they could find were two cavities in her molars. The last doctor she saw summed up the situation for her in one word: "nervous." But he slid over it as though he were almost ashamed to say it. "I think after you get married and have children it will be all right," he told her.

"If I can just live until then," Treasure thought desperately.

Things kept happening faster and faster. One Sunday at church service she found she couldn't take part in the duet she'd been scheduled to sing with a young man in the choir. She had to let him do it alone. She gave up the choir, but then found she couldn't attend church either. The first time she tried it she could hardly sit through the service because her heart was pounding so hard the whole pew seemed to be jiggling. She also stopped going to shows because the presence of so many people around her filled her with panic.

She still forced herself to work at the dress shop, but often now she would have to think up an excuse to get away from customers. She was the buyer for the store, but it was getting increasingly difficult for her to purchase the stock. She would walk round and round the wholesale houses before she could find the courage to go inside.

The worst of it was that she didn't dare talk over her troubles with anyone for fear she'd be judged insane. There was only one thing that could relax her at all—an alcoholic drink. She began to rely on those drinks to get her through the day. They were always just a few. She never could consume too much. Alcohol made her queasy.

Finally the long-awaited day of marriage arrived. It took place on the way home from the wedding of a friend in Cleveland, Ohio. Bill and Treasure just stopped at a minister's house. It was the way Treasure wanted it—a marriage as inconspicuous as possible. Even that would have been an ordeal for her if it hadn't been for the punch at the reception they had just left. It had contained enough alcohol to fortify her.

Even on the honeymoon Treasure's conscience began to trouble her because she hadn't told Bill how ill she was. Now she felt that at all costs she had to keep him from finding out. So she always insisted on stopping at bar-restaurants to get the life-saving drink that would help her force down her meal. And when the bar-restaurants weren't available she would start a little spat with her new husband and use that as an excuse for all kinds of strange behavior.

After this miserable honeymoon the young couple went to Minden City, Michigan, where Bill set up his office and went into general practice. By this time Treasure was in a state of almost continual panic. Even a visit from her brother and his new wife became a major ordeal which she could face only after having taken several drinks.

The doctor had been wrong about marriage, but he'd also said, "After you have children." And Treasure began pinning all her hopes on that.

3.

A year and three months after her marriage, Bill drove Treasure to the hospital in Detroit where he had interned, for her to have her first baby. That experience was one of the most horrible Treasure was ever to know. She, who couldn't bear the confines even of a theater or church, was now enclosed in a tiny delivery room. She lay there terrified that some of the hospital staff, the nurses and the doctors who knew Bill, would come and talk to her. And when they did, she felt like bolting in sheer terror.

The birth itself was traumatic. They had to knock Treasure out with anesthesia and take the child with high forceps. When she came to, Bill was walking up and down, up and down, and she was sure it was because he knew she was going to die. That night she insisted the light be kept on in her room until morning.

When Treasure was well enough, she and the baby, a boy named after Bill, returned to Minden City. But instead of being cured by the birth of a child she began to grow progressively worse. She lived in a horrible depression the whole time. And the child on whom she'd been pinning such hopes helped her only by providing her with a good excuse to live a withdrawn life. Now she could say that she couldn't go out because she couldn't get a sitter, or she was too tired. She was fatigued all the time anyway. While Bill was at work she would sit in the house, terrified that the telephone would ring or that someone would arrive at the door for a friendly visit. She didn't want to see or talk to anyone. And she yearned for midnight to come again—midnight that meant no more telephone calls or visitors, that brought peace for a few hours at least.

Treasure still couldn't bring herself to tell Bill that she found it unbearable to sit down to dinner with him. She made flu her primary excuse. She had learned how to fake the symptoms so well that she even deceived her husband's practiced eye. She'd lie in bed looking pale and drawn, refusing to eat until he left for the office. Then she'd jump up for a quick bite from the refrigerator, but she'd always be back in bed when he returned.

Sometimes she'd use hunger instead of flu as an excuse. "I just couldn't wait, so I've already had my meal," she'd tell Bill when he came home. So long as she knew she could get up and leave anytime she pleased, she was able to sit quietly at the table watching him eat.

After about a year and a half the family moved from Minden City to Brighton, Michigan. Bill was a busy man. With a growing practice, much of his time was spent in the office or making house calls. He belonged to a country club, too, and besides playing golf, he often joined the boys for a poker game.

Treasure, confined to her home and feeling the weight of her failure as a wife, began to develop an obsessive jealousy toward Bill. She wouldn't accept his explanations of his whereabouts.

Every time he left home she was convinced that he was going to carry on a clandestine affair with one of his women patients. She began phoning them to check on him. Sometimes she would drop in at his office, expecting to surprise him with one of them. She would go through his pockets and the car looking for evidence. When she thought she had found it, she would strike out at him furiously without explaining her reasons. Then she'd fall into a deep silence that might last for two weeks at a time.

4.

Finally Treasure realized she'd have to do something about her problem, which was now getting beyond all control. She contacted a hypnoanalyst. It seemed the easiest way—just to have the phobias hypnotized out of her. The hypnotist told her he'd take her only on one condition—she would have to tell her husband she was going to him. Treasure went home shaking. How could she admit to Bill all the terrors she had been concealing from him for so long? She was sure this would be the end of their marriage. But she was so desperate that she forced herself to talk to him about it anyway, and to her amazement he was very understanding and thoroughly approved of her seeing the doctor.

So Treasure went again to the hypnotist. On her second visit he was able to bring her to the drowsy state of pre-hypnosis. As she was slipping under, she heard him telling her, "One of your hands will begin to go up without your raising it."

Treasure watched her hand going up. But suddenly, to her horror, she saw that the last three fingers were joined into one. A frightful thing! Terror brought her quickly back to consciousness. She continued seeing the doctor for about a year. But after that traumatic experience, she couldn't be hypnotized and finally he sent her to a psychoanalyst.

Treasure went to the psychoanalyst faithfully once a week. Sometimes the sessions with him were so disturbing that she would come out with her heart pounding. It was just as though she'd been having an operation under local anesthesia, and the surgeon had been holding up before her gaze, one by one, the vital organs on which he was working. Only this was a surgeon of the psyche and what he was forcing her to look upon were the vital interior processes of her whole being, without giving her any hope or suggestion of what to do about them.

She'd drive home crying because of all the things he had dredged up—such weird, horrible things, such as she had loved her father sexually and wanted to commit incest with him, and she hated her mother. But the revelations, instead of relieving her, made her feel even more guilty. How could such an exceptionally horrible person as herself ever hope to get well?

After almost two years of consultation with both doctors, Treasure didn't feel she was any better. But then an idea came to her, and she said to Bill one day, "Maybe I am better and just don't know it. Why don't you take me to a restaurant in Detroit where I don't know anybody and see how I do?"

It was a freezing night and they drove in to Detroit with the car heat on, Treasure chattering all the way to hold back her fear. They chose a little out-of-the-way place, went in and sat down and ordered their meal. Everything seemed fine until Treasure happened to look over and see a woman whose face was flushed from the cold. The flushed face triggered Treasure's panic. She got up from the table and went to the rest room and cried bitterly. When she got control of herself she came out and told Bill it wouldn't work—they would have to leave. Despite the freezing night she was dripping with perspiration.

Treasure was so discouraged she couldn't face the psychoanalyst again. So instead she wrote a letter to him describing her demoralizing experience. His written reply was that in his opinion she would have to see him four or five times a week. He'd lower his fees, but he couldn't promise her an ultimate cure even then, because in losing this neurosis she might just develop another one. Even if a cure were possible it might take as long as ten years to accomplish it.

Treasure read the doctor's disheartening letter in a flood of tears. She was already paying him twenty-five dollars a session and feeling guilty about it because Bill was just starting his practice and they really couldn't afford the expenditure. Besides, they were expecting another child. If the doctor couldn't promise her anything concrete, what was the use of throwing away even more money on him? So she just stopped seeing him.

Treasure had read a book on natural childbirth and had faithfully practiced the relaxing exercises in it, so she had no trouble bearing the little girl, who was named Treasure Ann. But after the child's arrival she found herself sinking into an even deeper depression. She no longer cared about her physical appearance. Bathing had become such a dreadful chore to her that she seldom was able to find the incentive to do it. She wore the same pair of slacks most of the time. And she was swamped in self-pity. She would lie in bed unable to stir, and cry to herself for hours.

Of course the housework didn't get done unless now and then Bill got out the sweeper and did a little cleaning. Finally he wrote to his sister Shirley asking her if she could live with them and help out. So Shirley quit her job and came to stay with the family. She took care of the children and did the housework and was a companion to Treasure. She never talked to Treasure about her illness, but Treasure was always to remember with gratitude the warmth and comfort of Shirley's presence in that unhappy home.

5.

One day several months after Treasure Ann's birth, Treasure happened to be leafing through an issue of *Coronet*. Her attention was drawn to an article about an organization founded by a Dr. A. Low, a Chicago psychiatrist. Treasure read the article with quickening interest. Then she sat down and wrote a letter to Dr. Low, saying that she would like to be helped as others were being helped. He answered her personally, making no promises but telling her that she should come to Chicago and spend at least a week there and they would see then what could be done.

When Treasure told Bill about Recovery, he was dubious. It was, after all, a strange new technique and it wasn't approved by most other psychiatrists. But by this time he was willing to try anything, so he took Treasure to Chicago. They went by train and Treasure was so afraid of having to talk to people that when the conductor came to pick up their tickets she tucked her head down and turned her face away from him. She went without her noon meal, too, because she couldn't force herself to go into the diner and eat in front of other people.

The hotel where they were going to stay in Chicago had reserved a room for them on a high floor It was summer and there was no air conditioning in those days, so the window had to be kept open to catch any stir of breeze. Treasure stared at that open window in terror. For some time she'd been indulging in fantasies of suicide. She would meet a pleasant receptionist in her husband's office and think, "If he were free, he could marry her. She would be a good mother for the kids." Now she was desperately afraid that she would try to make it come to pass.

As quickly as possible Treasure got out of the room, and while Bill went to a ball game, she kept her appointment with the new doctor. The thing that Treasure noticed most as she walked into the consultation room was the understanding look in the doctor's blue eyes. He motioned her to sit down and began taking her history. Then he had her list all her fears. When she came to the end, he told her simply, just as though all her symptoms were really nothing remarkable, "Well, you will get well in Recovery."

Treasure wasn't satisfied with that blunt promise. It seemed to her she should know more about this man's thinking before she entrusted her mental health to him. Ever since her illness she had been an omnivorous reader of psychiatric books and had learned a lot of medical jargon. Now she asked, "Do you believe in instincts? What do you think about Freud?"

"I believe in instincts, certainly," he told her, "but I believe there is much a patient doesn't have to know about to get well. You can get well in Recovery."

"You can get well in Recovery"—he repeated it over and over, brushing off her questions with mumbled answers and coming out loud and clear only on that one phrase. "You can get well." And all the while he looked so sure of himself. How different in manner he was from the psychoanalyst who had told her he couldn't guarantee a cure even after ten years of expensive treatment!

It seemed to Treasure she'd been with him a long while, much longer than the hour she'd been spending weekly with the psychoanalyst. Actually her conference had lasted less than twenty minutes. At the end of it he said, "Why don't you go over to Recovery headquarters? I'm sure you'll be well-received there." And he ushered her out of the door.

Treasure went over to the headquarters, just two blocks away. Inside six or seven volunteers were folding and stamping the *Recovery News* for mailing. They were all chatting and laughing together.

"Ye gods," Treasure thought, "none of them are like me. They're all normal."

Then just as she was about to turn away, Gertrude Beres saw her and came over and took her by the arm. "Why don't you come in?" she asked.

She showed Treasure all the Recovery literature and told her about membership in the organization. It cost Treasure seven dollars to get the literature and her membership. She thought somewhat scornfully as she paid out her cash, "This is the gimmick. It's just one of those organizations that wants money."

All the same she sat down on a chair and watched the members working. Presently some of them started talking about their symptoms and Treasure became alert. Finally Gertrude turned to her and asked, "What are you afraid of, Treasure?"

Treasure began to enumerate her fears.

"But what are you afraid will *happen?*" Gertrude pursued.

"Well, I'm just afraid I'll go crazy," Treasure said.

"Did the doctor tell you you would go crazy?"

"No, as a matter of fact he said I wouldn't."

"What else are you afraid of?"

"I'm afraid I might die."

"Does the doctor say that?"

"No," Treasure replied. And then an amazing thing happened. The giant fear that she had been carrying around all those years suddenly seemed like a dwarf. As she gathered together the literature she'd bought and got ready to leave, the girls invited her to go out to dinner with them, but she didn't like to admit she was afraid of restaurants, so she told them she was expecting a long-distance phone call and returned to the hotel.

Bill wasn't back yet so Treasure lay down on the bed and started reading the literature, becoming more and more absorbed with every paragraph. Suddenly she jumped up and stood in the middle of the room, clasping the three volumes to her breast.

"Why this is it, this is it!" she cried out in amazement to the silent walls.

Bill had to go back to Brighton the next day to take care of his practice, but Treasure remained in Chicago. She revisited Recovery headquarters, and when the girls again invited her to go out to dinner with them, she accepted. So Ann, Gertrude, Annette, and a couple of others all stayed downtown to be with her, and Treasure found the courage to enter the restaurant with them and sit down. And they began looking over the menu.

"I'm not going to order chicken because I get symptoms every time I do," Gertrude suddenly announced.

Treasure stared at her. So other people had phobias about food too, she thought. Somehow it didn't make her feel so exceptional. That night she had no trouble eating. After the meal they all rode the El to a home meeting. Ann Landis was the leader and there were some fourteen other people present. Though there wasn't a psychiatrist in sight and the patients themselves did all the talking, Treasure got a great deal out of it.

For the rest of the week she was at the Recovery headquarters as much as possible and she saw a lot of Dr. Low during that time. One memorable day she had him all to herself, because he took her to lunch. His shrewd eyes didn't miss the fact that her fear of eating seemed to have disappeared, but he warned her that her symptoms would return once she'd left Chicago. To get rid of them for good she'd have to maintain contact with Recovery. Even though she didn't live in Chicago, she still could do that, he told her, just by starting her own group. Two made a group and he had the name of a woman in Detroit who had also seen an article about Recovery—this one in *Hygeia*—and had written to him about it. Treasure could contact her any time she pleased.

Treasure returned to Michigan by train. She felt so free and easy she was able to go into the diner and eat a big meal. When Bill met her, he was delighted with the change he saw, though he still wasn't convinced about Recovery. But Treasure's feeling of freedom didn't last long. Back at home, away from the other Recovery members, she was inundated again by the old symptoms. She couldn't even find the courage to phone the woman in Detroit, and she went through three months of agony before she finally did so.

The woman, whose name was Lillian, readily agreed to meet with Treasure. But she couldn't drive, she said, because she couldn't get a license, since her phobia was an inability to sign her name. So Treasure went in to Detroit and the two women held their first Recovery meeting in Lillian's apartment.

Treasure spread out all the literature she had bought at Recovery headquarters. The object, she explained, was to discuss pertinent symptoms. But she was still unaware that Dr. Low ascribed all tenseness with its ensuing symptoms, to temper—either angry temper directed outward or fearful temper directed at oneself.

"Do you have any temper, Lillian?" she asked.

"No, not a bit," Lillian answered.

"Well, I don't either," Treasure told her. "So we won't read these articles on temper."

"Exactly," said Lillian.

Treasure put all the articles on temper to one side and they began reading the articles on symptoms.

After the meeting Lillian served coffee and cookies. At the sight of food Treasure panicked. But she knew it was good practice to use the muscles and force the cookies down while she discussed her symptoms and fear reactions with her new-found friend.

Lillian understood Treasure's fears, though hers were of a different order. Since she couldn't write her name she not only couldn't get a driver's license, she couldn't even go shopping for fear she might have to sign a sales slip. She couldn't answer the door, because it might be the mailman with a registered package requiring a signature. She was as crippled in her way, as much of a recluse, as was Treasure.

So, bound to each other by their fears, these two desperate women started the first Recovery group in Michigan that September of 1947.

TWENTY-TWO

Treasure Rice's first months in Recovery were to prove among the bleakest in her whole life. Her session with Dr. Low, which had seemed so reassuring at the time, had in the long run appeared to worsen rather than better her condition. During that week in Chicago he had laid down the rules which she must agree to follow if she wanted to be his patient. She had to take him as her absolute authority. And as her authority he had told her unequivocally that she could be cured if she would learn to bear the discomfort it entailed.

He went on to explain the necessity for her having to depend on his authority as her physician. Her own crystallized conviction that she couldn't help herself, he told her, was preventing her from even trying. And this conviction was now so strong that it would be useless for her even to attempt to change it in the beginning. Instead she'd have to throw herself on his diagnosis that she could get well, and act on it.

Once more, as he usually did with his patients, Dr. Low described the situation graphically in terms of his twosome theory. Two convictions, hers and his, had now met and were engaged in battle. One or the other would win. Everything depended on her. If she would join forces with him by putting her determination on the side of his conviction, together they would succeed and she would eventually be healed.

It sounded simple, but it was far from easy. What had really happened was that Dr. Low, as her authority, had now barred the doors and all the escape hatches. She was left with only one choice

205

—to try to order her whole life on his belief. And his belief seemed at first like a hollow mockery to her. But then something even more devastating began to happen to Treasure. As she forced herself to practice Recovery she began to discover that, though it might be hard, she really could do things for herself. That meant Dr. Low was right when he said it wasn't a case of *could not,* but of *would not.*

During those days of her foundering, Treasure felt as though she were in an endless tunnel. Behind her lay the gray life of her semi-invalidism which had had at least some semblance of security, for how can you expect the ill to do anything for themselves? Now that she knew better, she couldn't go back there again. But the way ahead was long and black, and she had to grope sightlessly through it. Her only hope was the pinpoint of light at the far end, the light of Dr. Low's conviction that promised bright sunlight and freedom from fear in the end.

Fortunately Treasure was able to go in to Chicago from time to time, because though she and her brother had sold the clothing store at Bad Axe she was still employed as the buyer. Usually Dr. Low would take her out to lunch when she came and ask her all about herself. Treasure was impressed by his concern for his patients. Busy as he was, he always found time to bolster their morale when he felt they needed it. Just as he'd accompanied Caroline to the library, he'd led another timorous patient right into a grocery store when she'd been too terrified to enter it alone. Then there was the time Ann Landis had baked him some brownies to show her gratitude for all he'd done for her. Pleased because she'd moved her muscles to make them for him, he'd insisted on taking them as part payment on his modest fee. And there was the spring another of his patients, Elsie Nelson, had poured out a melancholy story of being unable to buy an Easter hat because of her family's straitened circumstances. When at the close of her consultation she'd tried to pay her five-dollar fee, Dr. Low had just shaken his head and smiled. "Keep it and buy yourself a hat," he had told her. "That's my prescription for today."

Treasure experienced that same compassion once when he asked her to make arrangements to go home by a later train so that she could stay for the Saturday afternoon panel session for more training. She told him she'd have to go over to the depot right away and change her reservations before the last-minute rush. Knowing how much of an effort it was for her still to face strangers, he told her encouragingly, "I'll go with you." And though it was getting close to two o'clock and he was expected to give his pre-panel lecture at that hour, he hailed a cab and accompanied her to the depot and waited patiently while she stood in line for about fifteen minutes to get her reservation changed. He didn't seem at all hurried when Treasure rejoined him, and yet somehow they arrived at Recovery headquarters at two o'clock sharp and he was there to call the meeting to order.

During her visits to Chicago, Treasure spent most of her time at the headquarters. But the astonishing relief she'd found there during her first visit had evaporated. Now even the presence of the other members no longer guaranteed her immunity from suffering. The sudden panics would attack her wherever she was.

Back home in Brighton they would come with horrifying and frequent regularity, until each day became a terror to get through. Symptoms and bizarre sensations of all kinds flooded her. Her heart palpitated, her pulse raced, often she felt that she was about to topple over. The most terrifying sensation of all was the feeling that her body was slowly thickening. She'd look at Bill and the children and they wouldn't seem real to her. It was just as though there was a screen between her and life. Then again she'd be walking down the street and meet a complete stranger and feel she had to hit him. The impulse would seem so strong that she would be seized with panic and would scurry on, shaking and distracted.

Treasure's salvation during those days was Dr. Low. Though separated from him by space, he was still as close to her as the post office or a telephone call. When some bizarre sensation would assail her she'd sit down and write him about it. Or if she felt she couldn't wait, he'd get a long-distance call. He always had time for her, taking the phone himself, answering every letter promptly, giving her detailed instructions on how to combat each terror as it came, most of all giving her encouragement. Over and over the refrain, like a litany, was drummed into her mind. "You will get well. You will get well. With the help of Recovery you will get well."

With the help of Recovery, her own little Recovery group—

Treasure clung to that thought. Despite her terrors she drove faithfully to Detroit twice a week and met with Lillian. They read from the pamphlets and discussed what they had read and, what was more important, did a great deal of practicing. Treasure kept forcing herself to eat cookies and drink coffee with Lillian. And, under instructions from Dr. Low, she got Lillian to start keeping notes during the meetings. As Lillian began conquering her fears, Treasure would send her special delivery letters that Lillian would have to sign for. Somehow knowing that Treasure was sending them made it easier for Lillian. Eventually she was able to write her name without too much trouble in front of other people as well.

2.

Treasure took the leadership of her little group of two quite seriously. She began firing a barrage of questions at Dr. Low, asking him all sorts of things about how to conduct her meetings. Even though many of the questions were foolish, Dr. Low always answered them promptly, or got one of his volunteers to do it for him. Treasure never wondered why the doctor should spend so much of his valuable time doing all this free counseling, and obviously he wasn't concerned about it either.

After six months the Michigan group began slowly to grow. Two people from Detroit joined it and Treasure's husband, as an experiment, sent over a young law student who was a hypochondriac. The recruiting of the fourth new member came about in a curious manner. One afternoon Treasure, coming home from the post office with a *Recovery News,* was walking along reading it when a woman whom she'd never met before stopped her and asked, "What is that paper you have?" Treasure was filled with confusion, but she forced herself to reply and haltingly told the woman about Recovery. To her surprise the woman's face brightened.

"My husband is having so much trouble," she confided to Treasure. "He's so depressed that he stays in bed all the time. Would you come and talk to him?"

In those days Recovery members visited ill patients in their homes, so Treasure went with the woman. She can remember how the man, now very prominent in Michigan, clung to her hand for hope that day. His wife was so impressed with what Treasure had to say that she started attending the meetings also.

Through the winter the four members from Brighton drove in to Detroit faithfully, through sleet and over snow. Treasure still wasn't able to go into a restaurant but she thought she was doing very well just by forcing herself to eat refreshments that were served after the meetings. Then one night on the way home, someone in the group suddenly suggested, "Let's stop off and get a hamburger."

Panic flooded Treasure. She would have done anything to get out of it. But she was boxed in by Dr. Low's authority that there was no danger. So she went into the restaurant with the others and ordered a hamburger and chomped on it, tearing off big lumps and swallowing them whole, perspiration streaming down her face, her hands shaking. But she got through the hamburger by telling herself minute by minute that there was no danger, no danger. In future years she was to remember it as a horrible experience, but a triumphant one too, though its effect didn't last long.

Recovery still couldn't bolster her the way a drink could, even though alcohol continued to have a toxic reaction on her body that made her deathly ill afterwards. But to Treasure the temporary relaxation she obtained was worth the suffering. With the group from Brighton she could drink without looking conspicuous because they always wanted to stop somewhere along the way, too, for a drink or two against the freezing weather.

Afterwards, passing through Brighton, Treasure would sometimes see Bill's car out in front of a bar. Fortified with drink she'd wait up for him and when he got home she'd fling bitter accusations of infidelity at him, because the jealousy was still working full force in her. Jealousy was a strange symptom, Treasure was to realize in later years, the one symptom patients don't like to talk about at Recovery meetings, one that you seldom ever hear mentioned there. Yet it is very prevalent. With Treasure it was directed at everything connected with Bill—his sisters and mother, the men with whom he went out to play golf, his patients, and his chance acquaintances.

She continued to be plagued by it even after months of Recovery training, but she was learning bit by bit from Dr. Low how to conquer it. "You have to starve it," he told her. "And you starve it through your thoughts and muscles."

So when the thought that Bill was being unfaithful came to her, Treasure had to learn to spot it immediately—trigger spotting Dr. Low called it—as just a nervous symptom and reject it, substituting the secure thought that Bill loved her. Then she had to bolster the secure thought by the use of her muscles.

Dr. Low pointed out that for years Treasure's muscles had been daily abetting her obsessive thoughts by rifling through Bill's wallet, his pockets, and the car, by checking up on him with phone calls and office visits. Controlling the muscles against the force of an obsession wasn't easy, Treasure quickly discovered. She would find her hand down in Bill's pocket, feeling around for the wallet, and she'd draw it out quickly. She'd get a jealous thought, go out on the porch, and be all set to continue down to the office, when she'd suddenly remember and jerk her head to get rid of the thought and tell herself it was nothing but nerves.

By this time Treasure had learned that she really did have a temper and a great deal of it—both angry and fearful. She and her son Billy seemed to be always at loggerheads. He was too full of nervous energy, too excitable to relax a single moment throughout the day. Finally she became convinced that he needed psychiatric counseling and asked Dr. Low about it. He only looked at her steadily and suggested, "Why don't you just see that his days are quiet?"

Treasure puzzled over that at first. Wasn't that what she had been trying to do for years? Then suddenly she realized what Dr. Low was really saying was to stop making issues out of everything, to stop her constant stream of advice: "Don't do this. Where are your rubbers? Have you lost your mittens?"

Treasure started practicing keeping calm herself and making an effort to communicate with the boy instead of berating him, and within two months Billy's hyperactivity had begun to disappear.

Treasure experienced other successes too. There was the evening at a friend's home when she felt Bill was needling her a little too sharply. She burst into tears and rushed home through sheets of rain to crawl into bed in her wet clothes. Bill came hurrying after her to find her shivering and crying under the covers. Full of remorse he began to apologize to her. In previous days Treasure wouldn't have accepted his apology. She would either not have spoken to him for weeks afterwards, or she would have lost her temper and started a fight. Now, through chattering teeth, she said, "It doesn't have anything to do with you, Bill. I have to conquer this. This is something wrong in me, not you." It was the first time she'd ever realized that she didn't really want the world to go tiptoeing around her.

Then there came the day that she first made use of the "inner smile" to keep herself from working up her temper. Bill, in a hurry to get off to work, found her keys in the car and flung them onto the gravel driveway, shouting at her to come and get them. Treasure picked up the keys and went back into the house and threw herself on the bed to have a good cry at Bill's brusqueness. But instead she jumped up and went over and looked at herself in the mirror. Her face, contorted into lines of exaggerated grief like the screwed-up face of a baby, stared back at her. "Boo hoo, boo hoo, boo hoo," she blubbered at the image. And all at once she started to laugh at herself.

These were all victories over trivial matters, of course. But Dr. Low stressed to his patients the importance of learning how to handle the numerous trivialities of their everyday living because it was their faulty responses to these trivialities, rather than the occasional big problem they had to face, that was making them ill.

Finally Treasure came to the biggest hurdle of all. She had to conquer stigma. By the summer of 1948, Bill, who was now an enthusiastic supporter of Recovery, had begun recommending it to some of his patients. And since his office was in Brighton, most of the people who came to him were townsfolk. So the little Recovery group became top-heavy with Brighton people, and it was decided that for their convenience the meetings should be held in the Rice home, with the Detroit people coming out to Brighton.

Treasure hadn't wanted it known in town that she was having trouble and she thought she'd done a good job of keeping it from them so far. But if she held the Recovery group meeting in her own home, and was the leader of it, they'd be bound to deduce the truth and start gossiping about her. At first Treasure felt thoroughly stigmatized, but as time went by she learned to laugh about it. She was getting so many benefits from her Recovery leadership that it was worth any discomfort to her social personality.

For the first time in her life she was developing a sense of responsibility. Week after week she had to be there to lead the meeting, to talk to the group when she didn't want to talk, to see that things were conducted in an orderly fashion. And week after week she had to listen to the experiences of others, some of whom were much sicker than she had been.

Gradually she began to realize that she was just an average human being after all and that the psychic vitals which the psychoanalyst had been at such pains to show her were really only the common heritage of the human race, not proof that she was a monster. She came to understand, too, that her angry tempers toward her son did not indicate that she was exceptionally cruel but that she was only suffering the emotions of many mothers who are worn out and frustrated by life. If all these responses were just average ones instead of overpowering impulses, it meant that she could control them with practice. That thought gave her a growing sense of security.

Meanwhile her little Brighton group kept fluctuating in size from week to week. Sometimes it would go up to five or six members. Once nobody showed up and Treasure had to conduct it for herself. One memorable night eleven people came. But no matter what the numbers, Treasure never skipped a week for six long months.

Then one weekend Dr. Low sent Annette Brocken and Gertrude Beres to Brighton to attend a meeting and see if things were up to standard. Shortly after they returned to Chicago a letter went out to Treasure telling her that the Brighton group had qualified and had been given official recognition. Nobody was more elated than Dr. Low over this new acquisition to his growing Recovery family.

3.

Step by step as the year wore on, Treasure had been making her way down the dark tunnel toward the light. The old symptoms and bizarre sensations were fading away. There were long periods when her thoughts would drift in and out instead of obsessing her as they had formerly. Once again she was beginning to experience some of the old spontaneity that had made life such a joy in former years.

Then without warning she was suddenly plunged into one of those inevitable setbacks about which Dr. Low was always cautioning his patients. Panic-stricken and despairing she rushed off to Chicago for counsel.

"I'm doing everything Recovery says to do and I'm still suffering," she told Dr. Low. "What's wrong?"

"Nothing," he reassured her. "You just have to wait for the accumulative effect of your Recovery practice to bring about the changes before you'll be rid of your symptoms permanently. And you'll have to wait for it patiently."

Dr. Low was glad that Treasure came in to see him at once. It was always most important to him to catch his patients' setbacks in time. A setback, if serious enough, not only affected the sufferer himself but the other members of the group. When Phil had broken down and gone into the hospital, Maxine had been so upset that all her old terrors had come back, reversing for several months the steady improvement she'd been making.

But the saddest tragedy to strike the original Recovery group occurred that year and caused a number of patients to suffer setbacks, some so severe that Dr. Low had to prescribe hospitalization and shock treatment. It was the death of Rosalie T., who for years had been a devoted Recovery member. To all appearances she had successfully curbed her strong suicidal tendencies. Then one day Rosalie either slipped or threw herself beneath the wheels of an oncoming train and was instantly killed.

Dr. Low himself never mentioned Rosalie's death to his group, but he doubtlessly grieved deeply over her in private. Again and again he must have asked himself what had gone wrong, how had he failed her. Then, as he often told his class he did, he must have remembered that he, too, could find help in the techniques he had forged for others, and turned to his Method to remind himself that he was after all human, and that human beings can never achieve 100 percent perfection.

Yet even with the help of the Method, Rosalie's death must have been very hard for him to accept. As Ann Landis' husband, John, was to say in a later year, "His patients were the most precious thing in the world to him. They were his jewels and he felt he couldn't afford to lose a single one." If Rosalie's death was indeed self-inflicted and not an accident, she was to be the only one among all his Recovery patients he was ever to lose that way.

TWENTY-THREE

"Always" was one word Dr. Low did not allow his patients to use. Should one of them say, "My husband always slams the door," Dr. Low, with his careful exactitude in the use of language, would correct her, "Don't use the word 'always.' It isn't 'always,' he doesn't 'always' do that."

There was, however, one instance in which his wife Mae was sure the word "always" could be aptly applied to her husband. It seemed to her that he was *always* losing the car.

On many days he'd be late getting home, just looking for that car in the Grant Park parking lot where he would leave it in the morning without ever noting its location. One Saturday he couldn't find it at all and had to take a taxi home. Sunday, when the lot was almost empty, Mae went down on the El and found it and drove it back. What was most exasperating to her, however, were the Tuesdays that she joined him for the group psychotherapy class, because afterwards she would have to take part in the ordeal of searching among hundreds of other parked cars for that familiar one.

One night, Mae, tired and eager to get home, suddenly exclaimed in exasperation, "You know in your lecture you were talking about 'always'? Well, this is one instance where I'll say, 'You *always* lose the car.'"

He must have been bone-tired, too, and chagrined as well, but he caught the humor of her remark and burst out laughing. "You know," he said, "you're right." And he promised he'd try not to do it again. Usually when he made such promises he was true to

215

his word. But it never seemed to hold good where the car was concerned.

In the spring of 1949 this periodic misplacing of the car was bound to have presented even more complications than before, because the Lows were preparing to move out of the city into a suburb. The lease had run out on their apartment and their househunting had led them to a charming old three-story house in Evanston. They chose this quiet suburb primarily for the sake of their daughters. Phyllis was almost ready to enter junior high school, with Marilyn only two years behind her. And Abraham and Mae felt it would be good for the girls to grow into womanhood in a homier atmosphere than the city provided. In March the family moved.

The new home was a spacious place. Downstairs there was a big foyer, a living room that extended across the whole front of the house, and a library behind the living room. Upstairs there was a separate room for each member of the family. Abraham firmly believed in such privacy—a place where a person could be by himself and develop his own individuality. The third floor contained Abraham's study, which the Low family called the Ivory Tower. He would work there in the evenings and mornings, arising early to write and study before going to spend his days in Chicago. Three days a week went to his private patients and the rest of his time was given over to Recovery, his work of love.

There is small wonder at Abraham's proud sense of proprietorship. This was the first house he had been able to call his own since, as a boy of eleven, he had lived with his parents in Strasbourg before his mother's death. To Treasure he wrote with an air of deep satisfaction, "I now have a house which Mrs. Low terms her dream house. I agree with her on this point and feel a real happiness in my new abode. . . ."

It was here that old friends still came occasionally to be served a modest dinner by Mae. The guest list was varied but always included Dr. Eugene Grosz, whom the girls called Uncle Gene. Now and then a new acquaintance might be included. And if he was of the intellectual type and bent on impressing everyone with his erudition, Dr. Low would have to practice his Method assiduously to control his speech muscles and remain silent. He had little patience with such showoffs—romanto-intellectualists he called them—and, had he cared to do so, he could have cut them to shreds with one or two carefully chosen remarks, for he could summon a rapier wit.

He still enjoyed best the evenings spent with his Recovery friends. He liked to point out that their training had stripped them of all false pretenses and had cured them of their need to be exceptional. They were people who had learned how to be themselves. Many were the evenings that he drove his "lieutenants" out to his new home to discuss Recovery business. Afterwards they would engage in simple homey talk and finally gather around the piano, where Phil Crane would play and everyone would sing, while Dr. Low sat puffing on his pipe and beaming proudly on them.

Still the ardent bibliophile, Abraham regarded the large house with its expanded space as an invitation to gratify his passion with abandon. The walls of his study were soon lined with shelves which were filled to capacity with books. Then the walls of the library downstairs, or book room as it came to be called, were provided with shelves and these also were rapidly filled. Finally one day a huge bookcase, ordered by Abraham, arrived and was set in the middle of the book room, reaching from floor to ceiling.

As row after row of heavy volumes began to line its shelves, too, Mae became alarmed because she knew there were no supporting beams beneath the floor. If the floor were to give way, half the room would go plunging into the cellar. Finally she called in an engineer to study the probabilities of such a catastrophe. The engineer confirmed her fears and Mae relayed his findings to her husband—no more books.

Abraham made only one concession to Mae's fears. He began to smuggle the books in. This was a difficult feat because he was a romantic man who liked to be sent on his way or greeted at his return by a show of affection. Of course when Mae embraced and kissed him she couldn't help feeling the package under his coat. Suspiciously she'd ask what it was.

"Oh, that's a box of cigars," he'd tell her.

Mae took his word for it but began worrying about the number of cigars he was smoking until one day Phyllis approached her with a whispered confidence, "Daddy's got another book under his coat, Mother."

"Whenever are you going to read them all anyway?" Mae asked him in desperation, though he was really doing a fair job of handling that situation. There were half-finished books lying all over the house with markers to keep the place. Wherever he chanced to settle down for a few moments of leisure, there would be a book handy for a snatch of reading.

Mae had to give up eventually and hope for the best, because the books kept on coming. They were almost personalities to Abraham, to be cherished and worried over. And in at least one of his panel lectures at Recovery headquarters he was candidly to confess his fear of what would happen to them should housebreakers enter his home during the family's absence.

Once he humorously quoted Cicero to a friend who was marveling over his library: "A room without books is as a body without a soul."

2.

Shortly after the Lows moved into their new house another member came to join the family. Her name was Lucky Girl and she was a little black cocker spaniel. Abraham didn't want a dog but the girls had long been begging for one. And now that they had a home of their own, they couldn't be put off any longer.

Lucky Girl soon became the most confused dog in the world. The girls spoiled her. Their mother took care of her, as is the usual fate of mothers where pets are concerned. The housekeeper, though she had a good heart, didn't waste any of it on the dog and treated her roughly. As for Abraham, Lucky Girl soon worked her way into his affections because he found that she made a good companion on his early morning walks. But there was one thing he demanded of her—obedience to discipline, a quality, in his opinion, all good dogs as well as all human beings should have.

He was just as concerned over discipline in his daughters' lives. And his standards, to their dismay, were stricter by far than their mother's. There was, for instance, the matter of the piano lessons. The girls had begged to be allowed to take them, and their father had been delighted, because he'd never forgotten the accomplished young ladies of his youth.

The trouble was that after about a year of daily practice both Marilyn and Phyllis lost their enthusiasm, and it became torture for their mother to get them to the piano. Finally she consulted with their teacher who told her candidly that neither girl had any musical talent. Armed with this information, Mae took up the subject with her husband.

"Having them continue those lessons, under the circumstances, is just pouring money down the drain," she told him.

"Well, I tell you," he answered. "I had hoped they would play the piano and learn something about music so that they'd be able to appreciate it. But even if they can't, they're going to continue anyway. It's teaching them self-discipline and that's money well spent."

He wasn't so adamant about the girls' schoolwork. Both of them did reasonably well and their father was satisfied. He never harassed them to get the highest grades, and though he accepted their "A's" he never seemed particularly impressed by them. It was his theory that really exceptional human beings were very few, and that it was the constant urge to be exceptional that caused tensions and eventually breakdowns.

"It's fine if you are just a good average," he used to tell his daughters. But even when they came home with a "C" there wasn't any real pressure. "Just try a little harder," was all he said to them.

He was also surprisingly lenient in his attitude toward comic books. He knew they were in the house and that the girls were reading them because there wasn't much he didn't know about their activities. But he didn't consider them a serious threat to the girls' welfare. And he even gave mild approval to those that depicted classical stories because he felt that the girls were at least picking up some culture, though in a diluted form.

Radios were a different matter. He detested them with their welter of advertisements and blaring music, as later he was to detest television and refuse to have a set in his house. The only time he himself turned on a radio was to catch an afternoon concert or the news when there was some discussion on political matters. But for his daughters, radios were out, because he couldn't believe their assertion that they could have the radio on and read and study at the same time. Despite his objections, Phyllis and

Marilyn each owned one which they kept in their bedrooms and played when their father wasn't around.

Going to movies, of which he also didn't generally approve, wasn't so easy for them. He seldom went to movies himself and the number of pictures he really enjoyed was limited. He found Groucho Marx hilariously funny and he loved Charles Laughton in *Ruggles of Red Gap*. Most movies seemed to depict violence though, and it was his contention that the nervous system suffered from being subjected to too much violence. So when he found out that one of these unsuitable pictures was being shown at the neighborhood theater the girls could count on a ban from him, even though their classmates were going.

Then all their tears and complaints about his callousness couldn't budge him. They'd long since learned that a temper outburst in their home wouldn't be tolerated. Control of temper lay at the very root of his Method, and since he was a man who did his best to practice what he preached, no member in his household was allowed to indulge in tantrums. If one of the girls so much as slammed a door in anger, she had to return and close it quietly. And if the temper outburst continued she'd be told, "If you can't behave yourself, go to your room until you can."

When he spoke to them in that clipped, stern tone of voice the girls knew better than to disobey him. But he wasn't always the stern disciplinarian. His feeling for the simple things of family life was one of his charms, and he savored to the full every precious minute of it. By nature he was a jolly man with a lot of spontaneous laughter in him, and he used to regale his daughters with all kinds of stories about the silly things that had happened to him when he was young. Those stories would send them into hysterics of merriment, and it was only later that the girls came to realize how much sadness there must have actually been in his early life. But they never once heard him speak of it.

By this time his humor over his own foibles had been honed so fine that he was able to accept and excuse as average the mistakes his daughters sometimes made. One day Phyllis, just learning to drive, attempting to put the car into the garage for the first time, sideswiped the brick wall and dented the fender. She got out crestfallen, expecting a stinging reprimand for her carelessness, only to find her father, his head thrown back, laughing so hard the tears were streaming down his cheeks. Seeing Phyllis staring at him in astonishment, he explained between gasps of merriment, "Why, that reminds me of me."

The girls were proud of their father, proud that he had been born in Europe and could speak seven languages and had read thousands of books, proud of his Viennese accent and of the awe he inspired in those who met him for the first time. They liked to brag about him to their classmates. But there was one discrepancy which they felt deeply. Their father's name wasn't in the American *Who's Who* and hadn't been for years. He'd been invited over and over again to send in his biography but had never done so.

When the girls took him to task for it, he didn't impress them with his humorous promise not to disappoint them should he be cited for the Nobel Prize with its large cash award and attendant publicity, which could be really useful in spreading the work of Recovery. Finally, however, bowing to what he called the "vanity of young ladies," he sent in his biography.

The girls' feeling for their father had deeper roots than mere pride. They felt complete security in the knowledge of his love for them. It was he, the earliest riser in the family, who at 7:15 each morning woke up his womenfolk, one by one, gently with a kiss. Whenever he was home, he was always accessible to them. If they had a personal problem they wanted help with, they had only to knock at his study door and he'd welcome them, push aside his pile of papers, and give them all his attention.

As the girls entered high school and began dating he gave them common-sense advice about the boys with whom they went out: "Don't settle for merely wealthy boys, pick those who come from good, solid families, families where the children are taught the basic virtues. And when you're going with a boy don't accept every single time he asks you. Go out with him once or twice, and then the third time tell him you're busy. Above all, when you marry, choose someone with ambition rather than money."

Regardless of whom they dated, he always insisted that the curfew hour be strictly observed. Once one of Phyllis' escorts earned her father's deep displeasure by bringing her home ten minutes late. He was up waiting for them. "Twelve o'clock is twelve o'clock, not ten minutes after," he observed dryly. Time was a commodity which he regarded with the utmost respect. Tardiness for an appointment, whether business or social, was to him ill-mannered and he would avoid the company of those who were perennially late.

Not all his advice to the girls, however, centered around the problems of living. Once Phyllis, having heard so much about her father's brilliance as a Shakespearean scholar, went to him for help with her Shakespeare assignments. Enthusiastically he accepted the role of tutor and begain painstakingly delineating each character in depth for her.

At first Phyllis enjoyed these periods with her father. But presently she found that all her new insights into Shakespeare's characters couldn't be used in the classroom, where the teacher was just skimming over the play. And she was getting less and less time for her other studies and none at all for the school's social activities. So her visits to the Ivory Tower for sessions on Shakespeare became fewer and fewer, and finally stopped completely.

There was one occasion, however, when Phyllis, instead of learning from her father, was able to teach him something. One day he came home to see her playing solitaire.

"Will you show me how to play that game?" he asked her.

Phyllis was delighted. She taught him the rules and he began using solitaire to relax himself after he'd been sitting at his typewriter working for long stretches of time. This went on month after month. Then suddenly he stopped playing just as abruptly as he had begun. When Mae commented on it, he answered, "Oh, wasn't that a waste of time?" That was all he had to say about a subject which had intermittently engrossed his attention for almost a year.

TWENTY-FOUR

Dr. Low's delight in his role of suburban householder didn't prevent him from crowding yet another project into his already tight schedule, though it cut into the little leisure time he had to enjoy his new home. He instigated this project primarily at the urging of an old passion—talking about Shakespeare, though his purpose was ostensibly to raise money for the Recovery organization. Beginning in the fall of 1948 and running well into 1949 he gave a series of lectures for members and their relatives and friends. He charged a small fee: $1.00 for a single lecture, $2.50 for five lectures to Recoveryites of six months standing, and $3.75 to all others.

The lectures were devoted solely to Shakespeare's *Hamlet,* which he read aloud, a few pages at each lecture, paraphrasing them sentence by sentence to put them into Recovery language. To Shakespeare he gave the highest accolade within his power to bestow: "the greatest spotter of them all." If Recoveryites would study the playwright more thoroughly, he told his audience, they would learn a great deal about how to spot in their own lives.

As the lectures progressed Dr. Low analyzed one by one the characters in the play, beginning with Hamlet. He described Hamlet as a rank intellectual who knew nothing about spotting destructive tendencies in himself and so indulged in sabotage throughout his short life. His interpretations were too literal. He was very temperamental, forever complaining and accusing others of being in the wrong and proclaiming himself in the right. "I" was always in the foreground; "he" and "she" were scarcely con-

sidered except to be criticized or ridiculed. Hamlet was also obviously suffering from both angry and fearful temper which almost
completely immobilized him. If he could have known and used
the principles of Recovery, he never would have been such an
indecisive character.

"Hamlet is just like my patients, except that he does not suffer
from the disturbing sensations," Dr. Low explained to his audience. "Shakespeare has given a masterly description of a psychoneurotic."

Subsequently he analyzed Laertes, the romanto-intellectualist.
"Laertes has no goals except his inclinations. He is for chastity,
but will seduce a girl he covets. He uses swollen diction. A person
who uses ostentatious language wants to impress someone, because
he lacks self-respect and has to convince himself that he is important."

He delineated the king and queen as tainted realists and Polonius as a fossilized pedant and a rascal with no true fatherly feeling for either of his children.

As for Ophelia, she was Dr. Low's favorite character. Perhaps
she reminded him of the sheltered girls of his youth, for he told
his audience, "Ophelia is the most genuine person in the play,
the epitome of loveliness. She is sweet and does not react with the
sensitivity of a tense person. She is naive and does not suspect
concealed meanings. She believes that Hamlet is in the abyss of
feeling for her. But true love is a pure feeling, and Hamlet is
incapable of real emotion. He impresses the naive Ophelia with his
theatrical affectations."

One lecture took up the famous soliloquy, "To be, or not to
be . . ." and the conversation between Hamlet and Ophelia that
followed it. Dr. Low pointed out that the soliloquy has always
been regarded as sublime poetry, and rightly so, but then he
proceeded to interpret its hidden meanings and to annihilate any
assumption that it might contain a deep philosophy. It was, he
said, only the mouthings of a temperamental person creating noise
and fury without much meaning, a verbal tantrum just like those
his patients themselves had thrown in pre-Recovery days. And it
was the innocent Ophelia who had had to suffer for it all.

Several times during the course of the lectures Dr. Low criticized
a famous early alumnus, the poet Johann Wolfgang von Goethe,

of his own former school, the University of Strasbourg. Goethe, he said, believed Hamlet was a noble spirit because the poet didn't analyze the play line by line. If she had done that, he would have been aware that the Prince, far from being sensitive of soul, was "magnificently psychoneurotic."

As Dr. Low revealed the motivations and personality of the Prince in the light of Recovery terminology and techniques, one wonders if he recalled how years before in New York he had delivered a similarly brilliant but psychoanalytic study of Hamlet before a group of his peers. If so it must have been with an indulgent smile for the romanto-intellectualism of his younger days.

2.

Shakespearean lectures to his patients weren't the only kind delivered by this unique psychiatrist. Twice a year he would give a lecture on sex to a mixed group of his Recoveryites. These lectures had little to do with instructions on the physical act of sex, since he expected his patients to use the Method to handle this area of life as well as all others.

Instead, the lectures were primarily for the purpose of correcting erroneous general concepts. Again and again in his work he had come across men and women filled with guilt and frustration over what they regarded as sexual inadequacies in themselves. And he was convinced that it was caused in large part by his colleagues' elevation of sex to the primal urge, governing all life's activities.

Conceding sex to be an instinct, he deplored the idea that it was the strongest or the most important one. He ranked the instinct for self-preservation, that is for food, shelter, and water, as much more vital, as did his contemporary, Dr. Carl Gustav Jung. And he concurred with Adler when he said, "With too many people, power is a much more important influence, for example the power money gives. The one who has it can suppress someone, boss someone—that is a powerful impulse in a human being."

But his greatest quarrel was with those colleagues of his who claimed that sex was not only the strongest instinct, but an uncontrollable one. "Instinctive craving," he told his audience, "that is precisely the point that made me scrap everything that I did with psychoanalysis. I scrapped it completely. I cannot imagine that human beings should be governed entirely by instinct. You must know what an instinct is, so you will be proof against this nonsense. You know what the breeding instinct is in animals—a machine. The migrating instinct, it is blind force, like a locomotive. I have nothing to do with this conception of instinct in a human being. It is unfortunate that this doctrine of human instinct is so dominant today. It works havoc. You know, for instance . . . the courts in the United States, and presumably outside of the United States, have adopted the doctrine of irresistible instinct, and murderers have been acquitted on it. . . ."

And he went on to explain: ". . . In an automobile factory you will find one car like the other. In Nature, everything is arranged in two small extremes, and one large middle ground—natural distribution of living factors. . . . If you have a thousand cars one like the other, then it is an unnatural distribution, an artificial distribution. That never happens in Nature, in living things. . . . There is not the slightest reason to think that sex is different from anything else. It has this natural distribution. What else should it have? Everything that lives has it. In a given population of a thousand people, ten percent will be strongly sexed, ten percent will be weak, and the remainder will be just average. . . . If it were true that sex is overpowering, that it governs everything in life . . . everything would be driven by this one impulse. There would be no natural distribution. Sex must follow the law of this natural distribution . . . there should be in every population a certain percentage of highly sexed people, a certain percentage of low sexed, and the remainder in the middle.

"In my thirty years of practice, I have only seen one man and one woman who could not really control their sex. It was as strong in them as the craving for drugs, with terrible physical reactions. I have never seen it except in these two people, one was a physician and the other a nurse. That is precisely what I would expect: ten percent strong sexed, ten percent weak sexed. Addicts are extremely rare. . . . Exceptional things in life are rare, as in sex. . . . This whole business of sex has been so outrageously oversold. Movies think sex is good business, so they promote it. . . . People accept it and . . . then get the idea they are frustrated in the sex feeling, they suffer and become preoccupied. Continual preoccupation with sex. I do not like this idea. If such an idea gets approval, you can get an idea of what it does to the human mind. It convinces the person he must express it at all costs, not frustrate it."

He himself would never admit of an "irresistible instinct" in a human being unless due to some physiological abnormality or illness. So he struck a blow for the dignity of free will, the human quality of choice, the foundation stone on which his Method was built. It was this will, he maintained, that could be activated to bear discomfort, to control all impulses, and eventually to bring the mentally and emotionally disturbed back to health. That simple truth was the secret of his success with his patients.

3.

Sex lectures were only a small part of Dr. Low's speeches. The meat of his philosophy was contained in the pre-panel and post-panel talks which he gave the year round. The stocky figure was a familiar one, striding to the front of the room, mounting the platform on which stood his desk with the gavel, pounding for order, delivering his talk. He insisted on absolute discipline during his lectures, though this was a high goal to set for the forty or more nervous patients who had gathered to hear him. He required that they sit quietly and refrain from talking and such other nervous impulses as coughing or repeated clearing of the throat which would disturb other members.

His lectures dealt only with the trivialities of daily life because it was these mundane events that his patients couldn't handle. Many of them lacked self-leadership and self-discipline in such simple activities as getting out of bed in the morning or taking a bath. So some of his lectures dwelt on the basic art of "moving the muscles" when the body felt leaden with mental fatigue, of making up the mind when it was torn by indecision, of forcing oneself to do the thing one feared to do, when that thing did not represent a realistic danger.

Sometimes the topic was his patients' tendency to question their own bodily functions—"stepping in and taking over" as he described the process. By doubting an organ's ability to take care of its own function after the doctor had declared it sound, he told them, they only interfered with the natural processes of the body, causing the intensification and prolongation of such symptoms as colitis, racing heart, headaches, and similar nervous manifestations. Dr. Low liked to point out that organs were designed by nature to fulfill certain functions, and that if left alone they would carry on very well.

"Trust the power of nature within you to bring about the balance in your life," he would urge. "The body, left to itself, is self-healing. You don't know how to digest an egg. Nobody knows. But your stomach does. If you leave it alone, it will do it for you."

Sometimes his subject was tenseness—two kinds of tenseness, he would tell them, one stimulating, the other frustrating. The negative emotions, such as envy, jealousy, hatred, self-pity, poured frustrating tenseness through the nervous system. When this happened on a sustained basis, and if the nervous system was weak, symptoms would crop up, all kinds of symptoms: phobias, compulsions, obsessions, depression anxiety, and many more. But no matter how many and varied the symptoms might be, they all sprang from the one source of frustrating tenseness, and were the result of an imbalance in the system caused by that tenseness.

To cure this imbalance and build up nerve resistance, he explained, his patients should grow chilly to the negative emotions when they were seized with them, refuse to give them the dignity of their attention, refuse to cater to temper. He had a ready answer for those patients who complained that holding back anger would turn them into dishrags.

"Oh, no, on the contrary, you'd have self-approval," he would reply. "It takes real courage to stop temper short, much more than to give way to it. That's easy. A dog can do that."

On the other hand, he told them, if they were seized with love or joy or any of the positive emotions, they should warm to them, keep them as long as they could, for they brought relaxation which allowed nerve resistance to build. But he also voiced a word of warning against too much of a good thing. The intoxication of joy, for instance, could be as undesirable a stimulant as that of anger because it, too, would create an imbalance.

He went beyond the popular school of "positive thinking" with his "constructive thinking" techniques as epitomized in the Method. And so it was natural for him to provide his patients with a tool for handling their excesses of euphoria as well as their depressions. They were to tell themselves, "Enjoy this moment, but remember that your mood is only a partial view of life. You will eventually come down from it and have to deal again with frustrations and disappointments."

He would have much preferred for them to be content with less dynamic moods. "Why won't you settle for something just this side of happiness?" he would ask them almost plaintively. "Be satisfied with peace and contentment."

Sometimes the theme of his talk would be a homily on gossip. Gossip, he pointed out, was indulged in because it relieved tension and boredom. But the stimulation it brought was harmful to the nervous system because it created frustrating tension. This kind of stimulus, in Recovery language, was labeled "undesirable stimulation," and was to be avoided.

At first one of his favorite themes was the subject of humility. Then one day he told his audience, "Maybe I shouldn't bring this in because I'm stepping into the clergy's domain." After that he stopped talking about humility. But he gave many talks on the theme of averageness, because his patients were always setting exceptional standards for themselves and then falling into deep depressions when they couldn't live up to them.

With a blackboard to illustrate his point he would draw a curve and relate it to the distribution pattern prevalent in nature. "Take a hundred trees," he would say. "You would find among them a few very tall—represented by one end of the curve—and a few very short—represented by the other. The rest of the trees would be of average size. So among human beings. Through the long span of history you would find only a very few truly exceptional figures. Most people fall in the average range, with average accomplishments and an average capacity for committing indiscretions and absurdities."

One day in discussing "averageness" he committed such an absurdity himself. He regarded himself, he said, as an average human being in every respect. The average height of human beings was five feet eight inches and that was about his height also.

A slight affectionate ripple of laughter spreading through his audience reminded him that in that one respect at least he had been guilty of wishful thinking, for he'd stretched his height by some three inches. He blushed a bit at the realization of his error—that habit which still troubled him in embarrassing or strange situations. Otherwise he maintained complete control and gave his audience a perfect demonstration on how to handle a trivial mistake by simply passing on to another subject.

Often his topic would concern the necessity of relinquishing the sense of self-importance because, as he told his patients, it was their fear that this self-importance was being threatened which caused them to panic in many trivial situations. The cure he advocated was simply an attitude of detachment toward self. "The more indifferent you are to a thing," he explained, "the less you can be insulted or scared by it. If I am insulted, then I have a feeling of having lost my reputation. You cannot have fear if you are indifferent to the thing that you are scared by. . . . Use your sense of humor. But you cannot use your sense of humor unless you are relatively detached. This means detached from fear and insensible to insults. The more detached you become, the less can you be insulted."

Over and over he was to tell them, "Humor is your best friend, temper your worst enemy. Cultivate the inner smile and use it on your own foibles and shortcomings." He described the inner smile, in effect, as a quiet realization and acceptance of one's own averageness.

4.

There can be no doubt that Dr. Low, in arriving at his form of therapy and his Method, made a thorough study of Alfred Korzybski's works and the new science of semantics with its emphasis on the part language plays both in individual and group behavior. But he was unique in seeing the value of evolving a special language that could be understood by all his patients, and providing them with to-the-point terms that could serve as tools to overcome their problems. It is no wonder that, in his phraseology, they "lapped up" this new language, often so quaintly, even humor-

ously expressed, and so tailored to their needs. Today, many years
after his death, it is this simple hopeful language that still appeals
to them.

Hopefulness was the doctor's keynote. Only a man as keenly
aware as he was of the great power of words to injure in a world
of increasing mass media would have spoken out so strongly
against the kind of crusades being waged for various health causes
by well-meaning organizations.

"There are too many efforts made today to strike fear in the
population, to constantly warn them of dangers without any
visible use and perhaps, let me tell you, without any visible advantage," he said in one of his talks. "To me there is nothing
advantageous in these associations that scare the population sys-
tematically. A hundred years ago people had dreadful fears but
they faded away in time. But today you are not permitted to let
your fears fade away. There is an organized systematic effort all
over to scare you, and I have to talk to you about it because it
scares particularly my patients. Patients under no circumstance
should be scared, even if you think you do them good. The end
does not sanction the means."

In semanticist circles Dr. Low's experiments and theories were
attracting a great deal of interest, which continued on after his
death. At Temple University in Philadelphia, for instance, Dr.
Harry L. Weinberg was to include Dr. Low's rules of therapy as
part of his course in semantics. And in his book, *Levels of Knowing and Existence,* which came out in 1959, he was to devote
almost a whole chapter to the Viennese psychiatrist and his brain
child, Recovery, Inc.

Even as early as that year of 1948 Dr. Low was singled out to
share the platform with a semanticist before a professional group
made up of speech professors, sociologists, and psychologists. The
semanticist was the well-known Dr. Irving Lee, head of the Speech
Department at Northwestern University and author of several
important books in the field of semantics. It was a memorable
program for all those present. First Dr. Low read a paper on one
of the mental illnesses. Then Dr. Lee discussed the same illness
from the viewpoint of semantics. Dr. Lee was so fascinated by
Dr. Low's ability to apply semantics to the field of medicine, and
most especially by his "spotting techniques," that he started at-

tending Dr. Low's Saturday afternoon talks and his group psycho-therapy classes, taking copious notes on everything.

There among Dr. Low's patients he could see living proof of the potent therapeutic power contained in the simple wording of the Method. So impressed was he that the following summer he asked Dr. Low to speak to his class at Northwestern on the use of semantics in psychiatry.

TWENTY-FIVE

The years from 1949 through 1951 were a period of such steady though slow growth of the Recovery organization that even the cautiously optimistic Dr. Low became enthusiastic. The two out-of-town branches had proved to him conclusively the remarkable capacity of Recovery to spread and grow, even without the stimulus of his immediate presence. Patients like Agnes Dumont were coming in to both these branches, brought by word-of-mouth and by an increasing spate of newspaper and magazine articles, and they were being cured by the Method alone.

A development of even greater importance to Dr. Low began when in March of 1949, Dr. Charles C. Graves, director of mental institutions in Iowa, became interested in Recovery through a former mental patient who had sent him some literature on it. Now he wished to investigate the new therapy with the idea of introducing it to Iowa state hospitals.

Referred by Dr. Low to Ernest and Viola Hoffman and their branch in Muscatine, Dr. Graves went to visit them and was so impressed that he came to Chicago for further conferences with Dr. Low. The upshot of it was that he decided to open his first Recovery unit at the Henry County Memorial Hospital in Mount Pleasant, which was only some sixty miles from Muscatine. In this way he could enlist the help of the willing Hoffmans.

Though the Iowa project was the answer to Dr. Low's twelve-year-long dream of making Recovery available to patients in state hospitals, his decision to encourage the experiment was accompanied by some anxiety, for it would have to be conducted far

233

from his own watchful eyes. And Dr. Graves, enthusiastic though
he was, had not been trained in Recovery techniques or principles.

In a letter dated November 12, 1949, Dr. Low wrote to Ernest
Hoffman of his fears and the reasons for them: ". . . I am very
jealous of everything that is done in the matter of expansion of
the Recovery program. I'd hate to see it watered down to the
level of a mere welfare program. Although welfare is a good
thing in itself, nevertheless, it is not what bears the name of
Recovery. . . ."

However, after some initial bungling, the project seemed to be
getting off to an auspicious start. Dr. Wayne B. Brown, head of
Memorial Hospital, assigned Phyllis Oberlin, occupational ther-
apist there, to work with Ernest.

The routine they evolved was a simple one. Once a week Miss
Oberlin drove a few about-to-be-discharged patients to Ernest's
home in Muscatine to attend meetings and become acquainted
with Recovery in the outside world. It was hoped that some of
these patients would eventually open Recovery groups of their
own to administer to other discharged patients.

Ernest Hoffman helped along the training project by making
periodic visits to the hospital to present panels. He found an
enthusiastic co-worker in Miss Oberlin and she soon became a
familiar face in Chicago, where from time to time she went to
visit Recovery headquarters to study the techniques firsthand and
talk to Dr. Low. Frank and Harriette, as usual, opened their home
to her when she came.

By March of 1950, a year after Dr. Graves' initial interest, he
was inviting Dr. Low to lecture at the Mount Pleasant hospital
before the members of the Iowa Board of Control. Since the Board
supervised all the state hospitals, this was a very important development to Dr. Low and he promptly accepted the invitation,
making room for it in his already crowded schedule. He gave a
two-hour talk, answered questions and sat in the next morning
when actual Recovery techniques were demonstrated to the Board
by a panel discussion put on by nine of the hospital patients.

A few days after Dr. Low's return to Chicago he received an
enthusiastic letter from Dr. Graves. The Board of Control officials
had been definitely impressed by what they had seen and one of
the members had promised to interest the governor personally

in the project of establishing similar groups in other state hospitals. Dr. Low was elated. Triumphantly he wrote to Ernest, prematurely as it was to turn out: ". . . I feel that from now on it will be smooth sailing."

2.

That year the American Psychiatric Association settled on Detroit for its May convention, giving Dr. Low the opportunity of visiting the new little branch in Michigan for the first time. Since he wouldn't be able to drive all the way to Brighton, Treasure and her group decided to meet in the apartment of a member who lived conveniently near the Book-Cadillac Hotel where the convention was to be held.

As the time drew near, Treasure became more and more aware that the sole responsibility for putting on the panel was hers, and all her old terrors were suddenly reactivated and she had to struggle to keep from being inundated by them. She was very grateful that she still had her crutch of alcohol to lean on. On May 4, The Day, she bolstered herself with a drink before driving in to Detroit with Bill to lunch with Dr. and Mrs. Low. They met Dr. Low in the hotel just as he came striding out of the morning session, shaking his head in disbelief.

"How was it?" Bill asked.

"Sterile," Dr. Low replied briskly and went on to explain. "They offered one interesting case, only one. They devoted a whole meeting to it. And it doesn't prove anything because twenty-five to thirty percent of the patients recover spontaneously anyway. But here's Recovery with an average far above that and they won't even investigate it."

Yes, he had the proof of what he was saying in the little group he was about to visit, but his colleagues didn't think it worth their trouble even to drop in to the next-door apartment and see what it was all about. As Treasure led him up the three flights of stairs, he felt a quickening of the heart that always came when he was about to witness a new unfolding of Recovery.

In the room sat some fifteen to twenty people eagerly awaiting him. He had never seen any of them before, yet they were there because Recovery had become a lifeline to them. He turned to Treasure, the one who had been responsible for it all. "Now you just go ahead and start your meeting," he said.

Treasure was drenched in sweat. Her mouth felt dry and her heart pounded. "Dr. Low," she gasped. "I couldn't say a word. You'll just have to do it yourself."

He smiled understandingly and took the meeting in hand. He started talking and asking questions and he corrected the members every time they used such terms as "introspection," "neuroses," and "introverted." "Now say that in Recovery language," he would tell them.

Before the afternoon was over, it was quite plain to Treasure how, with the best intentions in the world, her group had been lapsing into the learned jargon of psychoanalysis, obscuring Recovery's simple approach. She was so full of self-blame for her faulty leadership that it surprised and reassured her when she got the doctor's note of May 7. The doctor, never one to pick out flaws but to consider the overall picture, wrote: ". . . Your branch is undoubtedly a model for future branches. I wouldn't want it any better as [sic] it appeared last Thursday. The members are lively, well instructed in Recovery lore and as eager to keep well as I wish my patients to be. You may with excellent reason be proud of what you have accomplished with no outside support, all by yourself. . . ."

3.

For some while the growth of the Recovery organization had been making Dr. Low more and more aware of the need for a single textbook to replace the diffuse material now scattered through pamphlets, articles in the Recovery magazines, and mimeographed sheets run off by office volunteers. To provide such a book he had spent more than a year selecting and editing the best of the panel examples and his discussions on them. Since his purpose was to keep the book simple and plain enough to be understood by the layman, he had turned for help to Mae. She had the quality required—the thinking of a "good average" layman. There was no greater compliment in Dr. Low's terminology than this.

So Mae had edited her husband's work, page by page. Whenever she had come to a passage she couldn't understand, he had revised it. Sometimes he had had to make several revisions before Mae was able to say, "Now I see what you mean," and he could let it go.

Once it was finished he hadn't expected any trouble getting the book published, because it had not only been written for ordinary laymen, but for a particular segment of them—the Recovery members. And since it was to be their textbook, all of them would buy it. Surely the commercial value of such a project would be plainly understood.

But his early optimism faded as, one after another, the four publishers to whom the book was submitted rejected it. The reactions of each was typical. First there had been the enthusiastic response, coupled with what seemed a minor reservation, "Have to be approved by the medical reader." Then had followed the rejection on the familiar grounds, "Not enough public appeal." Dr. Low suspected that the fault lay in the medical readers' orientation to psychoanalysis, still the therapy of the day. Blind to the true value in the book's simple approach, they had rejected it immediately. Eventually, Dr. Low, giving up finding a sympathetic publisher among the commercial houses, had decided to pay to get it printed and had signed a contract to do it with Christopher Publishing House in Boston.

That July of 1950 the galleys came in for proofreading, and he spent a concentrated two weeks going through them. He must have chuckled over the foreword. He'd written it hopefully to jolt the profession into action of some kind. Using statistics obtained from Dr. Karl Menninger's published findings, he'd proceeded bluntly and conclusively to bare the fallacy of psychoanalysis as a curative power. The proof of its failure was in the statistics themselves, his stinging foreword pointed out.

Keeping that foreword hadn't been an easy matter with his publisher. He'd had to sign a paper releasing Mr. Christopher from all responsibility in case of a suit. Dr. Low hadn't quibbled over signing the waiver. He'd gladly pay the court costs. In fact he was in a mood to welcome a suit, not only because he was weary of the deadening silence of those who opposed him, but also because it would have given him a splendid opportunity to present the issue to the people. He had long since had demonstrable proof that an aroused public opinion could bring about social change and he was coming to the conclusion that this was the only way it could be accomplished.

It was November of 1950 when the first copies of *Mental Health Through Will-Training*, as the book was called, arrived at Recovery headquarters. The severe jacket and sober black binding revealed nothing of the sparkling contents they enclosed, for the pages inside were alive with the examples and discussions of long-time Recovery members. They were all there: three-dimensional beings, together with their lively doctor, dealing with the trivialities of everyday life, somehow conveying the adventure of their quest for health in vital episodes despite their averageness. But the book contained far more than rich delineations of human nature. In it were condensed all the rules, techniques, and insights, the quintessence of that extraordinary partnership over the years between doctor and patients—an enriching and ennobling philosophy of life applicable to everyone.

When in the following years Dr. Low's patients sometimes asked him anxiously what would become of them if anything were to happen to him, his reply was always the same, "It's all in my book. Read the book."

4.

That fall of 1950, the Muscatine branch celebrated its fifth anniversary. By this time Iowa was also represented by another little group organized by Miss Oberlin in Burlington for the benefit of patients discharged from the hospital. Other groups had been springing up in Evansville, Indiana; Louisville, Kentucky; Dixon, Illinois; and St. Louis, Missouri.

In St. Louis it was the Jesuit priest, Rev. Edward Dowling, a gentle man severely crippled with arthritis, who was responsible for Recovery. Together with an Episcopalian minister, Father Dowling had already sponsored Alcoholics Anonymous in his locality. And when he heard about Recovery he had gone to Chicago to investigate it. From that time on, in the affectionate words of

Dr. Low, "a close friendship sprang up between us two who seemed to share tastes and ideals."

After a brief training period in Chicago, Father Dowling opened the St. Louis group in one of the rooms of the Queen's Work, the Jesuit publishing house, and threw the meetings open to the public. This was an innovation in Recovery practice because up until then group meetings had all been held in the shelter of private homes where members were shielded from stigmatizing experiences with the public. Some of the more timid groups were carrying this farce of concealment to extremes. Equipping themselves with playing cards, they would hide the books under the table and bring out the cards whenever a neighbor dropped in unexpectedly. Father Dowling felt that such subterfuge was beneath human dignity. He provided a pattern which was presently to be adopted by the Recovery headquarters in Chicago.

5.

As the year of 1951 came in, the visitor that most roused Dr. Low's excitement was Dr. Harold R. Carter, prominent neuropsychiatrist from Denver, Colorado. He had come across *Mental Health Through Will-Training* only by chance, because the silence Dr. Low had hoped to break with his blunt foreword had remained complete and the book had not received a single review in the whole nation.

Dr. Carter was so impressed by it that he came to Chicago and spent two days at headquarters conferring with Annette and Dr. Low and attending panels, and when he returned to Denver he established the first Recovery group there. Unfortunately, shortly afterwards, he died in an automobile accident and the supervision of the group fell to Dr. Norbert Shere, his associate.

At the Recovery November Convention that year, Dr. Low, his voice shaken with emotion, delivered a final tribute to his dead colleague: "He was the first neuropsychiatrist to join in the Recovery movement. He had the vision, the warm interest for his patients, and the human feeling which, presented with the hu-

manitarian issue of Recovery, was bound to answer the call. . . .
After reading *Mental Health Through Will-Training* he became
convinced, he wrote me, that this was the most promising approach to the problem. He then added, 'It seems to me that your
techniques will solve the problem of how to give adequate care
to those of my patients who cannot afford my fees.' This was the
warm impulse of a warm heart, the enthusiastic response of a
mind geared to fellowship and service, the reflection of a spirit
whose kinship to Recovery found its most fitting expression in his
solicitude. . . ."

6.

The year was to close on an upbeat note for Recovery after all,
when a distinguished visitor from halfway around the world came
to the Chicago headquarters. He was Professor Paul D. Sivadon,
medical director of the Hôpital Psychiatrique de Ville-Evrard, a
psychiatric hospital in a suburb of Paris, France. He had already
introduced group psychotherapy to his hospital, because this
novel approach was just beginning to interest a few progressive
minds. But everything was so new and unfamiliar to him that he
felt it a godsend when *Mental Health Through Will-Training*
fell into his hands. Thoroughly impressed, he'd traveled all the
way to Chicago merely to study Recovery techniques.

Arriving on December 22, Professor Sivadon had intended
spending only two days in Chicago, but he stayed almost a week,
passing long hours at headquarters conferring with Dr. Low and
talking to patients. He attended a Saturday panel and a home
group at Frank and Harriette's house, and the more he learned,
the more enthusiastic he became. On the eve of his departure,
he told Dr. Low, "I was not sure whether I did it right. Now I
know how it should be done."

It was a simple but deserving tribute to the organization which
had been pioneering in group therapy self-help techniques for
years—a long lonely struggle with not much encouragement along
the way.

TWENTY-SIX

One evening in May of 1952, Dr. Low returned from his office complaining that he didn't feel well. All that night he was violently ill and slept only in snatches, but in the morning he was up, though a little later than usual, preparing to go to work. He was standing in front of the mirror shaving when he became aware for the first time of a weakness in his right hand.

Mae looked in and saw his flushed face and how he was struggling to get the shaving done, and she ordered him to bed at once. It was the first day of work he had missed in almost twenty years of practice. Despite Mae's remonstrances he was back in his office a day or two later, speaking offhandedly to his patients of a "weakness" in his hand. Maxine noticed how he favored it, using his left hand to pick things up. And on Tuesday night he asked her to take the registration, something he'd always before done himself.

By faithfully exercising his hand Dr. Low was able with time to restore it almost to normal, though he could never again write with complete ease. And the signature at the foot of his typewritten letters after 1952 shows a faintness and uncertainty of line in contrast to the former bold strokes. But there was nothing fainthearted about his spirit. If possible he became more energetic than ever, full of plans and decisions.

All about him lay the same discouraging scene where the state hospitals were concerned. In Iowa, after that first initial cooperation of Dr. Graves and the Board of Control, Recovery had made no progress. Dr. Low had little doubt as to the cause of the

241

blockage. He was to speak of it to his flock as "a sad tale of obstruction by certain forces which, hearing of the project, lost no time discrediting it in the eyes of the state administration and stopping Dr. Graves in his tracks."

But in a letter to his brother Sol he was to identify the opposition as being ". . . undoubtedly at the insistence of my ideological friends. They are against me because my ideology is against them. After all it is a fair exchange. . . ."

Even at Mount Pleasant there was a general air of apathy, though Dr. Brown still permitted weekly panel meetings in the hospital, led by outside Recovery members. But Miss Oberlin had resigned and left and all enthusiasm for Recovery had departed with her. The staff no longer studied the Method in order to coach patients in it. Unlike Miss Oberlin, they did not bother to transport improved patients to the groups in Muscatine and Burlington.

Despite these constrictions, Dr. Low had at first permitted the panel to continue in the hospital. But immediately following his illness that May he decided to bring the crippled Mount Pleasant experiment to a halt.

At the same time he began making important changes in the Recovery organization itself, restructuring everything along lines that would allow the program to be administered entirely by laymen. One of the first things he took up was the status of the leaders of the various groups. For a long while he had been concerned about the power he had granted them. Now he carefully redefined their role. They were no longer to be considered more knowledgeable than other members, and so they were not to give advice. They were told to spot only on the inner environment and above all not to intellectualize about Recovery techniques and tools, nor should they act as authorities in any way except that, as his lieutenants, they were to be answerable to him for the welfare of their members.

Next he redefined the nature of the organization. Until this time it had tended to be a closed one, for though the Saturday afternoon panel sessions at headquarters had always been open to the public, the home groups had been made up primarily of Dr. Low's patients. Any prospective applicants from other sources were first interviewed by the leader whose group they wished to join and were admitted only if found acceptable. Now, following Father Dowling's lead, home groups were to be relocated as quickly as space could be found for them in the facilities connected with schools, churches and synagogues, and other similar public places. In this way Recovery would fulfill its function as a free health service open to all.

But Dr. Low's more important reorganization concerned the panel meetings themselves. In the past the panels had been made up only of long-time members who were well-versed in Recovery. It was these members who gave the examples and afterwards discussed them while the rest of the group merely listened. Dr. Low now relaxed this rule to allow anyone to take part in the panel who had read at least some of the textbook, *Mental Health Through Will-Training,* and had attended several meetings.

For a long while he had been troubled by the tendency of the groups to intellectualize and had been working on a tighter format which would serve to prevent this. Now he presented it to them—his unique example-framework with its four-step format. From then on streamlined examples following this format were to take the place of the loose discussions. Each example was to be followed by spotting from the group using only Recovery terminology.

The example steps run as follows:

Step One describes the event which is to be reported as a panel example, mentioning the various things that were said and done, the persons involved, the time, and then the temperamental reaction.

Step Two describes the symptoms and discomfort the member experienced.

Step Three describes the Recovery spotting and practice.

Step Four describes what would have happened before Recovery training.

Like the expressions which make up the Recovery tools, the example with its four steps looks deceptively simple. Few perhaps would realize how much work actually went into the shaping of it. Each one of the steps was carefully designed to point up temper— always the root cause of the patient's illness, Dr. Low had found.

2.

The new format would require a more thorough training of leaders, and Dr. Low realized the necessity of schooling one of the Recovery members to handle this delicate work and later to conduct panel demonstrations for state hospitals. He had never given up the belief that sooner or later those hospitals would show an interest in his therapy, and he wanted Recovery to be ready for it.

It was natural for him to choose Phil with his pleasing personality, since he had been coming down to Recovery headquarters for so long that he was already well-grounded in the Method. All that was necessary now was to familiarize him thoroughly with the techniques of the new format. Three times a week Dr. Low turned over the panels to Phil while he himself sat back and listened and then later spotted on the faults in Phil's presentation.

"When you spot, don't try to give them the whole book, Phil," he would say. "Just give them a simple statement about how you would practice in that same situation."

Sometimes his criticism dealt with one of Phil's examples: "You make it too complicated. Just give one simple example at a time."

Directness of approach, too, came in for some attention. "Phil, you notice when I talk to someone I may only spend a few minutes with him, but I look him squarely in the eye, and I pay close attention to what he's saying right at that time."

As Phil became more and more efficient, Dr. Low's praise increased. Finally he was saying, "Phil, your technique is good. You bring out every step in the example plainly so that somebody who has been ten years in the state hospital will be able to see how he can help himself. Just remember always to keep it simple."

After Phil was well on his way, Dr. Low worked to train Ann Landis to act as Phil's assistant. Then, in line with his reorganization to make Recovery entirely a lay operation, Dr. Low began staying away from the weekday meetings—though he still led the Saturday afternoon panels—leaving Phil or Ann to handle things without any professional supervision.

3.

Until that fall Phil had been working on a volunteer basis, but now Dr. Low appealed to him to make a great sacrifice. Would he accept a job with the organization as director of leader training? He put it in his usual forthright manner: "Phil, you can't lose what you've gained in self-help through Recovery. But that's what will happen if it dies out. What will you do then? Where would you turn? Then wouldn't it be worth it to you to do everything you can to make Recovery live?"

Phil thought it over. It was a hard choice. For the first time in his life he liked his work and was making good money at it. If he gave it all up and took the Recovery job, he would have to live with his mother and depend on her for partial support, because Dr. Low was offering him only a meager wage. And Phil knew he couldn't expect more, for most of that money was coming out of Dr. Low's own pocket. But he couldn't in conscience turn down Dr. Low's plea, so in the end he accepted.

For eleven years Phil was to work for Recovery at substandard wages. It never occurred to him to ask for more. As he explains it today, "Dr. Low didn't want to establish a job market. If the membership isn't going to cooperate as volunteers, we might as well forget it."

4.

Despite his disappointments in Iowa, Dr. Low wasn't ready to give up his campaign to bring Recovery to the state hospitals. Over and over again he had found how valuable publicity was in getting the support of the public, and now he appealed to Maxine Kennedy to handle part-time public relations for Recovery. Maxine had given up her nursing work because of some difficulty with her eyes and was again employed as a hostess in a hotel restaurant. She would be able to juggle her hours to give Dr. Low the help he needed.

But Maxine was dumfounded at his request. She was too frightened of people, too timid for a job like that, she objected.

He only smiled and shook his head. "You are the right one, Magzeen," he told her. "It's all right if you blunder. If you do, you won't hurt Recovery. You can blunder a little bit."

So Maxine took the job. From two to five o'clock every day she did Recovery publicity work, for which Dr. Low paid her fifty dollars a month out of his own pocket. But actually Maxine gave Recovery much more time than this. She changed her place of employment to the Swiss Chalet in the Bismarck Hotel where she worked in the mornings from eleven to two and in the evenings from five to eight-thirty. The Swiss Chalet was a favorite meeting place of newspaper editors, political figures, and professionals, doctors included. Maxine, in her role as hostess, made an effort to become acquainted with all of them. The soft-spoken, disarming young woman with the friendly smile made many friends among her daily customers, and if they proved at all receptive, she'd talk to them about Recovery.

During the hours she worked for Dr. Low, she visited the people she'd met in the hotel and also others whose names he gave her. To each one she'd deliver pamphlets which described Recovery and explained why it was a more productive method than the psychoanalytic approach of the day. It offered help to the masses, while psychoanalysis did not. Psychoanalysis left out the hundreds of thousands of persons who could not obtain help because there were not enough professionals, and not enough funds to pay those professionals even if there had been enough of them. On the other hand Recovery was a free form of therapy that could not only save thousands of wasted lives but millions of taxpayers' dollars as well, since it had already proved effective in preventing relapses and therefore costly rehospitalizations among former mental patients.

Of course such public relations activities were unorthodox so far as the American Psychiatric Association was concerned. But Dr. Low had been orthodox for a long while in his attempts to interest the members of his own profession in Recovery, and had met with no success. Yet mindful of the censure he might incur for such activities, he still took care not to break the letter of the code whereby his profession was governed.

"Having turned over the campaign to the membership, I am an outsider watching the goings-on from the sidelines," he was to explain. "As a professional man I cannot engage in action against the state hospitals."

He did intend, however, to aid and guide the organization in its efforts to carry the story of Recovery to the world. He was constantly urging members in whatever state they might be located, to keep up a flood of letters to their governor and state legislators asking that Recovery be investigated as a possible after-care therapy. And he singled out two of his lieutenants—Treasure and Phil—to drill them on the history and purpose of Recovery and the obstructions it had encountered down through the years, so that they would have ammunition with which to carry on the campaign by word of mouth, person-to-person, over radio, or on television.

"Our target here is the state hospital," he was to tell them in words which later he was to commit to print in the *Recovery News* of February, 1954. "That's where the masses of mental patients are concentrated. If they improve they are sent home and—relapse in appalling numbers. The main reason for the many relapses is that neither the patients themselves nor the relatives are prepared for the task of prevention. If they were to be prepared it would have to be done with the aid of a working method, and the state hospitals have failed to develop any method of this kind. We have the method and are eager to offer our services to the hospitals. For some reason the state hospitals have shown no or little interest in our techniques with the result that countless thousands of patients sent home as improved have to return as relapsed. Our methods could prevent the infinite human misery which is involved and could at the same time reduce materially the over-crowding in the hospitals. They could also save the state treasuries the enormous expense for new construction to house the endless flow of relapsed patients from homes to hospitals. . . ."

5.

One day while all the work of reorganization was going on, Dr. Low got a call from an old patient who was suffering a setback. It was Elsie Nelson, now living with her family in Danville, Illinois, and her voice was shaken with panic. He recognized her need at once and told her to come up that Friday and see him. She came and poured out her fears to him, her utter defenselessness in the face of her terrifying symptoms and demoralizing panics. At the end of the session he rose from his desk and came around and put his arms about her like a father comforting a frightened child.

"Don't you know," he asked her tenderly, "I will always take care of you?"

A flood of tears was near the surface at his gentle solicitude. Yet why should she cry when she felt so secure? It was not until the following week that she suddenly thought to herself, "How can he always take care of me? He may die before I do."

Elsie had her reservations about the Recovery Method because it was too simple for her. For fifteen years she wandered through life seeking more profound answers to her panics. Eventually a religious experience came to her. Elsie took responsibility for it and in the light of it began trying to induce in herself feelings that she felt were appropriate. This was feeling corrupted by thought, and Elsie worked it up into a vicious cycle and developed a religious obsession. Then a series of crises came into her family life and Elsie tried to handle these in an heroic manner instead of recognizing her limitations as an average human being. The end result was that she fell into such a severe depression that she had to be hospitalized and given shock treatments.

One black night after leaving the hospital Elsie was lying awake in bed consumed with a terrifying panic, sure she was going mad, when she suddenly remembered Recovery and Dr. Low's words— that he would always see her as his patient if she needed his professional care. By this time Dr. Low had died, but now she saw another dimension to his statement. He had left her a legacy in the Method, and he had promised her over and over that if she practiced it faithfully she would get well and stay well.

Suddenly she saw that her halfhearted espousal of the Method while searching for other more esoteric answers to suit her intellectual tastes was the vanity of knowing better than Dr. Low. It was her desire for self-importance that had prevented her from really practicing the simple Method he had left her. This was at the root of her religious obsession.

Wracked by terror, Elsie managed to lie motionless as she had learned to do in Recovery, allowing her panic to reach its peak and ebb away. She also faced up to her vanity, though it was a painful insight to accept. But once she had recognized it for what it was, her fears began to subside. And she was filled with a sense of contentment, a true feeling of humility that can come only when personal vanity is controlled.

From that moment on Elsie began to practice Recovery faithfully and to participate in all its programs, not only for her own health, but to help others. She was to write: "Dr. Low was the finest person I have ever known and I loved him dearly, but found that my love and admiration meant nothing if I only gave lip service to his Method. I have never felt so well in my life, but continually keep 'averageness' in mind; that is, the balance advocated by him. . . .

"The one thing I have found is that whatever else it means, the light that has been given to me is Recovery. I feel my commission is to always expose myself to its discipline. . . . For me who indulged all my life in the intellectual temper of thinking, 'I know and I know best,' it is a blessing to have at my fingertips Dr. Low's dictum 'to spot is to know that I don't know.' "

TWENTY-SEVEN

In December of 1952, Charlotte Shamberg, sitting in the lobby of the large apartment building where she and her family lived, picked up the latest issue of the *Saturday Evening Post* and began thumbing through it. Suddenly her eyes were arrested by the title of an article, "They 'Doctor' One Another" by Jack Alexander. The subtitle read, "Members of Recovery, Inc., all former mental patients . . ." Charlotte, who didn't realize that the subtitle had erroneously grouped mental and psychoneurotic patients together, was forcibly struck by that adjective "mental."

For eighteen years she had been suffering from the dread of going mad. Looking back over those years she could see in them not even the faintest ray of light. It had begun that day years ago when her little six-year-old daughter contracted a streptococci infection in her blood stream and by nightfall was dead. It happened so suddenly that Charlotte went into shock.

For days afterwards she roamed the house in confusion, sure she was hearing her daughter's voice calling to her from every room. One day Charlotte found herself answering the child and this terrified her so much that she could no longer bear to stay in the house alone, so she went back to her old job as a stenographer. She left early with her husband when he went to work. He would drop her off at the El and Charlotte would ride in to the city and roam the streets aimlessly, waiting for her office to open. Sometimes an attack of nausea would drive her into a restroom to cry and vomit. Sometimes she would just sit on the curb sobbing her heart out for her lost daughter. But despite her confusion she was

250

still able to take dictation, transcribe notes, and type them. It was just as though she were two different persons, each going about her own business.

Presently other horrifying symptoms came: spells of dizziness, crawling sensations over her entire body as though millions of insects covered her. Sometimes she couldn't feel her legs and arms at all. At other times something seemed to be pulling her eyes back into her skull, then pulling them forward again. And suddenly she would find she had completely lost the sight of one eye. Sometimes she would have an agonizing awareness of her own breathing. At other times just the innocent flutter of a curtain or the movements of her own hands would send her into a panic.

Then the hallucinations began. Lights would flash on where there were in reality no lights at all. And she began to see figures standing in every doorway of the apartment. She was sure they were real people and locked all the doors and propped chairs under the knobs to keep them out. But the ghostly visitants just slipped through the walls and stood there staring down at Charlotte.

Night after night she would lie sleepless in bed, feeling herself sinking deeper and deeper into the black abyss, sure that at any moment a scream would burst from her throat—the sure sign of the onslaught of madness, according to her way of thinking.

And so the years went by. The Shambergs adopted a baby boy and then Charlotte had one of her own in the hopes that the children would help her. But they made matters worse. The hallucinations became more vivid and Charlotte developed an obsession about germs and dirt. Although her house was always spotlessly clean she was continuously dusting, vacuuming, scrubbing floors, washing woodwork.

Sometimes she felt a dreadful certainty that she would kill her youngest son and she would get on her knees and beg God desperately to save her from such a dreadful crime. Sometimes she thought of ending her own life by plunging a knife into herself, but since she was sure she was just a hollow tube without any vital spot inside for the knife to strike, she didn't do it. Sometimes she was convinced she was already dead and that nobody else recognized this because she didn't know how to lie down in the right position.

By this time Charlotte had become almost housebound because she was sure if she went outside, the buildings would topple down on her. She told her husband nothing about her mental torment, using excruciating headaches as her alibi for staying home. But she knew she had to do something about her condition so she began seeing psychoanalysts. She saw ten in all and went through her life history in depth with each one. But she was unsuccessful in freeing herself of her torturing fears.

And now here she was in the lobby reading about a new kind of therapy that was obviously helping people like herself. Charlotte put the magazine down and went up to her apartment and dialed Dr. Low's office number with a shaking finger. In the waning year of 1952, she became his patient.

At her first consultation with him, Dr. Low told Charlotte she must go directly from his office to the Recovery meeting. He was going to attend himself and expected to see her there. Charlotte went, but she sat with her head averted, afraid to look at those around her. She was sure they were all mad and that she must be on the verge of losing her mind, too, or the doctor wouldn't have insisted she join them.

As soon as the meeting was over, Charlotte rushed home and phoned Dr. Low. "How dare you do this to me?" she berated him through a torrent of tears. "You're making me even sicker and all I want is to get well."

His only reply was the firm litany which he repeated every time there was a break in her incriminations, "You will get well! You will get well! You will get well!"

It was the assurance in his voice that kept Charlotte coming back to him, though she was a thoroughly uncooperative patient, one of his worst, he told her. She refused to attend Recovery meetings and wouldn't follow his orders to do the things she feared to do. Nothing, for instance, could get her to go into a department store to dispel her dread of toppling buildings. Dr. Low was always telling her to stop playing games with her mental health and make it her main goal in life if she wanted to get well.

Charlotte contradicted him at every step. On several occasions she became so argumentative and hysterical that he got up, opened his door, and told her sternly, "I can't have you for a patient, because you won't cooperate."

That always brought Charlotte around. She still wasn't well by any means and really never expected she would be, but now, through Dr. Low's help, she was at least able to keep her head above the deep waters that before had seemed about to engulf her.

2.

Charlotte Shamberg was only one of many who responded to the article in the *Saturday Evening Post*. As Dr. Low had anticipated, calls began pouring into his office and new patients flocked to see him, presenting him with a staggering workload because he never could turn anybody down who was in real need. There were also more and more letters from people all over the country wanting to know how they could start Recovery groups.

In Michigan, however, Treasure Rice was still having problems just increasing the size of her one group. She'd tried to get new members by contacting physicians of her acquaintance and also several whom Dr. Low suggested, to ask them for referrals. They had all expressed polite interest in Recovery, but none of them ever seemed to find time to visit the group, and they certainly didn't send any patients.

Then two crises occurred in Treasure's life which changed both its course and that of Recovery in Michigan. The first crisis had to do with herself. One morning after a night of partying, Treasure awoke at four o'clock, feeling her heart beating so weakly that it seemed if she so much as turned her head it would stop completely. She looked up to see Bill sitting on the edge of the bed, feeling her pulse. He'd just given her a shot of adrenalin and now his face wore an expression of great patience and concern.

"Why, you simply can't drink," he told her flatly. "You could die in one of these spells."

So Treasure had no alternative but to give up alcohol, and the only way she could get along without that familiar crutch was to practice Recovery with more zeal than ever before. To her delight she found that as she did so she began making real strides toward completely regaining her health.

The second crisis was the illness of Treasure's mother, now seventy, who was suffering hardening of the arteries of the brain and had a mental breakdown. Treasure and Bill brought her to Michigan and had her committed to the geriatric ward at the state hospital in Pontiac, twenty-eight miles from their home, where she stayed for the last five years of her life.

Treasure, who often went there to see her, had to witness not only her mother's irrational behavior but also that of the various other patients who were in the ward with her. Since Treasure's major fear was that of mental collapse, she was highly suggestible to all these sights and sounds of insanity. But she handled her fears by using the Method and forcing herself to face the thing she feared.

She even began visiting the back wards where the worst cases of deteriorating human beings were kept. Since it was before the advent of the new medications, she saw all about her the unrelieved misery of men and women bereft of all reason. They cursed her with obscenities as she passed by, or they laughed or screamed aimlessly. In those wards the word "bedlam" took on graphic meaning for her.

The spectacle was so terrifying at first that her mind cowered before it, her heart pounded, and her thoughts raced. But despite her agony she continued to move her muscles, to force herself to look and listen. And gradually she was able to build up an immunity to the suggestion of danger. The secure thought for her was that even if she were to become insane and have to be hospitalized, Bill would take care of her.

There was a real benefit for Recovery in all the suffering that Treasure witnessed, because the experience spurred her on to work even harder for Dr. Low's dream of introducing the Method to the state hospitals so that the overworked doctors could utilize the self-help concept as an ally. This in turn would free them for the very important work that only professionals could handle. As it was, the patients, because of their great numbers, were seldom seen by the doctors at all.

Despite her zeal Treasure didn't have the slightest idea of how she could go about getting Recovery known and accepted. But she was ready to investigate every avenue, and when she found that at Pontiac the hospital staff had organized a relatives' group, she began going to their meetings and talking to the others about Recovery. Presently she had two new recruits, a young Detroit girl, Vera H., whose father had been in the hospital for twenty years and who was seeing a psychiatrist herself, and a woman from Pontiac whose daughter was in the hospital.

It was at Vera's suggestion that she and Treasure launched an all-out campaign on the three major Detroit newspapers to get some publicity for Recovery. She found that William Coughlin, Sunday editor of the *Free Press*, had seen the article by Jack Alexander in the *Saturday Evening Post* and had noticed that Brighton, Michigan, had been mentioned. He'd already made a note to look into it. Now he sent a young man named Norman Kenyon to cover Treasure's group. After attending a meeting Kenyon became so enthusiastic that he promised to do a feature story on it. And it was then that Treasure felt the old sense of stigma so strongly that she asked him to use a fictitious name when writing about her. So Treasure was referred to as Mrs. Smith and the paper gave the story a full page.

Treasure felt secure in her pseudonym until she paid a visit to Bad Axe and a relative of hers said, "Say, that was a description of you in the paper, wasn't it? Well, I'm certainly glad you didn't use your own name." Instead of experiencing relief at the relative's attitude, Treasure felt a tide of shame rising in her. She hadn't been self-led, as Recovery taught, but stigma-led. She made up her mind that in the future she wasn't going to hide any more. And from then on she used her own name in every news release, never veering from that policy in the years ahead.

3.

None of the Brighton group, including Treasure herself, had had any idea what local publicity would do for them. After that article two hundred and fifty letters arrived in the first mail. And more kept coming—some to the paper and others to Treasure's home. There were probably five or six hundred in all. Treasure called the group together and showed them the letters. "We've got them," she said. "What shall we do with them?"

The group went through the letters, reading them aloud to one another. Then they laid them out on a card table and composed a form letter and answered every one. The form letter told the

inquirers that three new groups were being formed and that they
would be put on the mailing list and would receive notice when a
group in their vicinity was available. Then the task of training
leaders for the groups began.

Treasure found she needed some additional training also to
master the new format Dr. Low had inaugurated. And on her
visits to Chicago she would meet with Phil. They would spend
hours together giving examples and spotting until Treasure had
learned how to do it his way—drawing out the timid members,
even if only for a few brief words, and interspersing this with
spotting from those who raised their hands and were willing to
talk freely.

Treasure found the new, simply-structured, four-step examples
most disconcerting after the pleasant intellectualizing in which
she had been indulging. There was nothing glamorous about
these simple examples, each one of which had to be dragged painfully from the most vulnerable area of everyday experience—the
darker impulses, the mistakes, the humiliating defeats—and presented to the group for its inspection. Sharing oneself with others
like this rather than acting like an authority meant developing
a rare and often painful humility.

There were other changes in Recovery techniques about which
Treasure hadn't needed advice. They had come about because of
the enlarging membership. One of these changes related to the
discussion of sex problems. Since Dr. Low made such a point of
speaking about sex only once or twice a year, Treasure had faithfully followed this pattern with her Michigan group. She had one
of his lectures in mimeographed form and when the time came
around she would read it aloud.

After the reading of this lecture, Treasure's group, which was
then small and composed primarily of married women, would
freely discuss their sexual problems. And many were the Rabelaisian "spottings" that followed. The favorite question by far was,
"What Recovery tool should I use to get a satisfactory sexual
relationship with my husband?"

"Your muscles! Why use your friggin' muscles, of course," the
answer would come back amid gales of laughter.

No one imagined that the growing numbers of people who were
coming in—some twenty-five to thirty at every meeting—would

make a difference in such discussions. Then one night the time came around for the reading of the sex lecture. Treasure introduced it to the large group and felt a sudden constraint. Discussion afterwards fell off lamely. They were all realizing the disconcerting presence of strangers. Intimate discussions seemed out of place among them. And they began to realize, too, that such discussions might even cause harm, for who could tell whether one of these strangers, instead of being helped, might not be roused to undesirable action.

By 1952, with the final development of his new self-help panel, Dr. Low himself ruled out sex, politics, and religion as topic matter for examples. This rule has been followed ever since, though, naturally members can discuss anything freely in the private conversations that take place during the Mutual Aid period with which every Recovery meeting closes.

4.

Treasure had at last found an ally in her efforts to spread Recovery. She was now being abetted by the editor of the Detroit *Free Press*, who had been made graphically aware of the appeal the organization had for his readers and was forthwith proclaiming himself its sponsor. From then on he printed stories in his paper periodically, bringing in a steady stream of new members. New members meant new leaders, and on one of Phil's visits to Michigan to see how they were conducting their meetings, he became aware that leadership training had to be offered on a continuing basis if these Michigan members were to become expert. Instead of having twenty-five to thirty people travel to Chicago, why not have one person, namely Phil, come to Michigan to conduct a leaders' training conference on the spot? Dr. Low gave his wholehearted approval to this idea and he and Phil mapped out the program. Then Treasure was notified and brought her leaders together for a weekend of training under Phil. This was the first Area Leaders' Training Conference, one of many to be held eventually all over the country.

By this time Treasure's own group had become too large for her living room, but help came from an unexpected quarter. One night the Rev. Andrew Howie and his wife visited a meeting. Rev. Howie was the pastor of the Presbyterian church which Treasure had joined when she came to Brighton. Only she wasn't attending anymore. She was bitter toward the church because she felt it hadn't done anything for her in her illness and was still ignoring all the thousands of other people who were suffering as she had.

But though Treasure hadn't been to church for a long while, her name was still on the church rolls. And it was natural for Rev. Howie, after reading the articles in the paper, to investigate what one of his old parishioners was doing. He liked what he saw, and finding things so crowded in Treasure's home, he offered a room in his church complex for a meeting place. The group quickly accepted, and presently Treasure began sending her children to Sunday school and attending church again herself. But that wasn't because of Rev. Howie at all. It was at Dr. Low's instigation.

One day she'd confided to him, "Dr. Low, Recovery is my religion. This is what I'm teaching my children. We learn not to judge. We learn all the things I've read in the Bible. But in church it's nothing but hypocrisy."

He listened gravely. Then he answered, "Don't ever say that, Treasure. There are so many evil forces in this world, this life, that draw men down. They are on every hand. The church is the one power that holds up perfection. Your children should be trained in this. Nobody ever reaches perfection, of course. But it is a force within life that draws men up. Send your children to Sunday School and church."

Dr. Low's belief in religious training for children was practiced in his own home. His daughters faithfully attended the First Presbyterian Church in Evanston where the well-known Dr. Harold Blake Walker was minister. On several occasions the minister and his wife were dinner guests in the Low home. And Dr. Low always welcomed exchanges of ideas with him, as he did with men of all religious faiths.

TWENTY-EIGHT

Few of Dr. Low's friends could understand the passionate zeal in this man to continue his fruitless efforts to breach the obdurate state hospitals' resistance to Recovery. Since it was bound to be a losing battle why did he persist in it, endangering not only his own reputation but his very means of livelihood? Wouldn't it be much better, they asked him, just to devote himself to his private practice and be content with developing Recovery only as an adjunct to it?

But, of course, Dr. Low could not listen to them. The thousands of mental patients in hospitals had troubled his conscience for almost a quarter of a century, ever since he had walked through the wards, stirred by their misery. It was for these that he had initially forged his Method, and he had seen it rehabilitate men and women who had been judged incurably insane. Now, no matter how widely Recovery spread or how many psychoneurotic people were helped by it, he would still feel a tragic gap until the hospital inmates had been drawn into the Recovery family too. It was the same fervor that in his youth had driven him across Europe campaigning for the Zionist cause. Now the scope of his zeal had been enlarged to include suffering humanity of all races and creeds.

Because he yearned so much to rescue those "lost ones" as he called them, he saw every crack in the frozen ice of his opposition as the harbinger of a thaw. He was pleased when Dr. Rudolf Dreikurs, an Adlerian psychiatrist and longtime supporter of Recovery, was able to arrange Phil's first self-help demonstration panel at the psychiatric ward of The Chicago Medical School. He was heartened, too, when at the 1953 American Psychiatric Association convention in Los Angeles he found an increasing number of psychiatrists becoming attracted to group psychotherapy and wanting to know more about Recovery. And he made full use of the opportunity he was given to tell them about it in depth when he was invited to talk before the American Society for Group Psychotherapy there.

Public Health departments in several states were also beginning to request lectures and panel discussions. And though it meant donating even more of his time, Dr. Low was so delighted with the whole promising situation that he wrote jubilantly to his brother Sol, "The only thing is that I have no time to reap the rich harvest. But things are moving in a very decisive tempo."

What most excited him was the cautious interest which the Illinois Department of Health and Welfare was again beginning to show in establishing Recovery in the state hospitals after long years of neglect. By early July he had received a firm request to help introduce Recovery to the eight-thousand-bed Manteno State Hospital. Two members of the Manteno staff came to headquarters and took intensive training under Phil and then began holding weekly meetings at the hospital.

2.

But with Dr. Low, as is common with most pioneers, his brightest expectations seemed to be always disappearing out of his grasp like fool's gold. There was, for instance, the little group which Dr. Carter had established in Denver and which was now still being supervised by Dr. Shere. Dr. Low, who was going to spend a very brief vacation with his family in Colorado, took the occasion to drop off and visit the Denver group. But what should have been a joyful occasion for him turned out instead to be one of the most disillusioning of his life.

Not that he wasn't welcomed wholeheartedly. A dinner was even given in his honor. And though he soon discovered that Dr. Shere had started to deviate somewhat from the Recovery Method, he would have tolerated this in itself in his zeal to get Recovery established. The one unforgivable sin so far as he was concerned was that Dr. Shere was charging members a fee to attend, while Recovery was based on the principle of a free self-help form of therapy.

Dr. Low objected forcefully and continued to do so after he had left Denver. But rather than make the changes required of him, Dr. Shere eventually simply withdrew from Recovery, and while continuing to use *Mental Health Through Will-Training* as his textbook, he formed his own organization which he called Security, Inc.

Back in Illinois Dr. Low ran into another even more heart-breaking disappointment. Manteno was languishing with the staff members complaining that they weren't obtaining results. Dr. Low sent Phil over to lead the panel himself and give a few pointers. But as soon as Phil got there, he realized that the situation was just as hopeless as it had been at Chicago State Hospital, and for the same reason. The patients weren't being screened and only one or two of them were sufficiently improved for the self-help therapy Recovery offered. So Manteno had to be dropped just as Chicago State Hospital and the Mount Pleasant hospital had been.

3.

Meanwhile, in Michigan a vibrant Treasure Rice, bearing little resemblance to the cowed young woman who had once averted her head from a railroad conductor for fear he would address her, now launched her campaign to get Recovery into the hospitals of her state. With the powerful backing of the Detroit *Free Press,* she contacted the director of the Michigan Mental Health Commission, and asked him to make an investigation of Recovery. He responded by sending a psychologist to her meeting. But though the psychologist returned with a glowing account of what he had found, months went by without any further action.

Next Treasure appealed to no less a personage than G. Mennen Williams, then governor of Michigan. Governor Williams granted her an interview and was so impressed with what she had to say that he requested the director of Mental Health to look further into the possibility of utilizing Recovery as part of the state hospital program, just as Dr. Low had outlined it to Treasure.

At its next meeting the Department of Mental Health discussed the question, but no one from Recovery was present to speak for the program. Instead, in November of that year Treasure received a blunt letter from the director informing her that on the motion of physicians, Dr. A. and Dr. T., ". . . the commission went on record as opposing any official recognition and participation in the movement known as Recovery, Incorporated. The motion was . . . unanimously carried. . . ."

In the *Recovery News* of February, 1954, Dr. Low was to comment on the situation with his usual succinctness: ". . . I know the views of Drs. A. and T. and know that, in the case of Michigan, Recovery was obstructed by these gentlemen. I have good reason, you will admit, to make the assumption that in Iowa and Illinois men with similar persuasion have done their part in opposing our efforts. It is worth noting that, in Michigan, Recovery was rejected without any serious attempt to study its procedure."

4.

But if the state hospitals of Illinois, Iowa, and Michigan had all slammed their doors on Recovery, there was an encouraging sign from another quarter, namely Ohio. In the late fall two visitors arrived from Cincinnati. One was a Catholic nun, Sister Marie Fidelis of the Good Samaritan Hospital, the largest Catholic hospital in Ohio. The other was Dorothy Kerchner, the clinical instructor in the hospital's small Psychiatric Department. Sister Marie Fidelis and Miss Kerchner had attended a demonstration panel put on for the hospital that summer and had come away so thoroughly impressed that they had traveled to Chicago to take leaders' training.

Dr. Low's eyes lit up when he learned that Miss Kerchner's brother-in-law, Dr. Douglas Goldman, was clinical director at Longview, the state hospital in Cincinnati. Would Dorothy talk to him about introducing Recovery to his hospital? he wanted to know. After seeing Dr. Low daily for a week both in private conferences and with his patients in the panel room at headquarters, Miss Kerchner readily agreed. Today, recalling her first impressions of this unique physician, she says, "Dr. Low was one of the most fatherly men I've ever known. True, he was very stern, but love was woven through his discipline. You felt it strongly, a very loving individual, a humanitarian. He had the kind of love most important to people who needed encouragement. His patients knew he would always be there, that he could be depended on. It was because he impressed Sister Marie Fidelis and myself so much with his dedication that we wanted to do something with Recovery—most especially for him."

So they went back and started a group for newly dismissed patients. They used a room in one of the hospital units, but they made it plain that what they were offering was a public service, open to everyone.

5.

By the end of 1953, Dr. Low could refer to no apparent success where the state hospitals were concerned, but he did achieve an opportunity to get the story of Recovery to large numbers of people when Miss Norma Lee Browning, reporter on the Chicago *Tribune,* became interested in the organization. Miss Browning had just completed a series of articles on psychiatrists and mental institutions, which had entailed extensive investigation in that field. When a letter from a Recovery member pointed out to her that her investigation had been incomplete because it hadn't included Recovery, Miss Browning became curious. One day shortly afterwards, she went down to headquarters to see what the organization was all about. She attended a panel led by Phil and was impressed by the directness of the panel approach. Afterwards, when she talked to the different members present and learned their stories, she couldn't help comparing their obvious progress with the negligible success she'd found among the patients of the psychoanalysts.

Finally Miss Browning read the book, *Mental Health Through Will-Training.* She was astounded by the clarity of concept and the simplicity of the Method. Here was no combing of the uncon-

scious for secret compulsions and complexes, no display of pun-
ditry with scientific terminology. Instead she found a philosophy
long discarded by the permissive school of psychoanalysis—that
man could and should govern his life by the use of his will.

Miss Browning attended several panels and then finally, one
Saturday, she heard Dr. Low for the first time. Nothing in her
encounters with other psychiatrists had prepared her for such an
experience. She saw this eminent doctor, trained in Vienna,
schooled in the Freudian method, repudiating the pedestal that
was the hallmark of his profession to talk to his patients as one
human being to others. She was impressed with his concern for
them, and his patients responded in kind. Who could help being
aware of the close-knit sense of fellowship that existed in that
room between doctor and patients?

Other surprises awaited her. When she asked him for an interview, he invited her to his home for dinner. No other psychiatrist
she had interviewed—and she had interviewed them all from
the Menningers down—had done so much. The home to which she
went was good upper-middle-class but not ostentatious. It was
obvious that this doctor was not enriching himself at the expense
of his patients.

But perhaps the greatest surprise was the doctor's wife, Mae
Low. She took an active part in the interview and was amazingly
knowledgeable on the subject of Recovery. She was the first psychiatrist's wife Miss Browning had met who, though not a professional herself, worked closely with her husband.

Miss Browning's enthusiasm, however, didn't prevent her as a
good reporter from probing mercilessly over and over again with
leading questions. But Dr. Low remained imperturbable, accepting the questions and interruptions, patiently making his point
clear, repeating it over and over: Psychoanalysis versus Recovery!
The stronger one, the one with more vitality, would win in the
end. That was the way of Nature, of all life, and he was sure that
Recovery would be the victor.

Miss Browning's article was printed on January 3 of 1954 and
given a full-page Sunday spread in the Chicago *Tribune*. This
time, Dr. Low noted with satisfaction, he had judged his reporter
well. Recovery had been fairly presented and he himself had not
been misquoted in any particular. In a letter to Ernest Hoffman

he was to say that it was ". . . perhaps the best and most forceful article on Recovery ever written. . . ."

The article was to be only the first of a series. The Chicago *Tribune,* like the Detroit *Free Press,* had such voluminous response that it, too, decided to sponsor the attention-attracting little organization. Miss Browning became a frequent visitor at the Low home as she mapped out ensuing articles. And it is a tribute to the Method that it stood up under this prolonged examination by one of the country's most critical reporters. Even more interesting was the fact that Miss Browning was well-equipped to pass judgment because she had made the field of mental health her special interest.

"I had been to Topeka and I knew the Menningers long before I knew Dr. Low," she says. "I had done many stories on them and they're tops in their profession. I've met all the leading doctors, I think. I did a tour of mental hospitals all over the country and I've watched practically every kind of treatment for mental patients —you name it, I've seen it. And I would say that I was more impressed with Dr. Low than with anyone else in the mental health field. My conclusion was that there wasn't anything that really helped the patients except Dr. Low's Method."

Miss Browning was also impressed by Dr. Low's forthrightness. "He spoke openly of the opposition he was getting, and then I admired him even more," she says. "There are only several big doctors who have bucked the Establishment in writing. And this is the kind of man Dr. Low was. He didn't care what the opposition said. This was something he believed in, and he obviously believed in it one hundred percent."

6.

Dr. Low was to describe the results of the Browning articles in an almost shocked letter to Treasure: ". . . Our Saturday meetings are now so overflown [sic] that we had to get a loud speaker for the surplus visitors which are crowded and huddled in our second room. This will soon be overcrowded. What we'll do then, I don't know."

The same phenomenon was occurring in his private practice:

"The flood of letters goes on like an inexhaustible torrent. Tele-phone calls are, of course, no longer counted. My appointment list has become a dragging waiting list, in spite of a raise in charges. . . . For me the development is a nightmare, for Re-covery it is a rare opportunity. . . ."

It was obvious he needed help and he didn't know where to turn for it. Finally he decided to appeal to an old Recovery mem-ber, Joe Janis. Following his internship the young doctor had obtained his first job, as a company physician for the CBQ railroad line. Joe had also been making housecalls for Dr. Low in his free time, and though he wasn't a psychiatrist, Dr. Low had found him very capable in his own field. He could be trusted with the purely medical side of things and that in itself would be a great help. So Dr. Low appealed to Joe and at his request Joe resigned from his CBQ position to join his former physician as an associate.

TWENTY-NINE

It was about this time that the Recovery members were able to persuade Dr. Low to start taping his extemporaneous speeches. Except for these providential tapes his voice and many of his insights would have been lost forever to future Recovery members. As time went by and the tapes began stacking up, Dr. Low decided to edit them and get records cut. Eventually four of them, each containing a one-hour lecture, were available to out-of-town groups at a minimum cost.

Meanwhile *Mental Health Through Will-Training* was already proving such a success that it had long since paid for its initial outlay. People from all over the country were writing in for it, and it had now gone into its third edition. The book sales were indicative of the new groups that were springing up everywhere. But in no place was the growth more phenomenal than in Michigan where, several years before, Treasure had made a vow to herself to blanket the state with Recovery. It had been a grueling, time-consuming effort for her and two faithful co-workers. First the two co-workers had gone at it a step at a time, using a map as a guide. They would pick a section and solicit publicity in the local papers. When they got a group together, they would take turns traveling there by train once a week to conduct meetings, sometimes getting back at three or four o'clock in the morning and then driving home from the station, often through blizzards. As soon as a leader was trained and the group firmly established, they would withdraw and tackle the next place.

In this manner Recovery got its start in Saginaw, a hundred miles from Detroit, then in Kalamazoo, another fifty miles farther. And still the circle widened, though as the women moved farther away from Detroit, things became more and more difficult for them. As soon as the groups had come into being, Treasure began traveling around the state visiting with them and conducting leaders' meetings. By that year of 1954 the combined effort had paid off and there were fifty well-established groups scattered over Michigan.

The groups in Michigan meant more work for Dr. Low in Chicago, but he welcomed the added burden. He was still as prompt as ever in answering Treasure's requests for advice on the members of her groups. And he would make room in his crowded day for the patients she sent to Chicago to consult with him in person.

Once at least he felt compelled to correct her concerning his fees, writing: ". . . You will not mind if I call your attention to the matter of my charges for consultations. Mrs. P. came with the impression that my charges are twenty-five dollars. This was correct some years ago. Today I have raised my charges very insignificantly. . . . But let me tell you that you have the privilege in special instances to recommend that the patient referred by you should be granted a reduction, let me say to twenty-five dollars."

But he even found ways to waive this fee in cases of extreme need, and some six months later he was writing concerning impoverished patients who wished to see him: ". . . I cannot afford setting a precedent whereby patients can take up my private time without compensation. You will understand that once this is established as even one incident in which I have agreed to give my private time free of charge, there may be subsequent candidates in large numbers. However, if the two [patients recommended by Treasure] come to Chicago, for, let me say, four or six weeks . . . then they can attend the daily meetings by Phil and can also attend my private Tuesday class, the fee for the latter being either waived or temporarily postponed. You can also tell J.R. that I will see him for brief periods of time before the meetings and after the meetings. In this manner we will keep in touch and on occasion I can ask him to come to my office without charge. This would not be construed I think as accepting a patient without compensation. . . ."

So he felt his way delicately around the issue, his purpose to bring help where help was needed. However, in cases of real hardship he had been known to send back checks uncashed. And he adamantly refused any fee from his "lieutenants." He wouldn't even bill them for relatives they sent him. When Treasure and her husband, now comfortably situated, tried to pay for one such relative the doctor wrote back firmly: "I will not make any charge to those people who are helping me get Recovery started."

Meanwhile, despite the flat rejection Treasure had received from the Mental Health Commission, she and her faithful groups continued to bombard both the commission and the governor with requests that the negative decision be reconsidered. They were joined by an impressive number of doctors who by now had become acquainted with Recovery and thought well of it, and who wrote letters asking the state to take a good look at the organization because they felt it had a lot of merit. Among these cooperative physicians was one of the psychiatrists who had treated Treasure in earlier years. At last the commission budged to the extent of sending Treasure a letter requesting her to make arrangements with Dr. Low to meet them in person.

But Dr. Low, disillusioned by his experiences in Iowa and Illinois, no longer had any hopes about such lukewarm invitations. If the people in charge were genuinely interested in Recovery, he wrote Treasure, they would contact him personally, and he concluded: ". . . By the way, the men seem to take the attitude that we are petitioners who request favors. That is the impression I have received both from their reactions and from the reactions of the men in Iowa and Illinois. It is necessary to correct this viewpoint and to suggest to the gentlemen we ask for nothing and offer our services to the hospitals without expecting any return of services or favors."

2.

Having been rebuffed so often by his own profession, Dr. Low had by this time begun to turn more and more to the clergy in his search for support. Father Dowling, who had never ceased leading his growing group in St. Louis, was taking an active part in spreading Recovery during his numerous lecture tours around the country. Up in Michigan Rev. Howie was continuing to endorse and aid the Brighton group. And the Rev. I. Paul Taylor, a Methodist minister from Detroit who had sponsored Alcoholics Anonymous in his district, had come with his wife to Chicago for a week's intensive training in Recovery leadership before opening their own group.

The clergymen's wholehearted sponsorship of Recovery was not without its hazards, for they, like some doctors, had a tendency to reshape the Method to satisfy their own viewpoint. Dr. Low must have winced to find his gentle old friend Father Dowling introducing parts of the Alcoholics Anonymous program into his Recovery meetings, including an opening prayer.

Father Dowling's example was being followed in Louisville, Kentucky, by Cleo D., the leader of the group there and a Catholic. Cleo, a dynamic and charming woman, was working with such zeal in the interests of Recovery that Dr. Low more than once voiced his admiration for her efforts. But he was unhappy about the delicate dilemma in which he found himself because of the prayers being offered at meetings.

Sometimes he discussed it with Treasure. "We might as well write off these groups because they will be religiously oriented," he told her. "But how would it look if I tell them they can't use a prayer? It would sound as though I'm against God. So I can't object too strenuously. But it is not my psychiatrically oriented Method, and it can't be accepted as the Recovery way. It is not the purpose of Recovery to save souls, but to rid patients of their symptoms."

He regarded this situation as such a serious threat to the Recovery Method that on one occasion at least he had taken Cleo D. to task in a letter dated March 30, 1951. It reads in part:

"My dear Mrs. D.: You will remember that I told you not to be afraid of making mistakes. Well, you made one and I want you not to be afraid because you *have made* a mistake. The mistake which I refer to is in reference to the interview in the *Courier-Journal* of 3/26/51. The article states that the Recovery practices are comparable to AA, and that religion plays a part in the program. These are mistakes which we wish to avoid in the future. Recovery, Inc., I feel, is so distinct and so radically different in method from other procedures that we do not wish to be made the object of comparison with similar endeavors. At any rate, religion is certainly no part of our program, except insofar as we frequently mention religious matters in private and even in public utterances. But that does not make religion part of our program.

"We do not by any means object to publicity, but it will be more expedient in the future to have any interview or other publicity matters submitted to Annette Brocken for approval before it is printed. . . .

"I hope you don't mind my giving directives in such detail. Again, remember: We don't criticize for mistakes, but we reserve the right to call mistakes to the attention of our workers asking them to avoid them in the future as much as possible. . . ."

The subtle dangers of mixing Recovery and religion were very apparent to Dr. Low as a versed psychiatrist, because of such patients as Ann Landis who were already suffering from religious obsessions. He saw a real danger of worsening their illnesses if Recovery were allowed to become even slightly colored with religious practices.

As for his own philosophy, he explained it even more thoroughly to Rev. Howie, who made a special trip to Recovery headquarters to try to get Dr. Low to add at least an opening prayer. "It would put a whole different tone to the Recovery Method," he explained. "It would be akin to faith healing. But the Recovery Method is a method of self-help. It all depends on the self, the individual. In AA they say there is a power higher than we are. But in Recovery we say we are average, which connotes we are under something."

Despite Dr. Low's firm divorcement of Recovery from Alcoholics Anonymous, comparisons between the two groups have persisted in the years following his death. Actually the only similarity between them is that they meet in groups led by laymen. Their differences are fundamental. Alcoholics Anonymous is founded on religious and psychological principles directed toward solving a one-pointed condition, while Recovery is founded in concepts running the whole gamut of psychiatric problems. Dr. Low was so keenly aware of the divergence of outlook that, while admiring the work done by Alcoholics Anonymous, he remained adamant against letting the simple Method he had evolved for his patients become adulterated by the more confining approaches of AA.

3.

Sometime in early spring Dr. Low received the long-delayed personal invitation to meet with the Mental Health Commission of Michigan on April 23. He permitted himself, as usual, a guarded optimism concerning it: ". . . I shall make every effort to be accommodating, and I shall definitely manage to approach them with an open mind. There is just a chance that they will be willing to appoint a man to come to Chicago for at least a full week to investigate the work done at headquarters."

But seeing the Mental Health Commission wasn't Dr. Low's only purpose in going to Michigan. The Michigan clergymen had become so enthusiastic about Recovery that they were organizing a public forum to bring it to the attention of numbers of people, and he wanted to discuss this project with them in person. Even more important, he was eager to meet with the Michigan Recovery leaders. So began his epic visit to Detroit. What optimism he had held with regard to his meeting with the Mental Health Commission was quickly dissipated. The discussion was polite, but it was soon made plain to him that Recovery would not be welcome in Michigan's state hospitals.

His conferences with the clergy were far more fruitful. But as he had expected, it was his meetings with the Michigan Recovery leaders that were the highlight of his stay. All his affection and whimsy for these "patients" of his, most of whom he had never seen before, came out as he addressed them. He spoke to them of the chain of command, reminding them, "I want the members in your group to look to you as the leaders, and I want you leaders to look to Treasure. Treasure will look to me as her leader."

He paused and then added smiling, "Never mind to whom I look."

He spoke to them, extemporaneously as always, on a topic of their own choosing: "Waiting"—the wait for the longed-for cure and the patience it required, one of the hardest and yet most necessary principles of Recovery to grasp. During the course of that classic talk, he emphasized the importance of self-endorsement, because he'd found it so often neglected by his patients.

"This is central to Recovery," he told them. "So why won't you endorse yourselves? Even God endorsed Himself. Do you remember when He said, 'Let there be Light,' and there was? And after each one of those statements the Bible says, 'And He saw that it was good.'"

Afterwards a professor of history at a Jewish college in Detroit pressed a small manual into his hands. It was an aid that would help Recovery people study the book, he said. Dr. Low inspected the carefully prepared manual. He knew from its thoroughness that the man must have worked long, hard hours to compile it and he praised it highly. Then firmly he shook his head. "No," he said, "It's a very fine work, but I don't want anything like this. I want my patients to get it out of the book for themselves." He never approved of aids in the use of the Method. The book was to be pored over, thumbed through, read and reread. There was no facile way to obtain a thorough training.

Others far less learned than the professor crowded around. Some asked for advice on pressing problems, but most were eager just to express their heartfelt gratitude to him. How could people profess so much love for a man whom they scarcely knew? he asked himself, visibly shaken.

Later from the depths of an overpowering emotion he answered that question in his letter to Treasure: ". . . I was simply overwhelmed with their [the patients] enthusiasm which was undoubtedly spontaneous. . . . It was, of course, a revelation to me of something that, in physics, is called distant action. If men and women can display deep feeling toward a person whom they hardly know concretely, that cannot be the result of mere magnetism, certainly not of literary tricks and oratorical skill; it is simply the result of feelings touched and responding. From the beginning to the end, my contact with the patients was a running display of a profound attachment in which soul speaks to soul. If that is the basis on which Recovery is resting, there can be no doubt that a vital and lasting value was bequeathed to those suffering minds. I have felt it, but now I know it."

At headquarters he told them simply, "It can go on its own without me. I saw it in Detroit. Now we can start to expand—expand the Michigan way—because the leaders can carry on by themselves."

4.

That June 4 Dr. Low returned to the rally in Detroit. Nothing
could have kept him away. For once he had determined before-
hand the subject of his talk. It would be "Patients Offer Help to
the State Hospitals." While stating the case plainly for Recovery,
he meant to avoid all inflammatory or controversial subject matter. This was to be a night of conciliation, not of battle.

With the help of the *Free Press* the rally had been well pub-
licized and the auditorium was packed with more than a thousand
people, while two or three hundred more had to be turned away.
The size and attentiveness of the audience moved Dr. Low, but
he was touched most deeply by an incident that occurred as he
was making his way through the hall to the podium.

A woman to whom he had given a simple piece of advice during
his last visit, shyly edged up to him and, sobbing with gratitude,
began to pour out her thanks as she told him how he had transformed her life. Then suddenly, completely overcome, she caught
up his hand in hers and pressed it to her lips.

"Let me kiss your sweet hand," she murmured through her tears.

The poignant incident, together with the numbers of eager,
earnest people packed in the auditorium that night hanging on
every spoken word, solidified his wavering determination, as later
he was to write to Treasure: ". . . After Michigan has definitely
gone on record as disapproving Recovery techniques for the state
institutions and after the Illinois Psychiatric Society has, in writing, refused to meet with me, I have no hesitation any longer to
announce, at meetings or in the press, that the state hospitals are
unwilling to do their duty to their patients. I feel that . . . tens
of thousands of patients are crying out to us to rescue them from
the danger of first admissions and subsequent relapses. We have
to heed this desperate outcry. It was perhaps a dereliction of duty
on our part to have waited seventeen years. It would be criminal
neglect now to abandon this army of sufferers to a cruel fate, now
that we know that the authorities refuse to save them, that they
are even reluctant just to take a look at the one method that
claims to have the method of salvation. . . ."

So he dropped his role as bystander in the Recovery publicity campaign and joined the battle with a deliberate frontal attack of his own. He was by no means ignorant of what this might mean to his own career. He wrote Treasure: "As concerns me, I am utterly indifferent now to the danger of being hailed before the medical authorities for possible disciplinary action. . . ."

He was not blind as to the form that action might take. In his talks to his private group psychotherapy classes, the warning phrase would slip from his lips from time to time, preparing them for the worst: "If my license should be taken away . . ." Always his concern in that eventuality was not for himself but for those whom he had served so faithfully for so many years—his beloved patients. Whatever happened to him, Recovery had to be kept alive by any means in his power. And so he urged leaders everywhere to forget the state hospitals for the present and to concentrate "on the great issue of winning over the churches." It was a desperate move based on the realization that the clergy were beyond the jurisdiction of his profession. They could nurture Recovery in case of disciplinary action to himself.

THIRTY

Over the years Mae Low had seen her husband carrying an ever increasing workload, but at no time had she found him so strained and preoccupied as in that summer of 1954. If only she could get him away from everything so that he could relax completely. He'd often spoken of wanting to see Lake Louise because he'd been told it was so like those lakes in the Swiss Alps upon whose shores he had had such pleasant outings as a young man. That summer the thought of it appealed to him so strongly that Mae had little difficulty persuading him to take a short family vacation at the resort town of Banff.

Toward the end of July he wound up his affairs at the office, and leaving his patients in the care of Joe Janis and Phil Crane, he set out with his family. They went by train because they all enjoyed this leisurely kind of travel. Dr. Low in particular reveled in the opportunity it gave him to catch up on his reading. However, he found the trip very tiring and he was bone-weary by the time they reached the hotel in Banff. That night illness struck with a soaring fever and delirium. Over and over Mae heard him moaning, "Oh, my poor patients, my poor patients. What's going to happen to them? And what's going to happen to Recovery?"

Mae called in a local physician and he diagnosed the illness as lobar pneumonia, a disease he had not observed in years. The small Banff hospital was too overcrowded to take him in, so Mae nursed her husband at the hotel and the doctor came twice a day to give him injections of antibiotics.

As the fever subsided and Dr. Low became lucid, he asked Mae

276

to write Phil informing him of the situation. The touching letter, dated July 28, concludes with an expression of sympathy and understanding for all those who would be so vitally affected by it: ". . . Dr. Low asks me to tell you that he knows that this complication will strike his patients both in Illinois and outside the state as a heavy blow. He asks you to assure them that he experiences the blow as heavily as they do. Also, Dr. Low asks you to tell whomever inquires that he cannot accept correspondence. The dictation of this letter alone has made him feel exhausted."

After a fortnight Dr. Low, though still very weak, insisted on returning to Chicago for a thorough examination by his old friend Dr. Grosz. Dr. Grosz, finding a great deal of fluid in the pleura, ordered bedrest, but his colleague didn't prove to be a very cooperative patient. After only a week or so he began importuning Mae to drive him down to Recovery headquarters to take care of the work piling up for him there. And when she refused, he made the attempt himself. By the time he reached the office he was so weak he had to hang onto his desk to steady himself while Caroline watched horrified. Nonetheless he stuck it out for several hours, looking after essentials, and then managed to get home again, still driving. But he could hardly creep into the house and he offered no resistance when Mae put him back to bed.

2.

For at least another week Dr. Low stayed in bed, but Mae couldn't help being painfully aware of how unhappy he was, like an amputated man. Part of him, the Recovery part, had remained in the headquarters on Michigan Avenue. So when presently he began insisting again that he had to go back to his patients, she agreed to drive him there and home if he would curtail his work to no more than three hours of counseling a day. He agreed to this, but gradually as the weeks went by he began to increase the hours and to resume his Saturday afternoon panels. To all appearances he was recuperating nicely.

Then one night he went to the hospital to see a patient. It was the first time since that day he had forced himself to go to the office that he had been out alone and Mae worried about him.

When finally he returned she was shocked at his appearance. He
was so weak he could hardly walk, and the next morning he asked
her to take him to see Dr. Mackay.

Dr. Roland Parks Mackay, a highly respected neurologist, gave
his colleague a thorough examination and then ordered him into
the hospital immediately. But Abraham refused. He needed a few
days to make arrangements, he said. Mae, who knew him so well,
realized that he was asking for those days of grace only to face facts
and prepare himself.

But even that little period of adjustment was to be denied him.
On the way home to Evanston, he suddenly collapsed against Mae
as she was driving down Sheridan Road. Fear and anguish gripped
her, but she kept her presence of mind. She needed help and
traffic police were the only ones who could give it to her, but she
would have to attract their attention. She kept driving out of line,
breaking rules flagrantly, all the while pressing her hand down on
the horn until its racket almost deafened her. People glared.
Others honked back. Some yelled, but no traffic policeman appeared. It was like a nightmare. Then finally she was home.
Leaving her husband slouched in the car in a coma she rushed into
the house and summoned the police. They came and carried him
up to his bed, while Mae phoned Dr. Mackay. Soon an ambulance
was speeding with her stricken husband and herself back to
Chicago and St. Luke's Hospital on Michigan Avenue. On the
way Abraham became conscious again. His whole right arm and
side were paralyzed but he still retained his power of speech.

In the days ahead neither Dr. Mackay nor the team of other
prominent neurologists, including Dr. Eric Oldberg and Dr.
Low himself, could decipher this strange phenomenon—a right-
side paralysis without any loss of speech, since usually such a
paralysis affects the speech muscles also.

Those were anxious days for the whole family. Phyllis was away
in Denver where she was starting her first year at the University
of Colorado. Marilyn was still at home, a sophomore in high
school, but she saw little of her mother who was now practically
living at the hospital helping to care for her husband.

Even there Dr. Low, handicapped though he was, continued his
work for Recovery. The letters were pouring in, letters from
patients and from Recovery members, not only those in Chicago

but in the outlying branches as well, letters from sympathetic doctors. Dr. Low sent for Caroline to take down answers to all these letters and also ideas for the upcoming November Recovery Convention. Once out of the fullness of her heart to cheer him up, Caroline exclaimed, "You know, Dr. Low, one can learn a lesson from you. And that is that you're carrying on the best you can, sick as you are."

Yes, he was very sick, how ill he himself recognized. Sometimes he spoke forthrightly to her about it, "Caroline, if I should be no more . . ."

"Dr. Low, don't say that," Caroline would cut him short.

But he wouldn't be deflected. "If I should be no more, I hope Recovery continues. It's all there, if only the patients use it."

Phil saw more of Dr. Low than anyone else those days. He was a daily visitor at the hospital where he would come after the panel was over to spend an hour or two at the bedside of the sick man. And he always brought a copy of *The New York Times* with him because Dr. Low enjoyed so much reading it.

Every day as Phil entered the room, Dr. Low would greet him with the old familiar question, "Well, how did it go today? Did you keep it simple, Phil?" Then over a cup of coffee Phil would tell the doctor all that had happened at the meeting and they would discuss the problems of Recovery in general. The affection between the two men was obvious. They enjoyed each other's company, but they worked also. Dr. Low had already taught himself to write with his left hand. And slowly and painfully throughout the day he'd scribble down material. Then when Phil came, he'd hand over the awkwardly written notes.

Some described fresh techniques and insights into the use of the Method. Others were points to bring out the great principle of the Recovery organization—the principle of group-mindedness that could not be allowed to become dimmed or obscured by time. Over and over again Dr. Low would remind Phil that Recovery could succeed only if the members realized its true mission was to bring health to disturbed people and worked together to that end, relinquishing their individual tendencies to sovereignty and vanity.

There, too, on his hospital bed, Dr. Low made his last effort on behalf of the patients in the state hospitals. It was in the form of a pamphlet entitled "Recovery Versus Psychoanalysis" and was allegedly authored by Phil. Actually it was dictated to him by Dr. Low, who used it to set forth bluntly the differences between the two modes of therapy and to illustrate the practical advantage of Recovery over psychoanalysis as a form of treatment. Dr. Low's hope was that wide distribution of this paper, ostensibly written by a former mental patient, would rouse the public more than any declarations by a professional, and set up a clamor that would eventually open the state hospitals to his form of therapy.

3.

Maxine was often on Dr. Low's mind during those days. She'd been a good and loyal worker in the public relations department, carrying out all his requests as he had known she would when he had selected her. The amount he'd been paying her was paltry in comparison to all the time and effort she had been putting in, and he was disturbed by it. One day he told Phil, "I want her to get a hundred dollars from now on."

He also wanted to see her. But Maxine, with her nurse's perception, felt that he was dying and simply couldn't find the courage to face him. At last one Saturday afternoon Phil said, "Don't you think that if I got a cab and picked you up and went with you, you would go?"

"I just don't believe I can . . ." Maxine began in a trembling voice. But as soon as she had said it she knew she would have to. She couldn't let him down.

That afternoon found her with Phil at Dr. Low's bedside. He'd lost a lot of weight since she'd last seen him, and his whole right side was so paralyzed that he had to lift his right arm with his left hand to place it where he wanted it. But he certainly didn't behave like a dying man. His mind and spirit were as energetic as ever. And he was so genuinely pleased to see Maxine that she was deeply touched.

It wasn't just a social visit. He gave her some letters he'd received and told her he wanted her to contact the writers and also to contact newspaper editors and the wire services to get them to do stories on the upcoming Recovery convention. Besides this he had several other important people he wanted her to approach. One was Dr. Walter Alvarez, the medical columnist. Dr. Low admired Dr. Alvarez for his integrity, and he hoped Maxine would be able to persuade him to help Recovery along by endorsing it in his daily column.

Maxine promised to carry out all his requests. What a fighter he was! Though he acknowledged that death was quite possible, he was far from resigning himself to it.

"Magzeen," he told her as she was leaving, "if I get over this, I'll come down to Recovery in a wheelchair if necessary."

Maxine was crying as she went down the hall from his room. Yet there was a lift to the day from having seen him, a sense of strength and purpose that dwarfed her own feeling of depression and gave her incentive. However ill she felt, she'd do everything he'd asked of her, she promised herself. It would be such a pleasure to be able to go back and let him know that things had been taken care of.

4.

One day a little more than a month after he'd been in the hospital, Dr. Low suddenly turned to his wife and said, "I want to go to the Mayo Clinic and see the men there."

The words filled Mae with a sense of dread. Once, years before, she had heard a doctor remark, "If I ever get critically ill I want to go to Mayo's, because there the department makes the decision, so no one colleague has to take the blame for it if I should die." Was that what Abraham was thinking of now? she wondered.

That afternoon Phil paid his last visit to the hospital. As he started to leave he felt he had to say something memorable that would cheer Dr. Low on his way.

"Dr. Low," he said, "isn't it a great thing that you were able to show the entire psychiatric profession all by yourself how this self-help method can be developed to prevent relapses or chronicity in former mental and nervous patients?"

Dr. Low didn't reply so Phil repeated it in simpler words—

words that would express his sense of gratitude to the man who
had led him out of the darkness of mental illness. "It's such a
great thing, Dr. Low, that you all alone could do this . . ."

He saw the familiar smile touch the haggard face.

"Yes!" the voice rang out clearly, acknowledging at the same
time the gratitude of this former patient and dear friend, and his
own frank awareness of the contribution he had made to humanity. It was this understanding of his unique role in life that
had kept him going in the face of all opposition.

The crisis at Mayo's came quickly. One afternoon shortly after
Dr. Low arrived there with Mae, she returned from a quick
shower in her hotel room to be greeted by his voice, once so strong
and vibrant and now turned halting and slurred. She stopped,
shocked to hear him say, "They're going to have to operate on my
brain, Mother." And he added, "Isn't it ironic that this should
happen to me—I who have devoted my whole life to the curing of
mental illness?"

Then he told her to get paper and pencil. With a numb heart
and a cramped hand Mae began to take down his slow, painful
messages. He was putting his affairs in order, she realized, preparing for the finality of death. The first request he made was
regarding his funeral. He wanted to be buried in his daughters'
church by their pastor, whose three sons were numbered among
the girls' good friends. Even if it meant going against the religion
in which he had been reared, he did not want to add confusion
to their grief or make them feel separated from him at the end
by choosing the funeral services of a faith strange to them.

Next came his final instructions for the welfare of Recovery,
his third child. One of the most important of these concerned the
little paperback book, *Lectures to Relatives,* which he earlier had
had mimeographed for the use of his patients. But after the publi-
cation of *Mental Health Through Will-Training* he had allowed
Lectures to Relatives to go out of print. This small book, containing the gist of his talks to relatives in the old Psychiatric Institute days, was actually a classic instruction on how to get along
with nervous patients. And Dr. Low, realizing its value, had been
making copious notes just before he was stricken to bring it up to
date. Now in his halting voice he asked Mae to locate those notes,
to make the revisions and additions he had indicated, and to get

the book published, a chore which she was subsequently to under-take, but only long after her first grief had finally spent itself.

From Recovery matters Dr. Low passed on to more mundane concerns—the auditor to be contacted in case he didn't come through the operation, the lawyer to be consulted. Finally there were notes to his relatives except Selma and Rebekka and Ben, all three of whom had already died. Slower and slower went his speech as he dictated. By the time the final instruction was given his voice had trailed away and Mae had to lean close to catch his words.

5.

In Chicago they had held the November Recovery Convention for which Dr. Low had been planning so enthusiastically. It had ended the Sunday night of November 13. The following day head-quarters received word that Dr. Low would be going into surgery on Tuesday. Before then, he ought to have a message about the success of the conference, Caroline thought. He'd been banking on it so much, but she was too upset to feel she could write it. So she appealed to Maxine.

"Well, Caroline," Maxine quavered, "I don't know whether I can or not either, but I'll try."

She sat down to compose the message. There were so many things she wanted to get across—especially the knowledge that Recovery would live even if he didn't pull through because she knew that would relieve his mind. At the same time she wanted to word it in such a way that he wouldn't get the impression that people really didn't expect him to live. The tears splashed down on the paper as she wrote. She described the convention and how wonderful it had been with all the representatives gathered from the various out-of-town groups. Several hundred had come, so many they couldn't all get into the National Headquarters room but had to stand in the hall outside. They had missed him, of course. But his absence, instead of making them disheartened, seemed only to give rise to an even greater spirit of cooperation. Everybody was rattling around trying to help everyone else, to raise despondent spirits. Nobody was breaking down. Recovery was proving itself a truly self-help program. Now they all wanted him to know their prayers were with him.

6.

The surgeons in the operating room still didn't know what had caused the strange paralysis but the loss of speech had at last pin-pointed the area of trouble and they knew where to look. The incision was made and the truth was revealed—multiple abscesses that had been slowly forming throughout his illness. Under the circumstances no operation could be performed. There was no hope. The surgeons closed the incision.

But still he lived on. For thirty-six hours after the attempted operation the strong heart continued to beat, though he lay in a coma and died without ever regaining consciousness. It was less than three months since he had contracted pneumonia at Lake Louise.

In a letter to Mrs. Low by way of post-mortem, Dr. Mackay was to state that after a thorough study of the findings submitted to him by the Mayo Clinic, he like them, believed "that his pneumonia was, in all probability, the actual cause of the abscesses." But in a private conversation with the widow he was to add that in his opinion the heavy doses of antibiotics which had been administered, together with Dr. Low's refusal to remain in bed and rest during those first critical weeks of his illness, had been a major factor in his death. It had enabled the poison to get into his bloodstream and spread throughout his body, causing the deterioration of vital organs.

THIRTY-ONE

Day by day during Dr. Low's illness Phil had kept the panel members faithfully informed of his condition through Mrs. Low, who had sent in frequent bulletins from the Mayo Clinic. The final tragic message was received over the telephone on Thursday by Caroline Philipp. He was gone, Mrs. Low told her.

"Do what you can in the office, Caroline," she continued in a voice that struggled to remain calm. "Carry on."

How did one carry on in the face of a catastrophe so immense? Caroline sat, white-faced and shaken. It took a great effort for her to get up and pass the word on to Phil, who was at that moment in the meeting room preparing for the Thursday afternoon panel. He and Caroline looked at each other mutely. Soon other Recovery members would be coming in.

"Shall we play a tape today, Caroline?" Phil asked uncertainly.

"I don't know, Phil," Caroline answered. "I just don't know."

Phil considered gravely and then suddenly he decided, "I think we should play it."

He set up the recorder and selected a tape, a short one so as not to force them to listen to that hauntingly familiar voice any longer than was necessary. At the same time it would help them to realize through example that Recovery was too important to them to let even death break up the familiar routine.

The tape he selected was entitled "Temper and Temperament" and it was only fifteen minutes long. But Phil had picked it for more than its brevity. It contained valuable techniques that would help them all through this ordeal. In Dr. Low's own words it pointed out that severe responses to outer events cannot be helped, but that one can and should control one's reactions to such responses. Let the grief come, not fighting it, but not enlarging on it either. That was the Recovery way, Dr. Low's way.

Phil waited until all the panel members had gathered before telling anyone the sad news. He simply couldn't bear to go through it again and again. When the clock pointed to one thirty he opened the meeting promptly, promptness being one of the dictums Dr. Low had laid down. Now, at last, he made his announcement, "Dr. Low has died. But we're going to carry on with the great organization he founded. That's what he would want us to do."

There was shock in that room at his words, exclamations of grief, and then a deadening silence. People sat motionless with tears rolling down their cheeks while the tape was played. Once again in their ears, the encouraging voice rang out. But he was gone. That was the knowledge that hung heavy in the room.

Then a sudden inexplicable thought came to Phil, a thought that cut through his grief with the surety of revelation. When the tape ended, he spoke it aloud, "Dr. Low will never die."

Now the panel had to go through the motions of being a panel— of giving examples and spotting on examples. How they got through that day, few could have explained later. It was like moving in a dream, a dream too painfully real.

Caroline sat in the office where she answered phones, greeted visitors, and took care of the paper work and where so often in the past she had taken dictation from Dr. Low. The murmur of the familiar voice floated down the hall and the realization struck her forcibly that she would never see him again. Tears were streaming down her cheeks, but she thought, "This is the real test. This is it. Dr. Low said use the Method, and I'm going to use it. I'm not going to get myself into a mess." And she began her sad task of notifying everyone.

2.

In Michigan the news that Dr. Low had died struck Treasure a stunning blow. Ever since he had returned from Lake Louise she had been concerned about him. Each time she had received one of his vibrant letters so full of plans for handling the future Recovery campaign, it had been hard to think of him as a sick man. Nevertheless, every letter had given her a sense of foreboding that had brought tears, despite the cheery tone of the writer.

One of the last letters was from the hospital in Chicago. It had expressed the hope that Treasure could come to the convention and that she would visit him at St. Luke's when she did. But of course by that time he was already at the Mayo Clinic. Now the telephone call brought home to her the finality of the death she had been fearing for months. In her grief she phoned Rev. Howie, who had known and admired Dr. Low so much. He would understand the depth of her loss. As she broke the news to him, she began to sob so that she could scarcely talk.

Rev. Howie came over to the house immediately and took Treasure's hand in his and said a comforting prayer with her. Then, because he knew that sometimes a little practical help is needed too, he offered, "I'll just go over and tell them what's happened and lead your meeting for you tonight."

The man who had given Treasure the Method by which she had worked her way through the dark tunnel back into the light was gone now. But she knew what had to be done and her Recovery training had established habits of control in her. She could have her grief, but she didn't have to act it out. She could bear it and perform as a leader where others had need of her.

"No," she said, "thanks, Rev. Howie, but I'll take care of it myself. Dr. Low has trained us to move our muscles."

Moving her muscles during those next hours was an excruciating torment for her. All that long dreary afternoon it was difficult for her to keep from giving in to her sense of desolation and just going to bed. Eating dinner was a chore she could scarcely get through. She kept bursting into tears, composing herself, doggedly shoving in another mouthful, bursting into tears again, while her little daughter Treasure Ann stared bewildered and upset by her mother's grief. Treasure would have liked to spare the child, but she simply could not stem the tears.

With the aid of Recovery techniques Treasure got through the day without collapsing. And that night, armed with a tape, she went over to the meeting. There they were all gathered, the people Dr. Low had called his "dear ones." Some of them had been to Chicago to be treated by him. Others had known of him only from his infrequent visits here, or just from his voice on the tapes. But all had loved him.

Treasure felt that to announce his death before the meeting would only be to disrupt it. They needed Recovery and Recovery practice more than ever now. So she forced her muscles to act and trusted her basic functions to perform properly and wore a mask, forcing back the tears and smiling, even laughing, though her heart was heavy. And so holding herself together, she managed to conduct the panel. It was only when it came to an end that she told them.

"Well, we have some bad news," she said gently. "Dr. Low has passed away."

Heads went down all around the table. There was the sound of sobbing. And the room seemed filled with a great emptiness. Somehow in that fellowship of grief it seemed a cement was formed to bind them more tightly together in Recovery than they had ever been before.

3.

The funeral, as Mae Low planned it, would be a simple one. Services would be conducted by Dr. Walker, the girls' minister, at the Hebblethwaite Chapel in Evanston. Mae had chosen the chapel because, being connected with a funeral home, it would keep the services from having any particular denominational flavor. She asked Phil to be chief pallbearer and to select five others from among the patients who had been closest to her husband.

Saturday was chosen as the day for the funeral, because it would enable as many of Dr. Low's patients as possible to attend. But she knew that both the funeral arrangements and the choice of day could not be approved by the Low family, since they belonged to the Orthodox Jewish faith. So she contacted them one by one to apologize and explain that this was in accordance with Abraham's dying wish.

Once the funeral was arranged it fell to Caroline to notify the patients. And everyone had to make up his own mind whether he could bear the shock of that last sad occasion or whether it would be wiser to stay away.

Treasure came in with the Howies. When she arrived at the chapel she found a large number of patients already there, with many more on their way. Most of the Lows had come from around the country. Who could have guessed that in the next two and a half years Abraham would be followed by all the remaining Low brothers, including half-brother Nutek, still only in his forties? Of the immediate family this would leave only Theresa, and Fanny who had gone to California and married Joe Alvarado, a widower, and was helping him bring up his daughters.

Nat's young attorney son Leonard, also from California, attended the funeral and was struck by the people he saw around him. There were several hundred mourners and they came from all walks of life. Private patients in furs and expensive clothes mingled with humble people in simple dress. But rich and poor alike were united in one common emotion, a deep sense of loss.

Most of them showed remarkable control as they filed into the funeral hall. But occasionally one or another would break down and have to be led away to compose himself before returning. Treasure and Maxine sat together, clasping hands for comfort. All around them others were clinging to one another. The little chapel was soon packed.

The service was simple. Now and then there was the sound of muffled sobbing, but otherwise the room lay in a deep hush. Treasure's gaze going from face to face alighted on Phil. He had been closest of all to the doctor, had seen most of him during those last days. Yet he sat there calmly subdued, full of an inner strength to which Treasure clung. Then, as she watched him, she saw a tear beginning to gather in the one eye visible to her. It welled up, broke, and ran down his nose and off his chin. He never bothered to wipe it away. Somehow to Treasure that tear expressed more poignantly than any other single event the emotion that pulsated in the silent room.

4.

During the difficult weeks that followed, Caroline Philipp remained true to the promise she had made to herself the day she had learned of Dr. Low's death. She wouldn't let herself get into a mess. She recognized she was in a setback. There was the old familiar depression hanging over her like a gray cloud day after day, so that she had to force herself to work. The head pressure was back, too, the feeling that her head was in a vise which was slowly being tightened.

But Recovery had taught Caroline that lowered feelings and head pressure were to be expected at such a time. Even an average person would suffer symptoms over the loss of a loved one. And she knew she could handle them all if she just didn't center on her own misery but thought of the others who needed her.

There were many of them. Often the phone would ring and a panic-stricken voice would come over the wire, "What am I going to do? I don't know where to turn now that he's gone."

With a calm she didn't feel, Caroline would reply, "It's true he is gone, but we still have the tools. Dr. Low left them for us." And she would spot for the callers, "Take the secure thought. Don't work yourself up. Come to Recovery if you can."

The answer would be a wail, "But will Recovery keep on going? How can it last without him?"

"I promise you Recovery will last," Caroline would reply. "I don't know just how, but we're going to go on."

Phil Crane was holding up, too, despite his grief. He never skipped a day but continued to conduct the panels in the same unruffled, unhurried manner he had learned from Dr. Low. He felt deeply that there ought to be a fitting memorial to the doctor in the room where he had given his talks every Saturday afternoon. So he kept the lecture table Dr. Low had used in its exact position, on the platform at the front of the room. On the table he placed a copy of *Mental Health Through Will-Training,* and the sheet giving the outline of the four steps of the example. That book and sheet of paper commemorated not only the man but the Method he had evolved—the Method that Dr. Low had always insisted was greater than he.

Phil hadn't exactly believed in the truth of that claim during Dr. Low's lifetime. He'd always had the feeling that over and above the Method he could rely on the doctor's judgment in a pinch. It was only after his death that Phil suddenly realized he'd been handling both his private life and the work at the office without help for several years now. And he'd been doing it through the Method.

Headquarters with its poignant memories affected people differently. Some Recovery members could no longer bear to come down and sit in that room full of so much of him. They would stop at the door around one thirty and look in to see if the panels were still going on. Just knowing Recovery was there seemed to give them some kind of comfort, even though they left at once. Others couldn't stand the strain and broke.

Maxine was one of these. She had been Dr. Low's most severe nervous patient and it was remarkable that she was able to hold herself together for several months until she had kept all the promises she had made him in St. Luke's that day. But by July of 1955 she felt the need of professional help and hospitalized herself in Passavant Memorial Hospital.

The other long-time members held up, however: Frank and Harriette Rochford, Agnes Dumont, Gertrude Beres, Ann Landis. Their sense of loss was agonizing, but they were able to recognize the difference between that grief which was genuine and the panicky thoughts and feelings which circled around it and which would have to be controlled.

5.

Shortly after Dr. Low's death a new face appeared at the Recovery panel meetings. It belonged to Charlotte Shamberg. During the two years she had been going to Dr. Low, Charlotte had consistently refused to have anything to do with Recovery. Then, a couple of months before his death, she'd gone into a severe setback and had stopped seeing him completely. Now she kept remembering how he had told her, "With the help of Recovery you will get well." The only other alternative was to see another psychiatrist and go through her life history in depth again. The thought was too sickening for Charlotte to contemplate, especially since analysis had never proved successful for her before. So one day she forced herself out of the house and down to headquarters.

Charlotte began attending panels three times a week and ducifully worked on "moving her muscles" and "doing the things she feared to do." But though she was able to prove to herself that she was as capable as those around her, she refused to relinquish

her belief that she was on the verge of insanity, so she went right
on suffering. Then finally, after two years of arduous training,
Charlotte woke up in the middle of the night to exclaim to herself,
"Why, of course I'm not going mad," and with that changed attitude her tensions faded and a complete cure came quickly.

Looking back at her experiences today, Charlotte says, "I don't
mean to minimize Dr. Low because I think he was a genius to
have understood the patients' needs and created a cure. But it was
not he but his system only that cured me. It was the completely,
totally self-help, self-discipline of his Method."

Other newcomers were dropping in at headquarters to prove
eventually the truth of Charlotte's statement in their own lives.
They had never known Dr. Low, and were being brought in by
the publicity the little organization had been receiving during the
past year. Even though Dr. Low was gone, even though they
would find only sufferers like themselves gathered in the headquarters room, they stayed and were helped. Recovery, bereft of
its medical director, was once again displaying that amazing
vitality which had always so astonished Dr. Low.

All the same the little organization was in a precarious situation. The directorship had lain firmly with Dr. Low and now that
he was gone an executive brain was needed to guide the organization into its new role of complete self-management. One person
had proved herself very capable along that line—Annette Brocken.
She had worked closely with Dr. Low through many years, knew
his thinking, and had organizational talents. When she had gone
into semiretirement from Recovery, she had promised, "If ever
I'm truly needed, call on me and I'll come back."

So they summoned her, and Annette contacted Mrs. Low because she knew she couldn't do the monumental work alone.
Would Mrs. Low join her on the Board of Directors and help
her steer Recovery through those difficult days? There was nothing
Mrs. Low would have enjoyed more than to retreat from the
unhappy scene and find peace and fulfillment in her daughters'
unfolding lives. But it was impossible for her to desert her "third
child" in its hour of need, and so she agreed to work with Annette
in the gigantic task of reorganization.

THIRTY-TWO

A whole volume could be written about the development and growth of Recovery down through the years that followed Dr. Low's death, beginning with Annette Brocken and Mae Low, those two valiant women who worked hours on end revising its structure along new, completely lay-oriented lines. They were an heroic and dedicated pair, each contributing her share to the project. Annette brought her genius for organization. Mrs. Low brought her intuitive understanding of Recovery and the stored wisdom of her husband's views, confided to her through their long marriage.

Their chief anxiety in those days was that leaders in the scattered groups around the country would overstep the bounds of a layman's knowledge in their conduct of meetings and bring discredit on the organization as a whole. They knew that such indiscreet behavior could very well cause the psychiatric profession to unite in a concerted action to crush Recovery, already the brunt of so much controversy.

Because the two women realized that mistakes would be made as they felt their way through the intricacies of reorganization, they personally handled all important correspondence that came to headquarters. Each letter was painstakingly composed. They must make no compromise with Recovery's integrity as a self-help organization, while maintaining cordial relationships with professionals and the public. The correspondence took hours and when it was judged complete it would be left at headquarters to be typed up by Caroline to mail out.

In 1956 Treasure joined Annette and Mrs. Low on the Board of Directors. To see how Recovery was doing outside Chicago she began traveling across the country with Phil, who was now being kept busy giving training conferences for the groups that were mushrooming everywhere.

Treasure was touched by the people she found coming so eagerly for help. There were psychoneurotics of all descriptions. Some had been bedridden or house-bound for years by their symptoms. Others were crippled with phobias of various kinds. Among them were pathetic young mothers suffering postpartum depression with its attendant dread of harming their children or of committing suicide. Recovery was also attracting alcoholics who through Alcoholics Anonymous had been able to eliminate their drinking, only to find that they still had major emotional problems. Improved mental patients recently discharged from hospitals were coming in accompanied by their relatives.

Like seeds in a wind, Recovery was being sown across the land and was striking root wherever it fell, for the need was great. Sometimes it was carried by leaders who had left their homes to take up life in new places and felt they couldn't get along without it. Sometimes sufferers, who had been forced to drive two hundred miles in a single night to attend meetings elsewhere, would go to Chicago for instruction from Phil and then establish Recovery in their own communities.

In January of 1961, the well-known writer Eleanor Harris, now Mrs. Jack R. Howard, wrote a stirring article about Recovery which appeared in the *American Weekly* and National Headquarters was swamped with some 17,000 letters of inquiry. Most significant of all, psychiatrists were beginning to voice approval of the organization's group psychotherapy format and the Method on which it was based, and were referring their patients to it as an auxiliary to their own treatment.

From all she observed Treasure realized there was no longer any need to fear for Recovery's life. It was growing stronger every day, and everywhere she went she found the same infectious enthusiasm that had from the first been a characteristic of Recovery members. Over and over again when she returned from her travels she would pour the wonderful news into the incredulous ears of her two co-workers.

2.

Even the most resilient human body can take only so much. The most unflagging zeal and determination must find its limitations. And so it was with that indomitable warrior, Annette Brocken. Ever since 1954 she had been driving herself mercilessly, handling two difficult jobs at one time. As 1960 approached, the weight of those past six years of work and harassment were resulting in a rundown physical condition.

She suffered a severe attack of flu and was given drugs to fight it. As was later discovered, she had an allergy to the drugs and they threw her nervous system into the old imbalance, bringing back all her former symptoms. Annette hung on as long as possible, but finally she knew she couldn't continue, and she had to resign from the Board.

Now Mrs. Low and Treasure alone carried on the work. Presently it became all Mrs. Low could do to drag herself to headquarters for a night of letter writing. A leaden fatigue had settled upon her and there was a tightness in her chest, which though she didn't suspect it at the time, was the beginning of lung cancer that in several years would require major surgery. Often now, after only an hour or so, she would have to stop with a plaintive apology, "Oh, I don't think I can stand it, Treasure. I'm going to have to go home. I'm so sorry."

"I'll just carry on here," Treasure would reassure her. And she would stay behind in the empty office until the last letter was answered and then turn off the lights, close the door and lock it. In the jet black outer corridor she would grope along the wall to the elevator.

On her shoulders lay the weight of her extraordinary responsibility, for she knew that Mrs. Low was too ill to help her much longer. But she kept thinking of the varied talents she had seen among the Recovery members she had met in her travels. There was Betty Keniston in San Diego, John MacDonald in Canada, Dick Bertke in Cleveland, Paul Rozay in New York, John Lozar in Milwaukee, Harold Eidelman in Detroit, Millie Scanlon in Kansas City. If she could bring all these people together to form one Board, Recovery would have invaluable counsel.

She and Mrs. Low discussed it. Money was the problem. Together they went over Recovery's slender resources, totaled up the figures, and found that it could be done. A Board made up of leaders from across the nation could be brought to Chicago at frequent intervals to complete the work of reorganization.

It would take many pages to recount the tumultuous meetings of that board. There were no "yes men" on it and when they got together sparks flew. But because everyone was using the Method to keep from pressing for "symbolic victories," they were sparks which benefited Recovery, and out of that creative melee the final work was done to refit the organization for its new role.

The Board meetings were only a fraction of the reconstruction that was going on. Treasure, utilizing John MacDonald's talents as a lawyer, had asked him to help revise the bylaws so Recovery could be structured along the lines of a democracy. Most of their correspondence was by tape, to save time, and everything they evolved was presented to the board members to be wrangled over and amended and finally approved.

Eventually Treasure was elected president, and Betty Keniston, chairman of the Board. These posts, like those of the Board members, were to be held by volunteers. But John MacDonald was asked to go on salary in the newly created office of executive director. At the same time the salaries of those two faithful workers, Caroline Philipp and Phil Crane, were raised to make them commensurate with salaries received for similar positions in the business world.

The increase in salary at last made it possible for Phil to ask Maxine to marry him. He'd been dating her for years, but he'd never allowed his thoughts to go beyond that because he was still semidependent on his mother's largess. So in a quiet church wedding Maxine Kennedy became Mrs. Maxine Crane.

3.

As Recovery continued to grow, one of the most important decisions it had to make concerned finances. Expenses were increasing at such a rate that it was difficult at times to make ends meet. Under such circumstances a grant either from private or government sources could look very tempting. However, after careful consideration it was decided not to seek one, for fear that restrictive clauses in such grants might hamper the freedom of the organization and corrupt the Method. So Recovery, determined to retain its unique self-help status, still depends for its support on nominal yearly memberships, free-will offerings, and outright gifts.

Another problem which Recovery has had to face since Dr. Low's death, is familiar to any large body made up of diverse human beings. This is the difference of opinion and clashes of personality which break out in various sections of the country, burdening the organization with its share of inner turmoil. Most of these differences have been resolved with the techniques Dr. Low left behind in the Method. However, it is normal for some disagreements to prove so irreconcilable that they ultimately result in a few splinter groups. The first to separate themselves from National Headquarters were the Louisville and St. Louis branches. Since then there have been temporary dissident groups in such places as Dallas, Buffalo, New Orleans, and Los Angeles.

For whatever reasons, breakdown in communications or organizational and administrative differences of opinion, the dissenter in Recovery in most instances demonstrates his own individualistic desire to be in power, as opposed to the more difficult and laborious task of group effort upon which the national organization is built. In spite of the fact that this organization was founded by Dr. Low, a psychiatric authority, as the repository of his proven Method, a dissenting member will sometimes find others who are likewise disposed and form a splinter group. Some have the unrealistic hope that in their organization all will go smoothly and differences will not plague them. Others have their own pet theories, or ideas borrowed from some other self-help group, which they attempt to graft onto the system of techniques worked out so carefully by Dr. Low.

Early members worried about the discredit such groups might bring upon Recovery. Today organization leaders have developed a more tolerant understanding. They realize that most of the dissenters, along with other temper-trapped associates, have only succeeded in exchanging one set of management problems for an even greater one. And at the same time, they have unwittingly separated themselves from the national organization that has earned the respect of the general public. Reluctantly, in some instances, Recovery is forced by circumstances to protect the public and referring professionals from the confusion brought about by the fact that often the dissenting groups trade on the name of Recovery, Inc.

Usually, however, the problem is a passing one, because it has been made apparent throughout their historical development that the groups that deviate tend to lose their vitality and eventually dissolve. This holds true even if such groups are under the supervision of competent psychiatrists. When legitimate Recovery came to Denver, Security, Inc., dwindled away and disappeared. And at least one well-known doctor has been heard ruefully warning a colleague, "Back Recovery, but don't meddle with it, because if you do, it won't work. I tried it."

4.

Throughout the years clergymen have continued their interest in Recovery. Many Jewish rabbis, Protestant ministers, and Catholic priests today recommend it to their troubled parishioners. It was a Protestant minister, the Rev. Robert Johnson, who started the first Recovery group in Cleveland, Ohio. And thousands of Catholics have been brought in by pamphlets written by Father Hugh Calkins, O.S.M., of Chicago, and the late Father John J. Higgins, successor to Father Dowling in Missouri.

One of the most interesting developments among the clergy has taken place at the Via Coeli monastery just outside Albuquerque, New Mexico, where the Society of Paracletes has a rest home for priests who have alcoholic or serious psychiatric problems. The superior of the monastery, Father John Feit, who several years ago suffered breakdowns serious enough to require three hospitalizations, testifies that he has kept his mental health since through the use of the Method. Accordingly he is holding two Recovery study meetings a week for the priests in his monastery. In addition the priests drive in once a week to Albuquerque, some sixty-five miles away, to attend the open meeting there.

In reference to religious groups special mention should also be made of the various Jewish philanthropic organizations in and around Chicago. Ever since 1953, when Dr. Low was first invited to speak to The Friends of the Mentally Ill, these organizations have been among Recovery's most loyal backers. Through the years fifteen of them, including ORT, have regularly asked for demonstration panels, and the Council of Jewish Women in particular has shown an active interest. In 1957, when the Council raised $50,000 to start The Thresholds, a professionally super- vised after-care organization, it began to encourage those who came to it to attend Recovery. Later, after Thresholds had expanded with a sister clinic called Thresholds North, Recovery was asked to hold regular weekly meetings there.

5.

In this modern day with its emphasis on group psychotherapy, Recovery has found innumerable new backers among sociological workers who are beginning to recognize it as a valuable adjunct to their rehabilitation programs. Professor Stephen Cohen, of the University of Chicago College of Social Service Administration, who requires his students to visit various psychotherapy groups, places Recovery along with Alcoholics Anonymous at the head of his list of musts.

"The students who take my course," he explains, "are those who will probably be going into psychiatric counseling. They should know about such an organization because the need is so far ahead of the available professional personnel that communities and patients and local people are going to have to learn how to help each other and not wait for the doctor to come and help them."

Recovery has proved itself so dramatically in its home city of Chicago that the local Mental Health Association is now honor- ing Dr. Low with a Dr. Abraham A. Low Volunteer of the Year Award. In recognition of Recovery's layman status this award is to be presented to the relative of a patient or former patient who has rendered outstanding volunteer service to the mentally ill in metropolitan Chicago.

Mental Health clinics in other sections of the country, too, have begun turning more and more to Recovery, because of a lack of professional help, especially as local and national funds become woefully inadequate to handle the growing need. In Portland, Oregon, Verne A. Davis, director of Field Services, expresses the feeling of many of these clinics when he says: "I am much impressed with the growth and service of the Recovery program in Oregon. Recovery 'self-help psychotherapy' has gained wide acceptance. Its service to communities of this state is unique and truly remarkable."

Casper, Wyoming, is a good example of what is happening. The Mental Health Committee there appealed to Lloyd Glasier, area leader in Denver, to get a group started in its community, offering to furnish $350, all it had available, toward the necessary expenses for plane fare there and back. Recovery supplied the rest, and over a period of six weeks several Denver leaders made the necessary sacrifice of time and effort to open up the new group and train a leader for it.

Usually Recoveryites themselves take the initiative in apprising mental health clinics of the availability of Recovery. When Dr. David Wade was appointed state commissioner of the Texas State Department of Mental Health in 1970, Irving H. Finkler, Recovery area leader in Dallas, wrote him a letter of congratulation and sent him some Recovery literature. Dr. Wade was so impressed that he arranged to have Recovery brought to the attention of mental hospitals and mental health and retardation centers across Texas as an available therapy for discharged hospital patients. Recovery was also invited to put on a demonstration panel for interested staff members in the auditorium of the State Department of Mental Health in Austin.

It was such a demonstration panel conducted by Phil Crane in Nebraska in 1969 that attracted the attention of Herbert Rooney, chief of the Citizen Participation Branch of the National Institute of Mental Health. Subsequently Mr. Rooney invited Recovery members to put on a panel and take part in a Citizen Participation Round Table discussion at the National Institute of Mental Health in Bethesda, Maryland. He has become a firm backer of Recovery and his estimate of its value follows:

". . . From my observation the Recovery Method seeks to supplement, not supplant professional assistance. It cooperates rather than competes with the mental health professions. In my view, Dr. Low developed a valuable Method, which provides useful techniques for people, based on an appreciation of their strength and abilities to help themselves.

" 'The mentally ill do come back' becomes a reality, not a slogan, when one has the opportunity to meet with and listen to Recovery members who indeed have come back to family, job, school, and community. . . . In addition to the help each member receives from practice of the Recovery Method, I feel the willingness of the members to speak publicly and personally of mental health problems truly represents the consumer as an educator for the general public's better understanding. . . ."

Another recent development for Recovery is the interest business concerns have begun showing in it, with the idea of setting up courses to train their employees in the Method, in order to improve relationships among them. Much of this interest is due to the demonstration of the Method by their own employees. In New Orleans, for instance, Recoveryite Bob Coke so impressed his employers at the Sears, Roebuck store that the personnel manager attended several Recovery meetings to see what it was all about and now advises employees who display emotional problems to attend Recovery.

6.

The small complex of offices in which Recovery headquarters is housed has recently been renovated at the members' expense, but there have been few changes in personnel. However, in 1968 John MacDonald gave up his position as executive director to work for the Canadian Government, though he was to continue serving Recovery on a volunteer basis. His place was taken by Douglas Elbert, area leader from Seattle, Washington. In 1969 Treasure Rice stepped down as president and Lloyd Glasier took her place, while Millie Scanlon, area leader from Missouri, took Betty Keniston's place as Board chairman. Then in 1970, because of serious illness in his family added to business obligations, Lloyd Glasier relinquished the presidency and was elected Board chairman, while Treasure Rice was reelected president. By 1971 the needs generated by the growth of Recovery had forced the Board to adopt an experimental plan for a year by putting in the field a second salaried leader under Phil Crane, national director of the department. Irving Finkler was chosen for the job.

Every year from all over the country representatives still meet for the traditional gatherings established by Dr. Low and the first Recovery members—the May Convention and the National Training Conference in November. It has been a long while now since National Headquarters has been able to accommodate them all and they gather at the Palmer House, the big hotel in the Chicago Loop, their board and room expenses paid for by the particular area from which they come. Even here they fill the large convention rooms provided for them by the hotel.

With each year the roll call has grown longer as the list of states increases. Today forty-five states are represented, besides Puerto Rico. And now Recovery's vision is beginning to span the Atlantic and the Pacific. The Society of Paracletes has established a study group for their priests in England and another in France. A number of years ago an unofficial Recovery group was formed in Australia, and recently two groups have been started in Ireland. Mike Shuster, formerly a leader in the Los Angeles area, and Robert and Rivka Gold, also from Los Angeles, have migrated to Israel and established a group in that country.

At the present time Recovery members are concerned about expansion in another direction—toward the youth of the nation. Treasure Rice's charming daughter Treasure Ann, a young woman herself now, has found the Method so valuable in her own life that she is convinced it should be brought to the attention of all her troubled generation. Recovery leaders, impressed with her effectiveness, are sending her on periodic tours to attract young people to the organization. And at conventions she is asked to conduct meaningful dialogues on means of reaching her contemporaries with the Recovery message.

7.

For more than a decade Mae Low was a familiar figure at the conventions. She had a great and understandable pride in this organization which had so wonderfully vindicated her husband's faith in it. And she enjoyed meeting new members and making them feel at home. But by 1970 a recurrence of her illness had so drastically curtailed her activities that she was unable to attend the moving tribute paid her at the November Conference. The event was tape-recorded for her so that she was able to hear and enjoy the messages from old and new members. There were citations too: from the mayor of Chicago, the governor of Illinois, and the President of the United States, who also sent a personal letter commending her for her valiant efforts on behalf of those tens of thousands of sufferers who had profited from her selfless efforts to preserve Recovery. Shortly afterwards, on January 20, 1971, Mae Low died, leaving behind two daughters, now married, and three grandchildren.

Of those early members who engaged in that remarkable partnership with their physician, two have preceded Mrs. Low in death. The first was Harlan Tarbell, who became national president of the Society of American Magicians before he died. The other, Ernest Hoffman, was killed in a hit-and-run automobile accident. But up until the time of their deaths both men had led healthy, active lives. As for all the others, once consigned to pass their days in hopeless invalidism, they, too, are vital, happy human beings. Some, having been cured, have left Recovery. Others, though cured also, continue to do service as volunteers. And one, Dr. Joseph Janis, having entered the field of psychiatry, supports and forwards the work of Recovery both with his patients and members of his profession.

New faces have joined the old familiar ones at Recovery meetings across the nation. And as these thousands of new members regain their health, many among them cheerfully take up their share of the responsibilities and workload of the now flourishing organization. It has been through the efforts of this army of willing volunteers over the span of years that the motto which Dr. Singer once bequeathed to Dr. Low has been fulfilled: "It had to be done and it was done."

THIRTY-THREE

"New ideas, if they are not just a flash in the pan, generally require at least a generation to take root," wrote Dr. Carl Gustav Jung. "Psychological innovations probably take much longer. . . ."

So it appears to have been with Dr. Abraham A. Low's Recovery, Inc., which roused such animosity in his own day. Yet a changing attitude was actually at the door when he died. With the passage of time, more and more doctors were turning from the long, involved Freudian analyses to newer theories and methods of treatment. And with the recognition of the therapeutic value in interpatient relationships, group psychotherapy started coming into its own, so dramatically that today even psychoanalysts are recommending Recovery to some of their patients.

Time has brought a change, too, among the heads of state hospitals where once Dr. Low battled so desperately to get Recovery, Inc., accepted. It began in Cincinnati and if Dr. Low had lived only a few months longer he would have seen the fruits of Dorothy Kerchner's visit to Chicago, for she did speak to her brother-in-law, Dr. Douglas Goldman. And in 1955 Phil was invited to put on a panel demonstration at Longview State Hospital. Dr. Goldman was so favorably impressed that he gave Miss Kerchner permission to start a group there. And ever since he has been a faithful supporter of Recovery.

In evaluating the reasons for its success with mental as well as psychoneurotic patients, he writes: "Dr. Low showed that by bringing patients who had benefitted from psychiatric treatment together, they could help each other reach an understanding of

304

psychologic, emotional and physical reactions within themselves through the processes of group communication, in which patients further along in their rehabilitation process would assist others in achieving the goals of resocialization and rehabilitation. Dr. Low's method included the development of a vocabulary of terms to label the kinds of symptoms that patients at this level of improvement from gross illness usually manifested. . . . Patients who are actually no longer psychotic find themselves to be like other people and not freakish or monstrous. This is particularly important for those who at the height of their illness manifested grossly deviant conduct and severely disturbed thought processes which are not entirely forgotten when the pathologic processes are terminated by good psychiatric treatment. Such individuals are particularly likely to be frightened by manifestations which they may interpret as the beginnings of recurrence or the residuals of the severe illness. Uninhibited discussion of these symptoms, particularly with the help of those who have gained a measure of control, helps patients to suppress automatically the subjective aspects of these reactions just as all people learn to suppress irrelevant noise in listening to the world around them.

"It is important for patients, for leaders of Recovery groups, and others interested in rehabilitation of formerly severely and chronically ill psychotic individuals to recognize that the group processes of Recovery, Inc. are not a substitute for psychiatric treatment, that psychopharmacologic and psychotherapeutic activity must be continued to maintain a solid matrix for the rehabilitation that is to be produced by the Recovery group. The Recovery group serves to re-introduce an individual into the working and social world and help make him self-sustaining and self-sufficient."

2.

When Dr. Low visited California in 1953 he was quick to recognize the bent of its citizens for novel approaches to life and was subsequently to state his conviction that its soil would be fertile for the growth of Recovery. Dr. Low's estimate has been borne out by Camarillo State Hospital near Los Angeles, because this hospital was among the first to introduce Recovery to its ward patients.

It began when Donald T. Lee, chief of the Social Service Department, became interested in the organization after reading about it in the early Fifties. By 1959 he was urging members of the Bureau of Service Work to look into the program as a means of helping patients on convalescent leave from the hospital. For several years Mr. Lee exerted every effort to bring Recovery into the hospital itself, and finally, in 1966, he was given permission by the head psychiatrist to start a Recovery group there. To conform with Recovery policy, Mr. Lee is now trying to get an outside group established in his vicinity, so that patients can be bussed to it, the system approved by Dr. Low at Mount Pleasant.

In evaluating Recovery as a therapy, Mr. Lee says, "Many times patients can't take things said to them by professionals, or they become dependent on professionals to work things out over a length of time. And there aren't enough professionals to do this, and never will be. But what Recovery shows us is that people can help themselves and help each other. And I feel professionals could devote more time to making it possible for this sort of thing to take place."

Another state hospital in California, Patton, near San Bernardino, has more recently begun bussing patients once a week to a nearby Recovery meeting. This was brought about by Dr. Orval Cobb, a long-time Recovery backer himself, when he took up residency in psychiatry at the hospital. Shortly thereafter he began campaigning to get Recovery recognized as a valid form of therapy. Within two years his efforts, backed both by insistent patients and enthusiastic hospital technicians, were successful.

In analyzing Dr. Low and his work, Dr. Cobb says, "He had a better insight as to what was going on within the patient than the average professional in the field. He not only grasped the causes of mental illness and understood what was necessary to cure the individual, but he also was aware of what was needed to maintain health once the cure was reached. It was no less than a new way of life, because if the patient went back to the old environment he would become ill again. Recovery enables the patient to establish that new way of life in his own inner environment."

In Wichita Falls, Texas, it was the enthusiastic staff members of the state hospital that brought Recovery to their town. The staff became so impressed by the improvement in a young woman named Billye H., a former hospital patient who for two years had been driving 120 miles to attend a Recovery group in Forth Worth, that they persuaded her to open her own group at home so that they could send patients to it.

At the state hospital in Norfolk, Nebraska, and the Nebraska Psychiatric Institute, Dr. Richard Sanders, the head psychiatrist, and Mr. Louis Moody of the Social Service Department, took a joint interest in sponsoring a similar group in their vicinity. Once it was established they began referring a constant stream of patients to it.

Even in once inimical state hospitals such as Fort Logan, Colorado, where in earlier days patients were actually forbidden to attend Recovery, the climate has changed. Now the staff at Fort Logan invites Recovery to put on demonstration panels there and makes many referrals of patients to local groups.

The same story is being repeated in many state hospitals across the nation, but nowhere have doctors and staffs become more enthusiastic about establishing Recovery groups for the benefit of their patients than in Dr. Low's home state of Illinois. The climate of the whole state is so ripe today for the spread of Recovery that the Coordinator of Community Relations for the State of Illinois Department of Mental Health has given Mrs. Mary Jane Maggio, area leader there, a letter of introduction to each of the state institutions in Illinois and has not only promised her his complete support but is urging her to step up her work of presenting panel demonstrations to state and veterans' hospitals because the full impact of Recovery is now beginning to take hold and the organization should not let up at this critical time of its development.

In 1969, after several panel demonstrations were given at Elgin State Hospital in Elgin, Illinois, the head psychiatric social worker and Mrs. Maggio held a lengthy discussion concerning ways and means of bringing Recovery to the patients there. The result was that a group was established nearby. The leader of this group is a former patient from Elgin State Hospital. And once a week, as in the case of the state hospital at Patton, patients are bussed to the meeting.

Dr. Werner Tuteur, the clinical director at Elgin State Hospital gives his estimate of Recovery in the following words: ". . . ever since I entered psychiatry during the early Forties I have been very close to Recovery and have been sponsoring the organization wherever and whenever I could. I feel that Dr. Low's concept of the "Internal Environment" was a stroke of genius and the past decades have proven that it is infinitely more important than all external manipulation."

Because of the success of the Elgin venture other Recovery groups are being developed near the community halfway-house hotels in central Chicago which are for improved but not yet cured patients. One such group is being established near the Psychiatric Institute to serve both the outpatients and the improved in-patients. With this group Recovery will have returned, after all these years, to repay its debt of gratitude to the Institute which first nurtured it.

Appraising Recovery, Dr. Melvin Sabshin, head of the Department of Psychiatry at the University of Illinois Medical School, where Dr. Low was on the teaching staff for so many years, says, ". . . I have had a recent opportunity to observe some of the work of this fine organization. In my judgment, the concept of ex-patients helping current patients is most often helpful and quite practical. The concepts embodied in Recovery, Inc., fit well with many of our modern ideas regarding crisis intervention and community psychiatry in general. I hope that your book will indicate there are many psychiatrists who support the concepts and practices of Recovery, Inc."

3.

When Dr. Don Verger, head of the Department of Psychology at Wisconsin State University in Platteville, was an undergraduate student in Chicago he used to attend Dr. Low's Saturday lectures. ". . . in addition to hearing Dr. Low's lectures," Dr. Verger writes, "I had the opportunity of approximately a dozen conversations with him. . . . One day he mentioned to me that he had offered to train Veterans Administration psychiatrists in Recovery techniques, but they declined his offer. . . ."

It took some fifteen years for Dr. Low's dream of introducing Recovery to veterans' hospitals to materialize. One of the first moves in that direction was made on the West Coast by Dr. Harold

Snow, chief of the continued treatment service at the Sepulveda Veterans Hospital in West Los Angeles, California.

It was sometime in 1958 or 1959 that Dr. Snow's attention was drawn to Recovery by an unusual circumstance. The daughter of one of his friends had developed an obsessive compulsive neurosis and the doctors were advising a lobotomy for the condition. Dr. Snow had recently been reading an article about Recovery which had stated among other things that Dr. Low had found the obsessive compulsive neurosis responded well to Recovery techniques.

In an effort to avoid the lobotomy, and at the same time to ascertain the accuracy of the statement, Dr. Snow recommended that the girl attend Recovery meetings five times a week. She did so, reading the book and practicing the Method assiduously over an eighteen-month period. During that time Dr. Snow gave her no psychiatric counseling, his only contact with her being to encourage her to continue her Recovery training. Yet when at the end of that period he repeated the psychological tests he had had her take when she first came to him, he found a 95 percent improvement in her condition.

Dr. Snow became so intrigued that he decided to do some research on Recovery through a controlled experiment. He established six Recovery type groups. The members, who were all volunteers, were examined before and at the close of his experiment, which lasted for almost a year. He also kept careful statistics on the types of examples which were given at the various meetings which he visited frequently for a period of three months. He discovered that true to Dr. Low's own observations, most of the examples and the subsequent spotting on them were concerned with hostility and methods for controlling it.

This experiment firmly convinced Dr. Snow of the value of Recovery and he began wholeheartedly recommending it to patients who came to him. Eventually, with the help of a Recovery group in West Los Angeles, he was able to get a group established at the Sepulveda Veterans Hospital. When he was transferred to Palo Alto in 1961 he again contacted local Recovery leaders and through their help another group was formed on the hospital grounds and remained in operation there until Recovery headquarters decided to adopt bussing to outside groups in all hospital situations.

Dr. Snow finds the Recovery Method so valuable that he is sure
it could be applied with profit in a far wider field than that of
emotionally disturbed people. "I have felt it would be the best
thing teachers could take," he says. "But then it's good for people
in all walks of life. I think the President of the United States, you
and I, everyone, would be benefited by Recovery."

4.

Estimates by individual psychiatrists of Recovery's usefulness have
come in to the authors in numbers from professionals in both the
United States and Canada. From among them we have selected the
following passages to show the various types of patients doctors
are referring to Recovery and the Method's effectiveness with a
wide variety of illnesses.

Dr. Rudolf Dreikurs, professor emeritus of psychiatry at The
Chicago Medical School says, "Recovery is one of the many groups
of what one can call 'self-help.' Dr. Low provided a framework
for such endeavors. The members of Recovery often exert a much
stronger and more effective influence on patients than psychiatrists
can do. The psychiatric guide for the members of Recovery is
provided by Dr. Low's book and tapes.

"One can only hope that the technique discovered by Dr. Low
and continued by Recovery will spread throughout the country
and provide help where such help is often unobtainable through
the established channels."

Dr. Beverly T. Mead of St. Joseph's Hospital in Omaha, Nebraska, says, ". . . all contacts that I have had with Recovery,
directly or indirectly, have left me very favorably impressed. Recovery is very useful in the treatment of a wide variety of emotional
and mental disorders. It is valuable when used as the only means
of therapy, and it serves as an excellent adjunct to other types of
therapy."

Dr. D. H. Moogk of Kitchener, Ontario, Canada, has discovered
that it "suits best patients with compulsive personalities who cannot work effectively in psychotherapy. Hypochondriasis, inade-
quacy also respond well."

Dr. H. J. Albers of Denver, Colorado, who has been sending

many patients to Recovery over the years and has found that those who attend at least six months all show some benefit, writes, "My high praise of the Recovery Method, besides, of course, its benefits to the patient, springs from two important factors: 1) It has given me a far deeper understanding of the nervous person's suffering. 2) It provides, in terms understandable to the lay person and most acceptable to a physician, a common ground for discussing nervous symptoms and Recovery techniques. There is no communication breakdown or barrier such as exists when the physician and patient cannot share a common language. Dr. Low's philosophy at the end of each chapter is the most realistic approach to daily living I have ever read. . . ."

Dr. Thomas P. Lowry of Kentfield, California, sees in Recovery ". . . a method by which nervous people find strength, growth, and mature comradeship."

Dr. Harold Caviness of Battle Creek, Michigan, writes ". . . I approve strongly of the method for patient self-help and symptom control in follow-up of hospitalized psychiatric patients. It seems to me about one-half to two-thirds of the patients I refer who give the method a fair try really benefit not only from the emotional support of the 'group therapy' but gain a positive philosophy of living effectively in spite of residual symptoms or only a partial cure by psychiatric professional treatment."

Dr. Jerome Hochwalt of Dayton, Ohio, says, "I stand in admiration of the program and continually recommend it for the proper patient."

Dr. Leonard E. Egerman of Pittsburgh, Pennsylvania, says, "I feel that Recovery, Inc., has a real service to perform. I would encourage more and more education of the leaders."

And Dr. Edward J. Delehanty of Denver, Colorado, who has been a backer of Recovery ever since Dr. Shere established his unauthorized group, Security Inc., there, writes, "Recovery has been a most valuable adjunct to me in my psychiatric practice. Since I am an advocate of 'Reality Therapy,' Recovery fits well into the philosophy of personal responsibility of the patient who must learn to 'live himself into right thinking rather than thinking himself into right living.' The knowledge that Recovery brings to the patient that he is not alone and that many others suffer the same nervous symptoms as he does and yet seem to make an adjustment to life is the most potent factor in Recovery's approach."

Dr. B. E. McLaughlin of Grand Forks, North Dakota, who claimed Dr. Low for a professional friend during the time he himself was a professor in Philadelphia, writes, "We have sent literally dozens of patients to Recovery here in Grand Forks since the movement started approximately two and a half years ago . . . one of the reasons I feel our unit here has been successful, is that it has been backed by the University of North Dakota and the various departments interested in mental illness. It is our experience that about one-half of the patients sent fit into Recovery, and the other half drift away. . . . Recovery lends itself particularly well here in this rural community because socialization is so much a problem in the scattered farms. We felt, in our developing mental health movement here, that it would be a very fine adjunct to the community services and has proved such. I feel that it will be a long-time adjunct to community psychiatric programs in this country and in the rest of the world."

Dr. M. W. Lathram of Methodist Hospital, Memphis, Tennessee, who had referred approximately fifty patients to the group in his city with "very high" results says, "I am probably one of your greatest admirers. Just keep up your good work."

Dr. Robert S. Carson of New York City, in a letter to a Yonkers, New York, area leader, after explaining the circumstances of his introduction to Recovery eight years earlier, writes, ". . . I have subsequently referred a large number of patients to the program. . . . In my personal experience as a psychiatrist, I have seen numerous examples where the patient's participation in the Recovery program has prevented hospitalization and other prolonged and expensive incapacitations. . . . I have been especially impressed with the language of Recovery. The terms are quite descriptive and tend to dramatize the problem areas in what I believe to be a highly effective fashion. With my own patients who have been active in Recovery, I have noted that as they become familiar with the language they instinctively begin to replace unhealthy patterns with healthier ones."

Dr. A. Finlayson of Brantford, Ontario, who has referred one or two patients monthly with 75 percent success says, "In my work as a psychiatrist, I find Recovery particularly helpful with many of my patients, particularly those who have had difficulties with interpersonal relationships. Although not suitable for all psychiatric cases, I find it extremely helpful in those cases where loneliness and insecurity have been factors in the reduction of their emotional symptoms."

Dr. Robert E. O'Toole, director of the Adult Mental Health Clinic of Youngstown, Ohio, says, ". . . The typical case I refer is an individual who has gained insight into himself but still reacts in an inappropriate habit pattern. I also feel that many people not suitable for insight-oriented therapy may gain significant improvement. I may place heavy pressure on a patient to initially attend a meeting but never pressure him to continue. . . . Many of my patients have responded very well to Recovery since it provides a system, answers, etc., which are lacking in usual therapy. It is certainly not for everybody but I know of no therapeutic system that is."

One of Dr. Low's most ardent backers in the psychiatric field prefers to remain anonymous. He writes ". . . since 1956 when I first read Dr. Low's *Will* book I have combed it through with a fine-tooth comb of scrutiny and criticism and I have come to the conclusion that, if any man deserves the Nobel prize, he does! I am serious about it. I sincerely believe the man knew more about psychopathology than anyone in history, and, what's more, developed a method to arrest symptoms and in many cases effect a *cure*. Who else anywhere has matched him? He is the only man I can honestly say I look up to, admire, and respect for the awful pioneer struggle he must have put up against odds. . . . Today . . . Dr. Low's followers, even from a book, continue to recover because he was so right. But not only his psychiatry. I was impressed with all he had to say from raising children to college educations, etc. God bless that man and I hope you people thrive and spread, for you all have much to give to a sick world."

5.

Doctors in fields other than psychiatry have long been aware of the psychosomatic nature of many illnesses and have been among Recovery's most faithful sponsors. Even during Dr. Low's lifetime many of his patients, such as Ann Landis, Harriette Rochford, and Caroline Philipp, came on the recommendation of their family physicians.

The best known of such physicians in connection with Recovery is, of course, Dr. William L. Rice, Treasure Rice's husband. Ever since those early years when he recognized the great therapeutic benefits Recovery had brought his wife, Dr. Rice has been referring many patients to the organization. In estimating the value of Recovery to such disturbed patients, Dr. Rice says, "Needless to say I was delighted with Treasure's progress. . . . Soon after the establishment of the Brighton group I referred a patient to it. He was from the University of Michigan, a young law student who had a long-standing nervous problem. The result was gratifying. He achieved good mental health and maintained it. Following that experience I began to refer more patients from my practice to the Recovery group. Some of these patients were actually psychotic, but with the advent of the new medications I was able to work closely with them, and get them started going to Recovery. One of these patients, who had continued to attend meetings after I stopped seeing her, came to my office one day with one of her children, and I failed to recognize her. She had a total personality change which had so altered her appearance I simply did not know who she was.

"I was quite selective in my referrals for the first few years. Later, because of the high percentage of good results, I offered Recovery to every nervous patient I saw whose symptoms were severe enough to justify such referral. Patients who required hospitalization for treatment of mental illness were referred to a specialist. But after discharge, I suggested they attend Recovery meetings as a means of preventing relapse. In very severe cases, where relapse did inevitably occur, I found that patients who had some Recovery training were able to cooperate better with professional treatment, thereby shortening the period of hospitalization in the majority of cases.

"I have been a general practitioner for thirty years. Living, as we do in a small community, I have been able to observe many of my patients whom I referred to Recovery, up to a period of twenty-five years. Almost without exception they have been able to maintain good mental health through application of techniques learned while participating in the Recovery program, all, incidentally, at negligible cost to the patient.

"Many people owe a great deal to Dr. Low and Recovery. I know Treasure and I do. We are very much aware of this indebtedness and we are truly grateful."

Another physician, Dr. John T. Brandenburg, with the Medford Clinic in Medford, Oregon, has, like Dr. Rice, experienced first-hand the great benefit which Recovery has brought to his own family. His wife, Muriel, is now the Recovery leader in Medford and he approves wholeheartedly and freely refers other patients. He writes: "When my wife, Muriel, first became interested I went along out of simple curiosity and was impressed, as I still am at any meeting I attend, by the warmth, the camaraderie, and the very real evidence of improvement that the patients exhibit. I know they are getting better because I have seen them in my office.

"Every year I refer an estimated thirty people to Recovery, many of whom have tried just about everything to make them feel better. I recall young women with chronic diarrhea so incapacitating that it entirely obliterated any social life, who are now well and have an increasingly outgoing attitude toward life; people with tension headaches necessitating heavy drug usage, including one girl with almost daily headaches for the past ten years who is now freed of the necessity for medicine and happier than she has been in years.

"As with any treatment, there are people who are unable to accept the rules. There are people who are repelled by the idea of group therapy of this kind in the first place, but I have discovered that since the existence of a Recovery organization in this town my labors as a specialist in internal medicine have been greatly lightened. I have a place to which I can refer the people; I know that they will be well taken care of. I checked out the standing of Recovery, Incorporated, with the American Medical Association, I have followed the reports of Recovery in official scientific journals where the reports, incidentally, become more enthusiastic every year.

"Last but not least I have seen the effects of the Recovery rules and system in my own family. My wife is an entirely different person, better able to handle her emotions, able to come back

from setbacks without falling into black despair, able to put aside
an increasing desire for alcohol indulgence, and in good control
of her temper. Thus our home is a far happier place than it used
to be.

"For myself, I have made frequent use of the Recovery principle, especially the non-judgmental rules, the rules of avoiding
the necessity for symbolic victory and the avoidance of any tendency to make moral judgments in family difficulties. Personally
I think Recovery has a great place still to fill in this country. As
part of my investigation of Recovery and during its efforts to
publicize its work in this town I secured an endorsement of the
Method from the head of the Psychiatry Department at the University of Oregon, who uses it in his work. . . ."

Then there are such doctors as Bernard P. Harpole, physician
and surgeon in Portland, Oregon. He got around to attending a
Recovery meeting after having heard about it for years, and was
so impressed that he decided his patients should know of its availability and usefulness. Dr. Harpole sends out a monthly form letter to these patients, and one of his letters was devoted entirely
to Recovery. After describing how a meeting is conducted, he
continues: "It's interesting and instructive to find out that a great
many other people have just about the same problems you have.
These groups demonstrate that there is, for them, an effective way
to handle their problems without getting too 'uptight' about them.
. . . I have many patients for whom I think Recovery, Incorporated, would be a great help." And he concludes with a list of
meeting places and the days of the week the meetings are held
there.

Dr. Harpole, some of whose patients have taken his suggestion
and joined Recovery groups and developed great enthusiasm about
them, concludes in his personal letter to the authors, "I think this
is an excellent program and I'm glad it's finally available to people
in the Portland area."

Medical doctors have also freely used Recovery in their own
lives. In San Diego, California, Dr. Raymond L. Klesstad, who
had been sending patients to Recovery for years, suffered a nervous
breakdown and after a brief hospitalization began to attend Recovery meetings and make use of Recovery techniques himself to

effect a complete cure. Today he likes to twit his psychiatrist colleagues about their inability to help him where Recovery could.

Wives and children of prominent psychiatrists and psychiatrists themselves, attending meetings as ordinary members, have also used Recovery to rehabilitate themselves, though, because of professional reasons, they have requested anonymity.

THIRTY-FOUR

⁓

It was with a solid list of achievements to the credit of their organization that in 1969 the Recovery leaders attended the American Psychiatric Association's convention in Miami, Florida. Here, for the first time since Dr. Low presented his ill-fated paper in 1939, Recovery was again brought before an APA convention and in a way that finally fulfilled his dearest dream. Recovery members were invited to put on a demonstration panel. The panel, which was well-attended by psychiatrists, was introduced by Dr. Hanus J. Grosz, professor in the Department of Psychiatry and senior clinical investigator at the Institute of Psychiatric Research at the Indiana University School of Medicine in Indianapolis.

"It seems to me that in the years to come, when the history of self-help movements in the United States, and particularly in the mental health field, is written, this meeting will surely be looked upon as something of an historic occasion," Dr. Grosz told his audience.

And he went on to explain that he had urged the Recovery leaders to put on the demonstration panel because Recovery "needs to become more active and come out of its relative isolation. Historically, the time has never been more propitious. What I have in mind especially is the rapidly developing trend throughout the country in the direction of comprehensive community mental health care and clinics. It seems to me that this is precisely the sort of situation in which Recovery can be of inestimable help.

"Besides being of benefit to the patients and helping them to learn skills of coping with trivialities of everyday life and making

318

them feel that they are assuming some initiative in helping themselves, Recovery would also provide a welcome check and balance
to the increasing dependence we note everywhere in the mental
health field on outside help and intervention."

As the panel drew to a close, Dr. Francis J. Gerty of Chicago got
to his feet. Dr. Gerty had been director of the Psychiatric Institute
at the time Recovery had been moved to the Loop and had since
then, in 1957, been elected president of the American Psychiatric
Association. Now he told his audience that the panel presentation
had been on his mind all day. He would not have missed it for
the world, and he went on to deliver a eulogy to his former colleague who had quit his safe berth at the Institute to guide Recovery through its bleak early years in the outside world.

Dr. Gerty was followed by other psychiatrists from all over the
country, each rising to give his endorsement of Recovery and to
tell what it was accomplishing among his own patients. One of
these psychiatrists even described how he extended preliminary
treatment to the patients waiting in his reception room by playing
Recovery, Inc. records of Dr. Low's lectures.

Among the psychiatrists extolling Recovery and Dr. Low that
day was Dr. Stanley R. Dean, clinical professor of psychiatry at the
University of Florida College of Medicine at Gainesville. Dr. Dean
was the first private psychiatrist to evince an interest in the
Method, as stated in a letter to him from Dr. Low.

Through the years Dr. Dean, an early pioneer in group psychotherapy, had continued his interest in the organization, eventually presenting its message to his colleagues in England. And
following the convention, he was to read a stirring paper on it
before the World Mental Health Assembly. This paper, which
was introduced into the Congressional Record of November, 1969,
begins with a general endorsement of the shift to group psychotherapy, "despite resistance from the parochial old guard," and
then limits itself to a thorough discussion of Recovery, Inc., in
particular. The organization's beginnings are described along with
its *modus operandi*. Then Dr. Dean follows with a description of
his own experiences:

"Over a period of twenty years I have referred some two hundred patients to Recovery, Inc. Most of them continued simul-
taneously under my care. In my opinion this concurrent group,

as a whole, showed better progress than nonparticipants. There was more rapid symptomatic improvement; less self-consciousness and embarrassment; a greater sense of pride, accomplishment, and degree of commitment; better coping behavior; accelerated social rehabilitation; and less tendency to decompensate under stress.

"Any fears I may have had about dependency and secondary gain were soon allayed by the observation that any element of *dependency* upon the group was more than compensated for by *responsibility* to the group and ultimately a social obligation to get well and become a productive member of society."

And the paper sums up: "Recovery, Inc., is effective because the group and the individual strengthen each other. . . . It deserves the support of everyone in any way concerned with the problem of mental rehabilitation."

2.

So at last the vision of the man who once lovingly referred to the Recovery members as "My Dear Ones" is now reaching its rich fulfillment in the acceptance of professionals. And the therapy that resulted from the extraordinary union of physician and patient to shape a Method and the organization in which to embody it is, as he predicted it would, curing thousands upon thousands of sufferers today.

Was it mere coincidence or prophetic vision that caused Bluma and Lazar Low to name their fifth child Abraham?—Abraham, which means "Father of Multitudes."

INDEX

⌇

Adler, Alfred, 17, 225
Air hunger, xi, 144, 150
Alcoholics Anonymous, xvii, 238, 270, 271, 294, 299
Alexander, Dr. Franz, 123
Alexander, Jack, 250
Alvarado, Mrs. Joe, *see* Low, Fanny
Alvarez, Dr. Walter, 281
Allgemeines Krankenhaus (Vienna), 17
American Neurological Association, 46, 87
American Psychiatric Association
  Low and, 235
  Recovery and, 83, 86, 235, 247, 260
  Singer and, 96
American Society for Group Psychotherapy, 260
American Weekly, 299
Anger, 29, 134, 153, 154, 182, 198
Anti-Semitism, 13, 15
Anxiety, depression and, 228
Anxiety neurosis, 185
Aphasia, 50
Aquinas, St. Thomas, 12
Archives of Neurology and Psychiatry, The, 46, 47
Army hospitals, 135

Association of the Former Patients of the Psychiatric Institute of the University of Illinois and the Department of Public Welfare, *see Recovery*
Averageness, 144, 229, 249

Bagby, Lorraine, 66–67
Benzinger family, 5, 6, 13, 20–21, 29
Beres, Gertrude, 150–51, 202–3, 212, 291
Bertke, Dick, 295
Bisno, Jules, 29, 37, 39, 50, 93
Bisno, Mrs. Jules, 32, 93
Breakdowns, 114, 164, 171, 194–95, 219
  schizophrenic, xiii
Brocken, Annette Tobin
  group psychotherapy classes and, 89–90, 92, 99, 100, 119, 136–37
  life of, 88–92, 295
  Low and, 89–90, 94, 117, 136, 292
  Recovery and, 92, 99, 117, 135–40, 189–90, 203, 212, 239, 271, 292, 293